BURDEN OF PAIN

BURDEN OF PAIN

A PHYSICIAN'S JOURNEY THROUGH
THE OPIOID EPIDEMIC

DR. JAY K JOSHI

HOUNDSTOOTH
PRESS

BURDEN OF PAIN

A Physician's Journey through the Opioid Epidemic

ISBN   978-1-5445-3732-0   *Hardcover*
        978-1-5445-3731-3   *Paperback*
        978-1-5445-3730-6   *Ebook*

FOR MY PATIENTS—YOU ARE MORE THAN A PRESCRIPTION NUMBER.

C O N T E N T S

PART 2: THE SOLUTION

INTRODUCTION

The day my life as a physician shattered, I felt an emotional intensity that left a permanent impression—an impression so vivid, so heartbreaking, that even today a passing recollection evokes sharp emotional bursts, spasms of anxiety.

The day that impression was made, I was no longer a physician, my patients were no longer my patients, and my employees were no longer my employees. A series of interpretations, instigated by something completely beyond my control, had transformed my life, igniting a journey into a new world filled with polarizations and accusations, a deluge of smear and slander.

In the world of the opioid epidemic, trust came from selecting a bias, sensationalism masqueraded as morality, and extremism represented the majority. Reputations were won and lost by the power of words. The words that accused me—written and spoken about me—all became pieces of my loss.

I found myself in that world, and I lost myself in that world. I had been a physician—until I lost my patients. I was a dreamer—until I lost my dreams. I experienced loss after loss, piece by piece, until I was left with only my identity. Soon enough, even that was taken.

But in losing everything, I became free to find meaning. However, that came later, after the losses. To understand how I found meaning in suffering, you must first know the details of my tragedy, word by word, and follow the coalescing crescendo as it culminates in the closing salvo.

Let us begin.

PART 1

THE STORY

CHAPTER 1

"THE CLINIC MUST BE HERE," I boasted cheerfully, looking out the window of the medical office space. In my enthusiasm, I gave a toothy smile as I surveyed the landscape. The town center sat across the promenade that led to the office's front entrance. In clear view stood the police station. The office itself fit snugly between a dental practice and a surgeon's office, all part of a larger complex of healthcare professional services just off the busiest street in the town of Munster, Indiana, and a block north of the region's busiest hospital.

It was the perfect location for my first medical office. The direct access from the parking lot, the overall ambience, and the easy, walkable entry for my patients had me swooning. The problem was the realtor and landlord knew how much I liked it, and they used my enthusiasm as leverage and my naïveté as grounds to set forth quite aggressive terms for the lease. In the end, the landlord and I needed a lawyer to parse through the terms, eliminate certain problematic phrases—including an attempt to lease out a few extra nonexistent square feet of space—and settle on an agreeable leasing contract.

It was an unusually contentious process for a small office property, though I did not acknowledge that at the time, focused as I was on my vision for the ideal primary care clinic. As a young physician practicing primary care for more than a year at another physician's office, I'd observed opportunities for improvement. I had formalized these observations into a model of primary care by studying industry trends in the field alongside research papers piloting new forms of patient care.

Newly married, and with the ideal professional space secured, I paraded through Northwest Indiana with unprecedented confidence and vitality. I touted my vision for primary care with my clinic model, enthusiastically turning my vision into a reality. I attended healthcare networking events and hosted seminars at town centers and health facilities—like nursing homes and assisted living facilities—explaining the clinic's model while demonstrating how it would help patients.

I believed in primary care as more than a discrete set of visits. I saw it as a continuous engagement between provider and patient—an ongoing relationship with open channels of communication. I planned to create a model in which primary care was less about patient visits, medication refills, and referral channels; and more focused on patient conversation, healthcare education, and shared decision-making between the provider and patient.

A diabetic patient, once oriented to this model, would participate in individual and group educational sessions. Those sessions would be reinforced through various channels of communication, such as sharing a daily food journal through email or texting about challenges complying with a diabetic diet. Between visits, my staff and I might also communicate through emails and phone calls. During visits, we might discuss issues such as implanting a continuous glucose monitoring sensor to track blood sugar.

For a hypertensive patient, we documented daily blood pressure values by phone or email and then graphed the values as trends correlating with stress or discontinuation of medication. By sharing these graphs with my patients, we were showing them the direct consequence a reaction or a decision had on their blood pressure. It proved to be far more effective than traditional consultations in changing patient behavior.

My staff and I also addressed patients' adverse behaviors. To improve smoking cessation rates, we piloted virtual reality simulators, complete with headsets, so patients could see the effects of smoking on their lungs and blood vessels through a series of guided simulation modules.

Complementing our primary care model with many innovative healthcare services, such as telepsychiatry, we became pioneers in the community. By tailoring the frequency and medium of communication for each patient, as defined by the patient's needs and preferences, we increased accessibility to healthcare for those who typically struggled to manage their health while simply living their lives.

I believed then, as I do now, that empowering patients to customize their healthcare gives them a sense of control. And as a result, patients invest more time and energy in their healthcare, make better medical decisions, are more compliant, and produce better outcomes.

Patients in my model are asked to commit daily to actively making decisions, large and small, to improve or maintain their health. They are asked to take every medication as directed, regardless of whatever else may be transpiring in their lives. They are expected to know what to eat and when to eat, as well as what not to eat and when not to eat. Their capacity and willingness to invest the necessary energy increases with increasing control. Patients develop a sense of pride, a sense of prestige. Hence, I named the practice Prestige Clinics.

With the right staff supporting and implementing the model with me, we would achieve accreditation as a top-tier healthcare clinic. But the initial staff was not the right staff, as I made major missteps with my first hires.

An acquaintance, a management consultant active in the local business community, introduced me to my first employee. She was a natural as a receptionist, with a friendly, personable, and professional demeanor. I trained her to perform clinically oriented tasks, such as using the medical record system, coordinating physician referrals, and completing the multitude of forms required by insurance companies, hospital systems, and other healthcare facilities.

After she became rapidly proficient in those tasks, I entrusted her to take on the role of office manager. Many staffing professionals in healthcare acknowledge it is rare to find a dependable office manager from the onset, when the clinic is still growing, so when this employee demonstrated reliability in her new management role, I grew to trust her judgment.

That trust proved crucial when searching for my second employee, a medical assistant to take patients' vitals and to assist in basic office duties. We cycled through assistant after assistant until I found someone I felt would be an agreeable addition. Initially, she was more pleasant than she was competent, mingling well with patients, though making more than her fair share of mistakes.

But she was an enthusiastic learner, performing the tasks of both a medical assistant and a phlebotomist. More important, she worked well with the office manager. Calculating that the positives outweighed the negatives, I hired her to a permanent position as medical assistant and shifted my focus toward developing the clinic.

It took a few months to realize my calculation was misguided. The holes that eventually sunk us did not appear immediately or in an obvious manner. Rather, they showed up as small leaks, quietly and insidiously.

One evening, after visiting patients at a nursing home, I asked a member of the nursing home staff to call my medical assistant to schedule a follow-up appointment in my office for a patient who was being discharged from the home. The staff called twice with no answer, and on the third attempt spoke with a gruff-sounding man who, before hanging up, tersely said, "Call back when we finish business."

When I inquired about what had transpired, my assistant insisted her brother had inadvertently picked up the phone while visiting her to drop off food. She seemed contrite, genuinely apologetic, and concerned with improving her communication skills and daily office tasks, which over time she did. I saw her mistakes as aberrations in her learning curve, minor deviations in an otherwise positive trajectory.

Minor incidents, such as missed phone calls, delays in relaying critical messages, and forgotten tasks, all tended to occur when the assistant was by herself. Yet, I never suspected anything other than an earnest employee making an occasional mistake. Sensing I might solve the problem by giving her more support, I looked for an additional employee to complement her efforts.

CHAPTER 2

THE CLINIC WAS HARDLY A FEW MONTHS OLD, but its growth was undeniable. The community took notice, granting us an award through the regional small business development center. Media outlets were eager to display the clinical services we provided. Because of this attention, a major in-state university and the state's health department inquired about our interest in collaborating on pilot programs designed to test new healthcare innovations. As part of the collaboration, we would have access to recruiting university students and state personnel as needed.

Through this collaboration, we found one intern through a marketing class in which we taught college students effective healthcare marketing strategies. He was an upperclassman, a military veteran returning to college after his service. He worked long hours, willing to perform laborious tasks that otherwise often fell to the wayside. I believed we had hired the ideal employee for our needs.

With this additional support, I deemed we were ready to

apply for accreditation awards. A healthcare system can obtain multiple forms of accreditation, and a variety of credentialing agencies facilitate that accreditation. We worked with the National Centers for Quality Assurance (NCQA) to achieve accreditation as a Patient Centered Medical Home, or PCMH, a recognition insurance companies widely acknowledge as the standard bearer of excellence in outpatient primary care. Many insurance companies offer select insurance plans, including plans designed to manage high-risk chronic care patients, to clinics that obtain this accreditation.

The documentation requirements were cumbersome, and the arduous application process took months to complete. We developed elaborate spreadsheet models to quantify points of patient engagement, record the net benefit in patient care per engagement, and provide visual representations of the clinical workflow, which we called the patient journey, through various customized engagements. I took the application process as a challenge, relishing documenting and detailing every aspect of the practice.

The employees took it as an unwelcome, additional task. They complained I was unfairly adding extra work to their day, but I assured them that once the application was complete, they would continue to do the same amount of work, only now with an added layer of transparency to document the clinic's activities.

Initially the backlash was modest. Still, I was taken aback by the fact that there was *any* backlash. In response, I became more assertive, more forthright with my demands, which turned the initial backlash into overt resistance, disagreements into verbal clashes, and calm waters into turbulent seas. If a first impression can mislead and lull you into falsely trusting, then a backlash can reveal what is hidden. In this instance, the office turbulence revealed far more than I had bargained for.

To inflict the most damage with a knife, you do not thrust the blade in with one giant stab; you inflict innumerable, precise slices, cutting ever so slightly, again and again, as the most subtle motions create the greatest effects. The same applies to deception, as select words can cut far deeper than even the sharpest knives. To truly mislead a person, you do not tell one blatant lie—you tell a series of little lies precisely coordinated to maximize effect.

A miscue here, a turn of phrase there, and pretty soon the gashes of lies spread all over. Like a fatal wound that has bled too much, once it becomes apparent, it is too late. When I faced the backlash, I had no way to imagine my initial reaction would prompt wave after wave of contention, arguments, and walkouts. But my employees had too much to hide, too much to lose, and from their perspective, no option but to escalate the conflict.

The medical assistant and intern were systematically forging prescriptions under my name, using photocopied prescriptions with my information and plastic molded templates of my signature. Only months afterward would I learn that while I was seeing patients in the office, they were forging scripts. When I visited nursing homes and assisted living facilities, they were forging scripts. When they asked for an extra hour to finish up paperwork, they were forging scripts. When they asked to work Saturday mornings, they were forging scripts.

What I had perceived as effort and commitment on the part of my two employees were actually guises for guile and deceit. Over the coming months, I slowly began to understand and learn the full extent of their activities. In my pursuit of accreditation awards, I observed their work more closely to measure productivity relative to efforts, and I soon identified periods of inactivity. I later realized such periods were anything *but* inactive.

When I first inquired as to why so many hours appeared to be void of any work activity, my employees denied any reason for concern and deflected to other matters. First, they complained I was too aggressive, so I questioned their work ethic. Then they said I was too demanding, so I adjusted the work schedule, shouldering a heavier load of the clinical work but keenly monitoring their activities. They became petulant, showing up late, leaving early, and complaining about work conditions and patients' demands.

Begrudgingly, I had accommodated their requests, unaware of what was transpiring. I'd hoped that, despite the growing tension, the pair would still support the accreditation application process. I adjusted the clinic schedule and the workload to best balance the practice, the employees' requests, and the demands of the accreditation application. The implicit trust we all shared was long gone, so while I addressed their concerns, the working relationship was now balanced on a pretense of trust rather than on a sense of genuine integrity. It was a balance that grew more delicate by the day, by the argument, and by the clinical task.

And then I received a letter in the mail.

The letter named my medical assistant and her prescriptions, including some I was allegedly prescribing her. The letter listed the names, mine included, of all physicians from whom she was receiving prescriptions and the types of medications prescribed. The timing of the letter, in the middle of the accreditation applications, pierced me as sharply as its words. It did not take long for the stab wounds to ignite an emotional storm, throwing my mind into a wild tailspin.

First came the questions: *How long has this been going on? How many scripts? Who else is involved? How did I miss this? Was I too trusting? Too friendly?* Then came the feelings: anger, doubt, fear, and betrayal. The stream of questions blended with the storm of emotions to form a cyclone of turmoil that left me emotionally paralyzed. I blamed my employees. I blamed myself. I made accusations. I made excuses. The times I forgave mistakes, I had enabled deceit. When I empowered my employees, they manipulated me. And on it went. But at the time, I had only one piece, this letter, and did not understand the extent to which the forgeries had occurred. I had just a glimpse of the storm, its full ferocity looming behind the horizon, hidden, unknown to me for the time being.

After my thoughts settled, I decided to handle the matter with an open conversation. I sent an email to the staff, who had left the office before I opened the letter, requesting a meeting for the following morning.

The next day, I was met with nothing but silence. The manager abruptly quit with only an email notice. The medical assistant did not show up for work but arrived later in the day in a fire of fury, vowing vengeance if I were to ever report the forgeries—she then left as quickly as she had arrived. Curiously, the intern reported to work on time, calmly discussed the letter, apologized profusely through vague generalities, and claimed he did not know anything of the forgeries.

The letter indicated my medical assistant, not the intern, had prescribed numerous medications for herself under my name without my consent. This was before I knew of the photocopies, signature templates, and infamous claim that I prescribed six thousand pain medications—information that impregnated the minds of an entire community.

I saw before me a plea for forgiveness and a face full of sorrow, and I chose to believe my intern. I do not know that I believed him like I would have before receiving the letter, but I distinctly remember believing him. Did I believe him because I wanted to believe him, because I was scared not to believe him, or because I was truly convinced of his sincerity? I allowed him to continue working in the clinic and on the accreditation application. Although I was fed up with employees duping me, I felt eager to move on and ready for a fresh start with a new staff.

CHAPTER 3

DESPITE THE RELIEF I FELT in believing all the conflict was behind me, I could not ignore the events leading up to the letter, my anguish in reading it, and the abrupt departures of my office manager and medical assistant. The former left in deafening silence, and the latter with overtures of violence and retaliation.

I knew I had to file a police report. I informed the intern of my intentions, giving him a chance to tell me if he had something to say about the letter or anything related to the forged prescriptions. I was providing him the opportunity to confess if he had any role in the forgeries. He repeatedly denied any involvement, first speaking calmly, then nearly in tears, pleading for me to understand his perspective. He claimed he knew nothing, that after enrolling in college late in life, he was focused on providing for his family. He would never do anything to jeopardize his relationship with his daughter, he insisted.

I sensed candor in his consistent responses and took him

at face value, not realizing the face only shows what the lies want you to believe. I went on with my day and began seeing patients with the support of two newly hired employees. I'd planned to file the police report later, anticipating it would take some time to complete.

But while I was tending to patients at a nursing home, the terminated medical assistant's brother came to my office. He reinforced threats of violence and property damage should I file a police report. In hindsight, it is obvious the intern tipped off the brother. But neither the intern nor I was present when the incident occurred. The intern was in school, and I was at the nursing home. When my receptionist, clearly shaken, called to tell me about the brother, I consoled her and cleared the rest of my day to file the police report. I now sensed the urgency of the situation.

The police arrived late, lacking the promptness I would expect from law enforcement agents documenting a report. But more peculiar was their line of questioning, oddly terse and vague. When I mentioned the forged prescription and subsequent threats, they questioned my integrity, asking me for proof. When I showed them the letter from the insurance company, they gave it a cursory glance. Posturing with indifference despite my pleas for help, they did not even take the photocopied version I had made for them. They challenged me on details, asking how I knew what I knew. They repeated questions in a way that seemed designed to elicit contradictions in my statements, rather than paying attention to the letter and the threats of violence.

Then, like that, the police left. Assuming the police would get back to me, I resumed working on the quality application. The new employees adapted to the clinic model, and within a few weeks, we regained our stride, managing patients with a coordinated balance of quality and efficiency. We introduced even more elaborate quality models, including customized interactions with patients through digital platforms. To improve patient compliance, we focused our technology on specific aspects of patient behavior, emphasizing the importance of health in their everyday lives.

We were in tune with the questions and needs of each patient as well as the broader trends and news of the community at large. Much of our clinic's success derived from understanding how each patient lived and worked within the community and customizing our healthcare approach accordingly.

Northwest Indiana is an all-American, blue-collar community that, like so many others throughout the country, fell victim to the opioid epidemic. You can read the statistics and study the facts, but until you've practiced clinical medicine in areas affected by the epidemic, you will not properly understand it. You will not know the shame of a person needing to work but unable to without pain pills, or the humiliation of having to choose between work or surgery, and often being left with only the recourse of pain pills as a viable solution.

Many of our patients were affected by the epidemic, directly and indirectly. We understood that impact on their lives. The pervasiveness of the epidemic made it a common topic of conversation. We talked openly and honestly with our patients. In doing so, we brought light to the dark, hidden difficulties in many patients' lives.

We integrated addiction medicine—the treatment of substance-use disorders and medication dependencies—into the primary care model. We also created specific questionnaires to address potential dependencies and addictions among our patients. We viewed patients with multiple chronic conditions and symptoms, including pain, as primary care patients, not exclusively as pain patients or addiction patients, paying attention to their other medical conditions as multiple parts of a whole person.

We monitored medications like opioids as we would any other medication. If we felt a patient's dose was too high, we tapered the medication through a mutually agreed upon process called micro-tapering. Rather than reducing the medications in large increments of thirty or sixty pills, we adjusted them in smaller increments. We closely monitored how the patients handled the changes, allowing our interactions to dictate the course of clinical care.

If it appeared the patient had developed a dependency or an outright addiction, we discussed lowering the dose or prescribing alternative medications. We established goals for each patient's health and lifestyle, setting short-term and long-term milestones. Communication and trust became the basis for our medical decisions and treatment. To ensure patients were properly taking their medications—that our trust was justified—we verified compliance with regular urine drug screens and imaging studies.

We found the balance between trusting and verifying to be effective in identifying and monitoring dependency and addiction. When concerns about dependency arose, we added telepsychiatry meetings. The time we invested in these patients led to mutual trust. Without fear of reprisal, patients were truthful with us.

One patient admitted he had told other physicians his pain was increasing, so he could receive additional medication, because previously he'd been arbitrarily given fewer pills without prior discussion. He was stockpiling pills in case that should happen again. But having built trust, we reduced the patient's medications without inducing the fear that had led him to hoard pills.

We shared this approach with many pharmacists and specialists in our referral channels. We discussed the clinical care plans, the justification for individual decisions, and the goals for patient care. Through our communication, we improved patient compliance.

One patient came to me after struggling with bladder pain for years. She had bounced from physician to physician, juggling pain-relieving procedures with medications, until her primary care physician deemed her to be too high risk. This risk was determined not by her compliance or medical conditions, but instead by the likelihood that continuing to prescribe her medically necessary pain medications would warrant unwanted attention from law enforcement.

We set goals for tapering her prescriptions and coordinating her procedures to minimize the need for excess medications. I informed her urologist and pharmacist of our goals, and I requested feedback on her progress. The patient appreciated this level of care and oversight, and she became more engaged in her care and compliant with treatment protocols. Within months her condition improved, in large part due to her active approach to her own health. She was the ideal candidate to benefit from the additional time and care we invested in patients. Other patients, lacking the motivation or inspiration toward self-improvement, found our approach unsuitable for their intentions and discontinued their clinic visits.

One such patient, a young woman with a type of attention disorder, was taking a high-risk medication her psychiatrist prescribed before she came to me. Since she had failed a urine drug screen, I prescribed her a lower dose and quantity than

I normally would have, as a precaution against medication abuse. After that initial, failed test, she became more compliant and passed subsequent drug screens.

When she later asked for her original dose, I told her I felt comfortable prescribing it only after she spoke with a specialist. I arranged a referral with her original psychiatrist, while initiating telepsychiatry therapy—a plan she decidedly refused. When I asked why she was refusing, she simply said, "I will just find someone else to prescribe me what I want." And she did find somebody else. In our final exchange, she was more honest about her intentions: she was not ready to address her dependencies and, therefore, not willing to continue participating in the quality model. As she left my care, I informed her of the risks and potential long-term consequences of her choices and wished her the best.

Often, patient care involves coordinating care through the community, including patients' family and friends, as well as law enforcement officers who get involved when concerns of drug abuse or illegal sales of prescriptions arise. In such a situation, I actively discussed patient concerns with the appropriate family member, friend, or law enforcement agent. Most often, the concerns arose because of a pharmacy alert or complaint from a family member. Such concerns were resolved by discussing the quality model—and the patient oversight we provided while prescribing pain medications—with pharmacists, family members, and anyone else who was involved in patient care.

Some law enforcement officers place huge emphasis on an initial impression, as if a snap judgment can capture the full patient history. Such an approach may work in traditional law enforcement, but it quickly falls apart when applied in healthcare. Each patient encounter is one of many interactions in a long, dynamic relationship, and evaluating patient behavior outside the context of clinical care produces errors of judgment and biases, which are disastrous for patient care.

CHAPTER 4

IT BEGAN WITH A SIMPLE PHRASE, beginning with three letters that came to define my life for years to come: "DEA is here, doc." Words uttered by the intern. Of course, it was the intern. It had to be him. The phrase caught me off guard, as it would any unsuspecting physician at the beginning of what would have been a routine day.

Before I could process the words, the main hallway doors slammed open and closed. I heard the thud of heavy boots coming closer and closer. The office entrance doors burst open with two shrill shrieks of rattling glass, one from the door slamming open and the other from the door slamming into the wall as it swung around on its hinges. I felt the gates of hell open. Disguised as law enforcement agents, every demon, ghoul, and goblin stormed in.

They brandished armored bulletproof vests and military-grade artillery holsters displaying weapons of mass destruction. They prowled around the office, inflicting fear with each step, intimidation with every menacing grimace. They howled, "Get down! Get down!" They cackled, "DEA." They taunted, "You're a drug dealer, a drug dealer." They warned, "Don't move," as they swarmed about.

Soon they broke into two groups. One watched over me and my employees, cornered in the waiting room. The other ravaged the clinic, sifting through patient files and medical supplies, throwing it all asunder as they looked for something, anything—invaders thirsting for plunder.

Our hands and feet were technically free, but our minds were instantly paralyzed with the primordial fear that arises only when faced with the imminent threat of death. We saw the looks of horror on one another's faces—the patients, my newly hired staff, and I. Almost immediately, I fell into a frozen state of disbelief, stunned into a stupor.

Those still capable of emotion cried in fits of discombobulation, while others shed silent tears, faces locked in a blank look of shock rapidly settling in—only to eventually explode in an onslaught of shock. We attempted to console one another as we were collectively herded into one large crowd in the waiting room. "Are you okay? Are you okay?" The empty words were spoken instinctively more than anything else, as we tried to process the atrocity unfolding around us.

My new receptionist, just weeks into her new position after being hired through an online job site, normally perky and attentive, crawled into a ball in a corner of the waiting room floor, her eyes lifelessly fixated on the ground directly in front of her. One of my patients, a retired union laborer and Army veteran, sat in silent obedience in a chair just a few feet away from me. He was conspicuously still and hardly recognizable with an unfamiliar, pained expression on his face.

The percolating shock took away my sense of time, my ability to process, to rationalize, and replaced it with the daze of confusion. I sat motionless, intensely aware of my inability to move, feeling extremely vulnerable and unsure of what to say or do.

After some time, two agents grabbed me, pinned me against a wall, and searched me. Their hands violently grasped parts of my body, but I stood helpless and detached, not questioning or resisting their actions. Any impulse to resist had disappeared. The agents took whatever I had in my possession—wallet, keys, cell phones. They displayed and passed around the items, multiple agents taking turns to rummage through them.

None of us understood what the agents were doing. Their search seemed to have no clear purpose. It seemed, more than anything, cruel and ruthless—and even today, it brings to mind mercenaries allowed to pillage a town after their conquest, to satiate whatever carnal instincts have risen during war.

Two new agents then approached and pressed me forcibly against the wall. Positioning their faces inches from mine, they stared at me, sizing me up and searching for any signs of resistance. When they found none, one agent grabbed my shoulder, instructing me to follow them out of the office and into their car.

As I stepped out, I saw the look of terror on my employees' faces. They were trembling and distraught. We exchanged the looks captives must give one another when one in the group is being singled out for an even worse fate.

I do not remember the car ride to the police station. I do not remember entering the police station. I remember only the heavy hands behind me, directing me into a small room equipped with an overhead light beaming directly over me. I was ordered to sit in a chair in the corner as officers positioned two other chairs to encircle me.

I recall only select moments, as the shock had fully overwhelmed my system by now, sending my mind into total disarray. For the longest time, all I could process were their stares. At moments when I was able to see clearly, I saw my reflection in their eyes. Each agent simply stared at me with the same look given when studying me up close in the office. The longer they stared, the weaker I became. I sat broken and motionless, feeling myself melting away—layers of thought, of proper judgment, were softening, weakening for what seemed a never-ending length of time.

Then the interrogation began. One agent spoke. "Would you like to have a conversation?" he asked, and, "Do you know you are being detained of your own volition?" He said it with an odd tone that was noticeable more for its calmness than its content. It was a tone intended to impose a statement through his questioning rather than actually obtain consent. All I could muster was a feeble nod, like a mistreated animal that knows when to perform and when to hide. I felt too fearful to disobey, too shocked to understand the consequences.

The questions came, and I answered. At least, I think I answered. What I answered, how I answered, I do not know for sure. My mind, now reduced to wildly fluctuating waves of consciousness, was fully submerged in a blustery sea of shock. Deciding which memories I retained, what to say, how to react, my mind batted helplessly between instincts and rationale. But within the swirl of awareness, I remember specific moments and questions with distinct vividness.

I remember discussing my former medical assistant, who, as I found out from the agents, had falsified her certification credentials, her lies beginning even before she started working for me. When I asked about her forgeries, the DEA agent asked why I had not filed a police report. I was stunned. *Why didn't I file a police report?* I had filed a police report with the Munster Police Department, having even provided them with evidence.

The shock by then was fully formed into trauma, and my traumatized mind did not possess the ability to ask the obvious—why my report had not been processed. At the very least, I should have repeated to the agents that I had filed a police report. That is the nature of shock: it overwhelms your ability to think effectively. But your mind, being your mind, is still consumed in some type of thought, no matter how chaotic. So you think thoughts that are clouded, incomplete, and scattered, attempting to rationalize an irrational state of mind.

But in struggling to make sense of the senseless, I perpetuated my own demise. I provided fodder for the agents, a semblance of perceived guilt out of genuinely pure innocence. In an otherwise normal state of mind, I would have realized the agents were manipulating the conversation, teasing words out of me only to later twist those words against me. In my state of shock, however, I simply acquiesced to their line of questioning.

They asked about my patients: "How do you decide what medications to prescribe?" "How do you verify the medical need for a medication?" "What tests do you order?" "What screenings do you perform?"

They asked about the clinic, about solutions to the opioid epidemic, about the quality model we were developing—ostensibly appearing to genuinely care about the quality of care I provided. But in reality, they were just fishing for evidence, a statement, an admission, anything to turn my clinical care into a crime.

It's nearly impossible to recapture in words the scorn in their approach. It was an agonizing interrogation, nothing remotely resembling a discussion—twisting words, manipulating facts, and turning patient care into a perceived moral failing of my own making.

When I told them I trusted my patients, they insinuated I

was complicit in selling illicit prescription pills, deliberately conflating the prescribing of medications with the selling of illicit drugs. When I discussed micro-tapering strategies, they intimated that I was enabling addictions and dependencies.

I knew they were wrong—medically incorrect—and afterward, I realized they were manipulating facts from my statements about medical care to contrive an admission of unsubstantiated illegal acts. But in the moment, my mind was too far gone, incapable of articulating measured responses or even wholly understanding what was transpiring.

They asked me about a patient named Todd Greenberg. He was a patient to me, but an undercover agent to them. Todd Greenberg was his pseudonym. He was a covert, Quantico-trained operative, whom the DEA had sent to investigate my clinic and determine what, if anything, could be construed as illegal. They were looking for specific acts that resemble what would ensue more so in drug deals than in clinical care.

This agent had presented with what he'd claimed to be cramp-like pain in his lower extremities, stating he had a history of taking moderate-strength opioids. He portrayed himself as a truck driver who had recently relocated for work. He provided all the requisite documentation, stating he wished to continue his medical care with me. When asked if he had a history of addictions or was currently addicted, he documented "no." When asked if other physicians were providing him treatment, he said "no." We believed him and verified his information through the state of Indiana's prescriber database.

During his appointments, we discussed his job and television shows he enjoyed. Throughout our visits, in my observation of him, I deemed him trustworthy. This makes sense; an agent who intends to—and is trained to—deceive and falsely gain the trust of a caring physician will likely succeed.

During the initial encounter, I lowered the opioid medications based on what he had said he was taking to a dose I was more comfortable with, below the threshold level at which addictions are shown to form. He agreed, which to me served as a sign that I could trust him. During his visits, we asked him to complete a urine drug screen and to provide his medical records when they became available. I prescribed non-opioid alternatives, as well as other medications to address the potential root cause of his pain. We discussed the risk of addiction and the impact of long-term opioid use. I ordered an imaging study to inform him of the effects long-term opioid has on bone density.

None of that mattered. What mattered was that I prescribed anything at all. Communicating with patients, trusting patients, and establishing goals for patients were irrelevant, subservient to the act of prescribing opioids alone, irrespective of the clinical context. The absurdity of this perspective only exacerbated my shock—a clinically harmful approach to patient care touted as the legal standard to determine criminality. I felt a need to explain to the agents the harm that can arise from such a limited perspective to patient care.

But when I tried to explain, the words I needed were elusive and fleeting, leaving me scrambling as I pleaded for them to understand that you cannot isolate one specific act in the continuum of patient care—prescribing medications—take it out of context, and then label it as a criminal act.

I did not understand then how the interpretation of the law creates the crime and defines the criminal through an ever-changing set of subjective criteria. I thought being a good physician should suffice—that fulfilling my duties and being dedicated to my patients were more than enough. But they were far from enough.

The mercy of time brings all things to an end, and when the agents finished questioning me, they presented a set of documents for me to sign. I do not know how the topic was even introduced—or what was in those documents, for that matter. I remember only that documents were placed in front of me, and I was told to sign. "It'll be good for your patients," one agent said, goading me. In my shocked state of mind, I actually accepted his words, that I should willingly resign my ability to prescribe controlled substances at the insistence of DEA agents, without once considering the effects it would have on my patients and my practice.

The prolonged trauma over hours of detainment had disconnected my thoughts to the point of deterioration, reducing my mind to a state of childlike obedience. I obeyed, not because I understood what I was signing, but because I was not capable of anything else. I was like a toddler mimicking commands, desiring to please, unable to understand, but complying nonetheless. The moment the pen in my hand signed the papers, the documents were swept away, collated, and shared between the two interrogating officers—presented as a trophy of their victory. I stood there, unclear on what to do or say, too dazed to react, too stunned to understand that a silver tongue and sleight of hand had beguiled me.

The agents moved quickly then, having obtained what they were seeking, and were left with nothing to do but orchestrate an exit. They released me from my detainment and ferried me across the promenade from the police station to my office. The ride was short and straightforward, but merely a reprieve that belied the enormous legal cataclysm in which I would soon find myself.

I walked into my office and into complete devastation—the scattered cinder of abject destruction, a once organized clinic now with papers scattered about and medical supplies thrown in disarray. The residual embers of violence recently passed were still fresh, festering throughout the clinic. The air was drenched in palpable misery, and the trauma, etched deeply upon the faces of everyone present, spoke louder than any words could.

In the waiting room, patients who had scheduled appointments at the time of the onslaught sat interspersed with my employees in a haphazard arrangement of chairs. Agents continued scouring about, looking for anything to justify their continued presence. My patients and employees had every reason to leave, to take flight at the first opportunity available, but they had all stayed.

They stayed because they believed in me, and together, we supported one another. Despite law enforcement agents threateningly recording their information, inscribing their names into a veritable scarlet letter, they stayed. Their belief in me gave me confidence, a faith no fear could dispel, renewing my mind with a vigor that overcame the fear. I determined to press on. But the steps needed to move on would quickly prove heavy and cumbersome, as the scars inflicted left indelible marks of terror on the minds of everyone present…with deadly repercussions.

If one person embodied the true scale of trauma inflicted, it would be a young woman who came to the clinic that day for a follow-up telepsychiatry appointment. I was gone with the agents when she arrived, but when I returned, she was lying on the floor, on her side, curled in a ball, trembling in fear, a DEA agent lording over her. I pleaded with the agent to leave her be, and eventually, I escorted her into a patient room where she could recover in silence.

After the onslaught, I went to console her. We cried

together, finding solace in the madness, in sharing our misery, our trauma. She made me promise I would never abandon her, never let anything like what just had happened ever happen again to her. I dutifully obliged, unsure how else to respond, and we shared an embrace.

In due course she left, only to return the next day, equally hysterical, still bearing the fresh scars of trauma that had not yet begun to heal. But they would never heal; the scars were too deep, the trauma too severe. Within a few days, she committed suicide, just before her young daughter's birthday. Her mother called to share the news. My employees and I cried together, her death serving as a painfully sharp reminder of the wounds we all suffered that day.

From the day she became my patient and forever after, I will be grateful for the time we shared while I was her physician.

Her name was Megan.

CHAPTER 5

WE CONTINUED TO SEE PATIENTS at the clinic, but something felt different, like living in a home after the death of a family member. The items and arrangements all looked the same, but the perception was unmistakably changed, and the resulting sensation felt like cognitive dissonance.

We made our best attempts to move on from what happened, as if by moving on we could somehow lessen its impact. But the ensuing ramifications never dissipated, as reminders of the event and its effects on patients and their families kept appearing. Despite trying to move forward, my mind kept coming back to that day, particularly the last few moments when I got back to the office before the agents left.

I had informed my patients that we would resume clinic after the agents left, and I thanked them for their patience. At my utterance of these words, the agents became visibly upset, inflicting another round of threats and invectives, and casting fear and intimidation through facial expressions. Instead of seeing my dedication to my patients, they saw defiance. Upon my saying, "My duty is to serve my patients; I will not abandon them," one agent approached and directly threatened me, warning that I should never upset him.

"That would be bad," he said before walking out to his car. I can still vividly picture the animosity on his face, the glare in his eyes, and the snarl on his lips. It feels as chilling now as it did then, but I did what any committed physician would do. I continued to serve my patients until I was literally prohibited from doing so.

Word spread throughout the community. From the beginning, we were transparent about what had happened as we understood it. We welcomed and appreciated the outpouring of support from community members and other physicians.

We formalized a referral network of supporting providers to treat patients who required medications we could no longer prescribe due to the restrictions imposed by those DEA documents I had signed. But the wait times for patients to see new providers amounted to weeks, sometimes months. I believed it was my responsibility to help my patients as long as they remained mine, and I sought solutions to transition their care while they waited to see their new physicians.

We found alternative, non-opioid medications for some patients; and for others, we planned to hire a nurse to oversee the transition of care. The nurse would have the ability to prescribe opioids and other controlled substances as necessary. Together, the nurse and I would determine how to continue care for patients until they could see their new provider.

We hired a nurse, who was willing to work part time, from a neighboring hospital system. She and I reviewed the quality model, set goals for each patient, and discussed all that had transpired with the DEA.

My two newly hired employees continued to work for me

because they believed we genuinely provided good quality care to our patients. But fear from that traumatic day, and from threats made by DEA agents vowing to return, moved them from being cautious to outright suspicious of some patients. We ordered more drug screens, required more imaging studies, and, at times, refused to see patients who were not able to complete certain imaging studies.

Trust had been eroded, something our patients keenly noted through our additional demands for tests and uncharacteristically firm tone of communication. Patience began to reciprocate our distrust with commensurate distrust. Our clinic's methods, which previously flowed effortlessly through mutual respect, ground to a halt as patients received clinical care focused more on provider self-protection than patient outcomes.

My intern, the most fearful—and with the most to fear—began acting erratically after the DEA onslaught. He reached out to patients and affiliated healthcare facilities, trying to solicit any negative information against me and to compile evidence that didn't exist. He also solicited the nurse's input toward his efforts. Realizing what the intern was doing and fearing her possible liability should she end up a target like I had, the nurse quit on the spot.

When I learned what the intern was doing, I fired him immediately—an action long in the making. In turn, he became violent, needing to be escorted out and ranting with an eerily familiar set of threats and promises of retaliation I'd first heard months ago when my first medical assistant had left.

While the intern contributed his share of drama, we faced a different kind of drama through a constant barrage of phone calls that prevented any sense of stability from settling in. Patients called to inquire how law enforcement agents, who were cold-calling and asking about their prescription histories, had obtained their medical records and contact information in a brazen violation of patient privacy laws.

Pharmacists called, unsure of what prescriptions to fill in light of the newly placed prescribing restrictions. Police officers called, covertly asking employees about the patients who had come to the clinic that day so they could look up any prior criminal backgrounds among them. During one of these calls, a newly hired employee intentionally gave illicit access to medical records.

We became a toxic environment, afflicting ourselves and affecting anyone who joined or helped us. Any attempt to bring in a nurse or a physician partnership imploded. We rapidly grew a distinct miasma around us—an aroma of suspicion, doubt, and eventually, abject fear. Good intentions instantly turned negative, and the legal ramifications of prescribing superseded the medical need of prescribing.

Physicians offering support now needed formalized agreements to help. Referrals to partnering physicians now required letters of termination and reinstatement, formalizing patient referrals into a set of contractual agreements. Any possible solution fell apart, potential partnerships disintegrating no sooner than they had materialized.

With the office in such disarray, I made my own misstep—an oversight in adhering to legal formalities in securing prescriber support, whether with another nurse or another physician. As a result, a select number of patients received prescriptions without the required, valid collaborative agreement. Since I had lost my ability to prescribe controlled substances, I was no longer permitted to engage in collaborative agreements with providers who were able to prescribe controlled substances.

My ignorance of this policy proved a costly misstep that

law enforcement agents were eager to exploit, to create the presumption of criminality when none had previously existed, contriving a narrative that turned my commitment to my patients into willful complicity.

We were doing our best to focus on and treat the patients coming to the clinic. We were hobbled but nevertheless committed. We continued to provide unparalleled quality of care for our patients, exhibiting a persistence that would eventually be recognized. We reached arguably our greatest milestone at the time, the formal designation as a National Committee for Quality Assurance (NCQA) certified Patient Centered Medical Home (PCMH), two months after the DEA raid.

It was a validation of our dedication to quality patient care and determination to overcome the obstacles we had faced. Under any other circumstances, this milestone would be celebrated as the best of times. But just one week later, this blip of success would become only a precursor to what would be the worst of times.

CHAPTER 6

GLIDE YOUR HAND over a piece of velvet and you notice the
smoothness. You feel its aggregated smoothness, not the individualized roughness of each fiber. Each fleeting fiber, a prick
of truth, is nullified, synthesized, and then magnified into the
silky fluency of general perception—propaganda containing
within it a concoction of ambiguities and assumptions, cooked
with a splash of outright lies and a dash of truth. This is to
ensure the intrigue rises to a level that is just right, just unbe-
lievably believable. I experienced this dish, served in all its
varieties with all the flair and pomp, until I could eat no more.
And then the dish forced its way down my throat.

My first taste came during my last days of seeing patients. On
a Friday, I received a call that indicated I was to be indicted. I had
to first search the term to verify its definition, and even then, I did
not grasp its immense implications. I was not yet able to process
that I was being accused of a crime. I continued seeing patients
the next day, Saturday—a physician until the very end. I reported
to the federal courthouse in Hammond, Indiana, on Monday.

The courthouse is a truly impressive building in an otherwise dilapidated neighborhood. I suppose there is symbolism in that contrast, but I was too consumed with my own symbolism to pay that contrast any mind. The legal proceedings were brief, surprisingly polite, and more ceremonial than judicial, with none of the fanfare one might expect in what was—or perceived to be, at least—a high-profile criminal case. That soon contrasted with the virulent propaganda in which I was immersed—article by article, drop by drop.

The first news article, a harmless drop in an otherwise empty bucket, made its presence known through a transient *splash*...followed by a moment of silence. And the moment was over, disrupted by another drop and then a rapid series of drops, until they were no longer drops, but a stream. A rumbling, noisy stream of news and hearsay overflowed from the bucket, spreading out with accelerating aggression to permeate the minds of readers, gossips, and rumormongers. Then the stream turned into a flood, a deluge of destruction, ensuring its presence was felt and its impact known.

News reports claimed I gave pills to relatives and acquaintances of federal agents and coordinated a multistate drug operation. Those who followed the flood as closely as I floated in it likely learned what was written about me at the same time I did. We learned I was the top prescriber of opioids in the area I practiced, and one of the top opioid prescribers in the state of Indiana. We even heard I was impersonating another physician from another state.

The articles grew to be so numerous they competed for attention with one another. The crafting of each article became a coordinated dance, a bid for attention between reader and writer. These writers used scandal to attract readers, twisting key facts, deliberately introducing ambiguities to create an air of suspense in an evolutionary process of journalistic adaptation—attention being the competitive prize.

The outright dishonest articles soon went extinct, leaving articles more successfully fit—in the most Darwinian sense—for navigating the ever-blurring distinction between truth and fabrication. Each article's competitive advantage came from the selective use of sensationalistic terms or buzzwords and phrases appearing regularly as to warrant the familiarity of trust but unique enough to captivate with the thrill of novelty.

Soon the words danced from article to article, displaying different styles and techniques, sometimes subtle, sometimes crude. The dance became as enticing to the reader as the underlying content. In such a dance, some readers create their own perceptions as much as they respond to what they read. The coordination of perception and reaction continued, increasing in fervor, inside the minds of my colleagues, friends, and family—manifesting the most acute responses with utmost subtlety.

I noticed them all: the double looks, the unnatural pauses, the off-kilter body movements, the side-to-side eye sprints, and my favorite—the tight-lipped, blank-faced stare of someone trying but failing to hide emotions, as though by forcing silence, that person can avoid an unwanted conversation. The articles written were rarely discussed aloud; most people maintained a muted silence. But I could feel every word they'd read, line by line, from the looks on their faces.

While most simply avoided discussing the situation, not knowing what to say, some reveled in it, taking liberty to lash out with biting remarks, taunts, and jeers. Others saw opportunity at every twist and self-promotion at every turn.

Many physicians, some within my referral network, turned on me to designate my practice as the epitome of the opioid epidemic in healthcare gone awry, conveniently substituting allegations for facts and suppositions for hard data. They printed inflammatory materials and wrote scathing articles in local newspapers and on their personal blogs discussing my case, while keenly promoting their clinical practices, hoping their efforts toward social justice would net a pretty penny in the process—holding true to the saying, "Never let a good crisis go to waste."

One pain specialist I had referred patients to self-published a scathing editorial, contrasting my indictment with the experiences of physicians who had suffered physical attacks from patients for refusing to prescribe controlled substances. Though these attempts at self-righteousness were thinly veiled self-promotions, they still hurt, and the closer the previous relationship, the more personal the wound.

Hysteria emanating from the opioid epidemic affects how we discuss and understand it and causes extreme responses. The more we simplify the conversation about how the epidemic grew to what it is now, the more we gravitate toward extreme, sensationalized interpretations around its beginnings and who is to blame. By now the terms "irrationality" and "misinformation" define the epidemic as much as the words "addiction" and "fentanyl." When hysteria overtakes rational examination of the epidemic, the conversation is reduced to a never-ending array of accusations.

In this extreme environment, the deluge of articles produced an ensuing storm of words, which led to a war of names, and that gave rise to a lawsuit concerning the right for me to use my own name. The suit was brought by a physician practicing in another state—a physician with whom I have in common the name Jay Joshi. In a world defined by hysteria of the opioid epidemic and the name Jay Joshi instead of John Smith, such a lawsuit is not summarily shelved but instead widely broadcast and displayed to everyone's bewilderment.

Tragedy and comedy bear each other's mark; and what initially appeared as a comedic, frivolous lawsuit tragically aggravated the already polarized criminal case, escalating my case to political pandemonium. The physician filing the lawsuit behaved much like the other physicians who took advantage of my indictment, though his behavior was far more extreme.

He filed a civil lawsuit in federal court, alleging that I was using his name and physician information for financial gain, thereby causing him undue harm. The lawsuit was based upon a trademark statute reserved for corporate conglomerates fighting over brand assets with significant material market value, though he had none of that, which was obvious to all except him.

He was an effective marketer, probably a better marketer than physician. Utilizing his abilities to promote his clinical practice to create a physician brand—and brandishing himself as a physician identity theft expert—he leveraged the publicity of my case to make up for his unsuccessful attempts at securing television shows and media appearances he so desperately sought.

He leveraged political support and marketing firms to promote his lawsuit on major media outlets throughout the country. He then wrote a letter, a verbal tirade, to the judge overseeing my criminal case, lashing invectives and outright insults at me the likes of which boggle my mind. His efforts were remarkable, and if I were not the target of his ire, I would have likely believed some aspects of the lawsuit on the merits of his effort alone.

But interpretations tend to have an air of fleeting imperma- nence. Normally a lawsuit with no merit, no actual evidence, falls apart quite quickly. But he didn't need evidence; he needed only to present an interpretation of a law—and a media campaign to uphold his interpretation. I learned that, in both civil and criminal cases, with the right interpretations, there is no need for actual evidence.

I first tried to dismiss the lawsuit. However, based on the novelty of the legal interpretation, the judge decided against dismissal. The other Dr. Joshi thought this signaled a preliminary victory, issuing another round of articles and press clippings to flaunt that. His goal from the beginning was to secure a settlement, which some might describe as extortion, sadly a bitter reality in today's healthcare.

Newly emboldened, he escalated attempts at a settlement, issuing extension after extension, hoping a protracted legal battle would relinquish any desire to fight legally. He knew the longer the lawsuit drew out, the more audacious the publicity, the greater the chances of a settlement. His attorneys filed a wide array of extensions, some requesting more time to compile evidence, one citing a medical ailment that prevented them from working on the case. Eventually the lawsuit turned into a machination of motions and filings with no explicit intent but to sustain the case.

By introducing new interpretations of law, the other Dr. Joshi influenced the legal proceedings of the case, thereby obtaining undue legitimacy for an argument that had no basis to begin with—in effect, creating the pretense of a possible legal outcome and then using the pretense as an argument for that outcome. This sustained the frivolous lawsuit with no factual basis for years, until a judge finally dismissed it.

CHAPTER 7

IN ANY ATHLETIC COMPETITION, the most observable difference between an amateur and a professional is the level of skill displayed, the former appearing obtusely clumsy and the latter elegantly nuanced. Though the two may be playing by the same set of rules, the contrast in skill levels creates the impression that the athletes are playing two different games. If, in this analogy, the Joshi v. Joshi lawsuit is the amateur, then the DEA and federal prosecutors are the professionals, elegantly navigating the nuances of legal interpretations and court machinations to influence the outcomes of legal proceedings.

After federal prosecutors had completed their investigation, they indicted me on four counts of prescribing outside the scope of medicine, though their initial impressions were based on artful deceptions and subtly contrasting shades of truth and fabrications. Hearing their portrayal, one would assume all manner of colorful conjecture—that I was running a covert drug ring or selling pain pills to undercover agents.

To understand how they got away with painting this portrait, we need to return to the nature of fear.

Fear slithers and slides, glides onto and grows in any patient, healthcare provider, or pharmacist, slides into the interactions that involve opioids, growing seeds of doubt, eroding trust, and creating suspicion. Fear slithered into the minds of my landlord and neighboring tenant when they grew concerned about the outward appearance of my patients, thinking the way a person dresses signifies their likelihood of addiction. Fear slithered into the minds of local and federal law enforcement when they sent undercover agents, one after another, and patient interactions did not validate the interpretations they sought to create. Fear of failing to validate their initial suspicions pushed the investigating officers to become increasingly more aggressive.

Fear grows in the most instinctive parts of our brains, the regions wired for trust; and as fear grows, so does our reluctance to trust. Harmless aspects of a routine day can easily turn into a cesspool of hidden clues and innuendos pointing to every patient as a potential lurking addict. A steel worker still in work clothes seemed to be transformed into a homeless drug addict when visiting my clinic. An elderly woman with lupus and fibromyalgia was denied her prescriptions because she appeared anxious at the pharmacy counter. We regularly encounter such situations in healthcare, where an initial impression, nothing more than a flash pseudo-clinical analysis, goes on to influence decision-making—often without our even realizing it.

When a pharmacist from a local branch of a large pharmacy chain called with concerns about a patient, we discussed the patient, formulated long-term solutions, and even invited regional corporate leaders to discuss pilot programs on medication adherence. When my landlord called to follow up on a patient complaint from a neighboring tenant, we invited her to meet our patients. We even invited the landlord's management representative to sit in our waiting room to observe our patients and the care we provided.

We took an active role in educating the community on safe opioid-prescribing practices and spoke to community leaders and chamber of commerce officials. We engaged in frank conversations with local law enforcement officers about risks that arise when patients file police reports for prescription pills that may or may not have been stolen. We valued community engagement, deeming it integral to comprehensive patient care. We were eager to combat any nascent fear or misunderstandings community members had about our patients.

This makes the heightened focus of law enforcement all the more curious. Despite our making a strong impression in the community and quickly addressing any minor issue that arose, negatives have a way of overwhelming positives, and two factors likely piqued the attention of law enforcement. The first was a patient—a middle-aged man with a history of obesity, diabetes, hypothyroidism, insomnia, and substance use disorder—who presented to the clinic, looking to enroll in the quality model.

While the patient was a complex mix of primary care conditions, law enforcement clearly viewed him only by his addiction disorder. Knowing he was a high-risk patient, we integrated his father into the care plan. But after only two visits, we discovered he was attempting to see multiple physicians. We determined his high-risk behavior was not a good fit for our model. Unfortunately, the patient later overdosed on medications provided by another physician, and numerous illicit substances were detected in his body at his time of death.

We were one of many practices involved in his case, and after sending our medical records to authorities, we assumed the matter was closed.

The second factor that had me on the radar of law enforcement was the scale of counterfeit prescriptions my medical assistant and intern had written. In retrospect, it seems incredulous that I was not aware counterfeit scripts were photocopied and distributed on such a mass scale. I had been overly trusting to a fault.

When I received the letter revealing the scripts the medical assistant had prescribed to herself, I was not aware of the scale of her activities. I believed filing a police report would be sufficient to address the issue. I found the script templates and photocopied scripts long after filing the police report, and long after my indictment. When I attempted to present this evidence to the prosecutor through my attorney, it was withheld as evidence in the case.

Somewhere along the course of the few short months my clinic was open, a series of incidental, isolated events that most would perceive to be part of a normal clinic coalesced into a criminal investigation that created a vastly dark interpretation of my clinic and patients. I cannot differentiate any one incident as an instigating factor, but the counterfeit scripts clearly piqued the interest of law enforcement and subsequently became the focus of their investigation.

After I filed the police report, law enforcement agents went on to question the medical assistant, not about her forgeries but about my clinic, my patients, and me. They asked her wide-ranging, open-ended questions, more to validate their preconceived perceptions than to collect meaningful evidence about her forgeries.

The agents asked her to confirm whether my patients were

drug addicts, as though she were qualified to make such a judgment. They asked her to specify which patients were addicts, and she provided a list that included many who had legitimate medical conditions but at one time or another had frustrated her. Back and forth they went, asking to verify what they already believed, and she answered willingly, giving them the responses they sought, perjury be damned.

Subsequent to her encounter with law enforcement, the medical assistant recruited patients to testify against me. She reached out to patients, encouraging them to make false statements against me to Munster police officers, sometimes even inviting patients to her house. This was all done to create the impression she was an unwilling employee in a criminal pill mill enterprise—a false impression the Munster police were happy to support.

If you repeatedly stroke a paintbrush on canvas, over and over, the hue naturally darkens, making the contrast between the color and the blank canvas more extreme. If investigators perpetuate an investigation only to look for what they seek to find, inevitably they interpret what they find as what they were looking for. Law enforcement sent multiple undercover agents, posing as patients, looking for something—anything—to substantiate the impressions they had already formed.

When they found nothing, they pursued my clinic all the more aggressively, tilling the soil for further grounds of investigation. Their growing aggression compelled them to take extreme measures, and like phases of matter changing under extreme pressure, select pieces of evidence were changed, manipulated, or outright disregarded.

The police report I filed conveniently went missing when the DEA detained and interrogated me. When the report was submitted into evidence, it had been tampered with, to state the forgeries were never mentioned. False statements became true when it was necessary for them to be true, and true statements became obsolete when that was convenient. Soon, a mound of evidence was built upon false statements from the medical assistant, police reports that had been tampered with, and deliberate misinterpretations of patient care I had provided. This would have been a flimsy pretext in any other time, but during the era of the opioid epidemic, it was the basis of evidence presented to a grand jury that indicted me.

CHAPTER 8

A POLARIZING LENS selectively permits certain rays of light to enter while reflecting others away, manipulating what can be seen. With the right shading, any desired interpretation can be formed, any set of unrelated facts and events can be correlated, and any half-truths or direct lies can be transformed into testimonies.

My indictment was based on a statute called the Controlled Substance Act (CSA). This act mostly addresses the distribution or possession of illicit drugs, with severity of sentencing based on the type and quantity of the substance, or the amount of cash found in presumed possession to purchase the substance. In other words, the crime and punishment center around the substance and the quantity.

When applied to healthcare, the law becomes a series of interpretations, primarily of the prescriber's behavior relative to that of the patient. Therefore, the basis of the criminal act is defined not quantitatively, as it would be under most circumstances, but descriptively. In the healthcare world, adhering to CSA requirements depends on whether the prescriber's behavior fits the perception of the investigating officer. When the perception does not match his or her interpretation, it's deemed that the law has been violated.

Past interpretations of the law add to the ambiguity by using broad, poorly defined language that confuses more than clarifies. According to prior legal interpretations, if a physician prescribes a controlled substance over the "course of clinical care, as part of a bona fide medical practice," then the prescription is valid. If not, the law has been violated.

If a patient obtains a controlled substance to "relieve the suffering incident to an addiction," the prescription is valid; but if a patient obtains it to "cater to the cravings of an addict," the law has been violated. But describing sufferings or cravings easily differs, depending on who is interpreting the behavior and on its underlying context.

Determining a patient's addiction cannot be done objectively. In the past, this revolved around a changing array of subjective assessments that depended on the case, and on the biases of the investigating officer. With no firm basis to define lawful or unlawful activity, previous cases have looked at other aspects of each encounter for context. But for investigating law enforcement agents, regardless of what transpires during an encounter, prescribing medication is not perceived as simply one component of patient care but the center of *all* patient care. This effectively recontextualizes the patient encounter to create biased, inconsistent interpretations that can be harmful to the patient.

Historically, the frequency of convictions utilizing this law in healthcare reflects the different drug epidemics that have come and gone over the past decades, with various medications targeted by law enforcement, changing over the course of time. During the 1960s, law enforcement focused on medications with psychedelic effects in the same way law enforcement focuses on opioid prescriptions during the epidemic.

These convictions target encounters in which a patient received a prescription for a controlled substance that was justified, and they are based on a specific behavior or act during the encounter that could be interpreted as falling below the standards of good clinical care. Factors might include the time spent with patients, the documentation during the encounter, the presence of a physical examination, the amount charged per visit, or whether the compensation was directly related to the quantity of medications prescribed. Deeming that behavior, that specific transgression, as representative of the entire encounter, turns the whole of patient interaction into a crime and places the prescription outside the scope of medicine, and therefore illegal.

In my case, the interpretation included elements outside of the patient encounter—the number of counterfeit scripts and the false statements made by those counterfeiting the scripts. There was also a reinterpretation of my physical exam—not the lack of a physical exam, but the interpretation of my musculoskeletal examination of the pseudo patient, the undercover agent.

DEA agents claimed that, during the first visit, I did not examine the legs as comprehensively as *they* deemed necessary—despite my observing no structural damage and noting the patient was able to place weight on the leg. They created their legal argument with the notion I had not done enough of a physical examination.

Based on that interpretation of the patient encounter—their perception of, not the absence of, a physical exam—coupled with the excessively high number of prescriptions (though they were not counting them as counterfeit), the DEA set about reinterpreting all aspects of my clinical practice. The undercover agent was no longer posing as a patient but a drug addict. He was not a hypertensive truck driver with cramp-like leg pain, but a drug addict with whom I was complicit. By tapering his pain medications, I was enabling an addict.

When I ordered a urine drug screen, requested medical records, reviewed his prescription history, and prescribed non-opioid alternatives to address the root cause of his symptoms, I was enabling an addict. When I ordered an imaging study to assess for long-term bone damage to help him understand the effects of long-term opioid use on bone density, I was enabling an addict. When he requested additional pain medications, to which I responded by tapering and adding non-opioid alternatives, I was enabling an addict.

With such inaccurate interpretations of the law, clinical care disintegrates into a set of acts, each viewed in isolation, each vulnerable to a variety of perceptions. Healthcare providers make a series of decisions in parallel, based on clinical data, as they appear. In law, facts are placed in an arrangement to create an argument, well after the alleged incident has occurred.

Healthcare is dynamic, and every patient encounter has a substantial amount of uncertainty. Good clinical care thrives on making optimal decisions in the face of uncertainty, as patient care changes with new information, and clinical decisions adjust with new facts. An "addict" as perceived by law enforcement, through the right therapy and medication, may just as easily become a "patient with an addiction," a substance use disorder—just as a "patient with an addiction" as perceived by the medical community, through distrust and abrupt discontinuations of medications, may easily become labeled an "addict."

What defines part of a whole changes when the whole is still developing its parts. Specific elements in a patient encounter cannot define the full essence of ongoing patient care. Absent any clinical knowledge or background, law enforcement agents interpret clinical actions through what is familiar to them. They view the patient encounter as the setting for a drug transaction, reducing the patient care decision-making into a discrete set of actions that can be interpreted and manipulated from the perspective of individuals trained to see drug deals. As a consequence, legal interpretations have now come to define the standards of clinical care.

Any change in legal interpretations creates a cascade of clinical changes, setting new standards and perspectives. Any provider deviating from the legally defined standards is met with suspicion; and for many providers, the fear of being suspected or targeted leads them to project their fear onto their patients, and soon fear fills the patient encounter with suspicion and paranoia. A strange resulting pattern forms between provider and patient, each too fearful to do anything that may be interpreted as criminal, each willing to sacrifice good clinical care at the altar of fear.

Physicians justify discontinuing medications, delaying prescribing medications, or requiring an imaging study or urine drug screen prior to prescribing medications—in effect, transacting legal risk for additional, unnecessary medical tests and imaging studies that may help the provider avoid legal scrutiny but adversely affect quality of care. If the quality of clinical care is to be defined, and subsequently restricted, by the legal interpretations set by law enforcement agents, who keenly watch the actions of physicians, then who is to watch the watchmen?

We accept rule of law because we believe it sets a firm

standard for moral conduct, the law serving as a proxy for good behavior. But when the interpretation of law becomes extreme, it no longer represents the public. It represents only itself, existing for its own sake, as a necessary evil that is no longer necessary. The original purpose of the law is lost, shifting rule of law to abuse of power.

CHAPTER 9

MY DECISION to enter a plea bargain never felt like a real decision, but instead a foregone conclusion. Though hardly ever stated explicitly, the understanding was that if I were indicted by a grand jury, then it was presumed I did something wrong. Under that perception, the indictment was not an opportunity to explain and defend myself, but a tragedy to accept and mourn. Any attempt to fight the inevitable was considered merely a stage in the grieving process.

I felt trapped and manipulated, my ability to defend myself weakened as my legal options dwindled to nothing but inaction. I felt defiance and disgust that my identity—as a physician, as a person—could so quickly give way to the extremism that engulfed and defined me. Soon enough, any attempt to justify or rationalize was met with tacit silence, pressed lips, and expressive eyes balancing sorrow and condemnation. Perception became my harsh new reality, defined by the prosecutor who selectively created the impressions needed to obtain his desired outcome.

The prosecutor obtained a grand jury indictment by focusing publicly and overtly on the undercover agent's visits, as well as on the actions and perjured statements of my medical assistant. To coerce a plea agreement, he impressed upon me directly and covertly the regulatory violations of the collaborative agreements I had used in the patient transitions. He claimed the regulatory policies could be considered criminal, and that he would superimpose additional charges if I were not to plead guilty.

Two separate legal strategies—one public, the other private; one to indict, the other to convict through plea... This was the prosecutor's desired intent from the outset. The pressure to enter into a plea bargain grew heavier with every article, every motion, every misrepresentation gone unchecked, and every legal interpretation twisted and perpetuated, until I stagnated into a state of helplessness, weighing whatever limited options I had left.

After my indictment, I thought, naively, that I could resolve the matter like I had resolved other issues in my clinic, through open and honest communication. I called the police station, where I had been detained, to schedule a meeting to speak with the Munster police officer leading their opioid awareness initiatives. Surprisingly, he invited me to meet later that day.

We discussed the clinic, the quality model, strategies for patient care, and opportunities for physicians and police officers to work together in managing high-risk patients. We spent a significant amount of time discussing how trust in the clinical setting is essential for high-quality, cost-effective medicine. The meeting went well, and the officer invited me to future community events. I left the meeting feeling content, decidedly confident that the officer had the right impression of me.

Then my phone rang.

My attorney blasted me for doing something apparently so reckless, so foolhardy, that to the interpretive eyes of the prosecutor must have been an attempt to manipulate the police to my advantage. I quickly realized there were no upcoming events or collaborations; there was only the legal case and its interpretations. From then on, I knew the die had been cast. The stain of criminality had left an indelible impression that could not be removed as long as the legal proceedings continued.

At that point, defiance became delusion, and I was left with no legal recourse and no ability to speak the truth. I stopped fighting. Anger became arrogance, so I stopped getting angry. Sadness gave way to acceptance, and I agreed to accept the plea agreement.

My eyes grew heavy under a lingering shame that overtook my face whenever I looked at my wife and now six-month-old son, feeling the sorrow of unconditional support in every broken smile.

My mind never agreed to what my hand eventually signed. I never believed I'd committed a crime over the course of patient care—and, to be honest, I believe I was entrapped. Entrapment consists of two parts: inducement and predisposition. Inducement is when law enforcement directly forces a person to commit a crime, and predisposition is when the government influences a person to behave out of character, thereby committing a crime. How is this anything but an attempt to induce me into a crime? When no crime could be induced, law enforcement imposed intense pressure that led to administrative oversights in the collaborative agreements.

I provided good care to a patient who claimed to have a history of leg pain and behaved as if he were a compliant patient. He was agreeable to lowering his pain medication and to imaging studies once his insurance coverage was activated. This led me to believe he was a patient with legitimate medical issues.

The prosecutor argued that prescribing any opioid medication was illegal, and that by trusting the patient, I violated the law by violating my duty as a physician. He cited the phrase that represents a physician's civic duty: "Do no harm." Prosecutors and DEA agents take this phrase and interpret it to mean any prescription they believe is medically unnecessary is immediately illegal, regardless of context. In my case, they used the phrase to imply that I blindly trusted an undercover agent by prescribing medication based on his presenting symptoms rather than requiring verification before prescribing any medication. They turned my trust of a patient into a criminal act.

Blind trust is irresponsible and simply bad medicine. However, so is immediately distrusting and requiring the patient to verify medical conditions before treatment is administered. In finding a balance in trusting and verifying, I performed my duty to someone I had every reason to believe had legitimate medical conditions.

I believe I chose the right balance of verification and trust. I believe I was induced. But what I believe matters less than what they interpreted. And that made all the difference.

CHAPTER 10

THE DAY OF SENTENCING was long overdue. After numerous motions to delay and defer under vague, poorly defined explanations, it was months in the making. By then, the acute apprehension of anticipating a sudden event had dulled into an emptiness in which the uncertainty of waiting overtook the fear of any potential ruling. However, it was not dull enough to remove the emotions of each delay and each period of waiting for motion after motion to be addressed. With the weight of existential dread, I felt a heaviness that progressed into a gravitas of suspense.

While dread lingered in the back of my mind, front and center was this odd feeling, an unusual sense of lacking—not worthlessness, but an absence of feeling, a nothingness that had come to fill my thoughts. I completed my morning routine, solemnly focused on each action in front of me, keenly noting the toothbrush in my mouth and the razor against my face.

But I was not capable of thinking about anything, the thoughts just not forming. I hardly recognized what I saw in the mirror. My face, once proud and beaming, looked withered and wrinkled, lined with the crevices of stress. Somehow, I mustered just enough clarity to make it to the courthouse with my family.

When we arrived, my state of mind proved prescient. I had sensed in advance what was obvious when we walked in. Long gone were the pleasantries, the cordial exchanges of courtesies among law enforcement, court officers, and my family. These were replaced with a stern, determined look on the prosecutor's face, like that of a soldier lining up for battle, with the probation officer following in step, bracing themselves for the carnage.

The prosecutor initially assigned to my case was now accompanied by a second federal prosecutor. When I approached the courtroom, the two were huddled together, stealing intense glances in my direction. When I inquired as to why the government needed a second prosecutor, I was told the first prosecutor was busy with other cases—contradicting the reasoning for all the delays and motions that had been requested to give the initial prosecutor additional time to prepare for the case. But when law is interpretation, reason and contradiction are interchangeable. I knew the most likely reason—intense media scrutiny—yet that was never explicitly stated.

I sat on the right side of the defense table. From my point of view, I could see the judge's bench just off to the right. To the left, closer to me, was the prosecutors' table. My family sat in the pews—my parents, wife, and in-laws. I could see them only by turning my head fully to the left. I saw my reflection in their faces. I saw the shame. The sense of hopelessness that had long been imprinted on my face after months of toiling through legal proceedings was now firmly imprinted on their faces, too.

The probation officer sat directly behind me—a fitting location, as I felt his presence breathing down my neck at the most critical juncture of the sentencing. Aside from the court officers and clerks, the room was relatively empty, a symbol of the underlying emptiness at the heart of the media spectacle populating the internet for nearly a year and a half.

In the plea agreement, I agreed to plead guilty on one count, one visit, nominally the last visit—though the exact visit I pleaded to was never explicitly defined and was interpreted differently depending on who you ask. This was based on the premise that instead of tapering the medications gradually, I should have terminated the medications entirely, in spite of that being a horrible recommendation in clinical care.

But after the plea was submitted, the prosecutors reinterpreted my plea to include every prescription medication I'd prescribed to the undercover agent. This was now quantified by the pill count over the course of the agent's four visits—and every pill prescribed to patients during the transition period. So, anything involved in my case, however remote or irrelevant, became very relevant and somehow legally permissible.

Every pill I prescribed to the undercover agent was calculated into a number based on a sentencing guideline normally reserved for calculations in traditional drug-dealing crimes. What was intended to be a prescription for a limited, one-month supply of medications per visit became a massive month-long supply of drugs tabulated into a set of guidelines equating one pill of Norco to kilograms worth of marijuana.

Any patient who received medications during the transition period, regardless of whether the medication was crucial to an underlying medical condition, was automatically perceived to be an addict illegally receiving drugs. How much of the patient care was interpreted as a crime, versus how much was clinically necessary, became the main point of contention in the sentencing.

The sentencing began in a way befitting the theatrics of the past months, with a series of video clippings—scenes from when the DEA detained and interrogated me. These were proudly portrayed, as if by displaying the detainment, the events would not only become legally justified but also become evidence of my culpability. The scenes said much of nothing, yet screamed loudly and dramatically, and were clearly intended to intimidate me.

As the video footage was shown, the courtroom devolved into a vulgar display of the extreme investigational tactics that constituted the prosecutor's argument. One scene showed me crying hysterically, begging the agents to understand that I was a good physician. Another showed the agents blatantly deceiving me under false pretenses into signing documents that restricted my prescribing abilities.

While viewing the clips, the shock and horrors of that day resurfaced, renewing my shame and humiliation when I needed to be alert and vigilant. But on it went, until the videos became nothing more than a Kafkaesque display of prose-cutors publicly humiliating me, passing taunts and insults as arguments in the absence of any evidence or solid claims.

I was visibly relieved when the videos ended, but I should have known the worst was yet to come. I should have heeded the warnings of Kafka's doorkeeper; I would have realized that the videos, though painfully humiliating, were "only the low-liest." What came next was far more heinous: testimony from the highest-ranking DEA agent on the case, one of the two agents who had detained and interrogated me.

The agent had a cold, derisive smile that grew into a toothy grin upon seeing me, revealing his Machiavellian sense of justice, exposing his desire for draconian punishments. He'd played many roles during the investigation and would now play a role during each stage of sentencing. He first sat with the prosecutors, advising them while the videos played. He then walked directly to the witness stand, shapeshifting from an adviser to the prosecution's first witness in the sentencing hearing.

He weaved a fancy tale and spoke with a deliberate cadence, meticulously parsing his words to maximize their effect while minimizing the risk of being held liable by them. He was vague when necessary, specific if possible, and made wide-ranging statements to encompass truths, half-truths, and outright lies, all interlaced.

When asked how many patients I saw in a day, he replied, "thirty to sixty," knowing I saw up to thirty patients a day but including an upper range to make sure the total prescription count so proudly disseminated would fit within the daily patient tally he stated. He had obtained illicit access to my medical records and knew I typically scheduled twenty-five to thirty patients per day. By skewing the numbers to an outer range, he deliberately created the impression I saw more patients and wrote more prescriptions than I did.

When asked how he first came to investigate me, he cited some esoteric database but left out details on how it functioned. He was keen to sidestep providing an answer to the original intent of the question, substituting an insult by calling me a crooked physician. This struck me as a peculiar thing to say, considering that when the agents deceived me into signing the prescriber restriction documents, they had appealed to my concerns for my patients' well-being—an odd tactic to use on an allegedly crooked physician.

When asked about my medical assistant, the agent lied and

said they attempted to investigate her but that I had not been cooperative—transforming the police report to outright lies, to no police report, to obstruction of justice. When he stepped down from the stand, he returned to his seat next to the prosecutors, and again shapeshifted, this time from being a witness to coaching a witness.

The witness he now coached was my employee, at least for a day—the nurse I had hired to help my patients transition their clinical care. After talking to the intern, she had grown afraid she could be targeted as I was, so to protect herself, she helped the intern compile evidence against me. Just a few weeks after leaving my office, the nurse spoke with the DEA agent, who coached her as a witness for the trial with instructions to answer questions a certain way.

She was told to answer "yes" when asked during sentencing if I had prescribed medications outside the scope of medicine—meaning for no legitimate medical purpose—to patients she and I had seen together. She happily did so, knowing she was being asked to lie, but too scared to refuse. In her attempt to balance honesty with perjury, she interpreted the phrase to mean something else entirely—outside the scope of medicine, and for my practice only, not in general.

She reasoned that the patients had legitimate medical conditions with real clinical needs. They needed the medications prescribed, but only if they received their medications elsewhere. The irrationality of this stance became even more evident in the cross-examination.

When asked in broad terms if I was prescribing outside the scope of medicine, the nurse testified that I had. But when asked about specific patients, she admitted that the patients cited had legitimate medical conditions and needed the medications given within the course of their clinical care. Back and forth it went, a different answer for the same question, depending on who asked it—the prosecutor or my attorney. Truth disintegrated, and every person in the courtroom witnessed the dissolution, particularly the judge. He grew more incensed with every contradictory response, each display of doublespeak, eventually boiling over and venting his frustration by denouncing the speculative nature of the prosecutor's argument. The judge then abruptly left, fuming, through the chamber door, prolonging the already prolonged sentencing into a sordid two-day affair.

CHAPTER 11

THE SECOND DAY OF SENTENCING did not arrive until a month later, sending my family and me back into the abyss of existential dread, the vastness of the unknown, of uncertainty, submerged in the hollow heaviness of waiting.

The first day had revealed glaring incoherence in the legal case against me. Arguments hinged on various conjectures from dubious sources which, when analyzed closely, could be reduced to speculation and contradiction. Prosecutors selectively interpreted specific events at specific levels of granularity. If too broad, the interpretations had no relevance; if too focused, they showed the quality of patient care I provided, revealing all my efforts to prevent diversion and address abuse potential.

If the first day of sentencing revealed how fragile and vulnerable the prosecution team's legal arguments were, the second displayed their seething anger in learning how fragile and vulnerable their argument turned out to be. Day two began with another witness called by the prosecutor—an attorney representing the state's medical licensing board. He was peppered with questions that effectively restated the same premise: the prescriber collaborative agreements were invalid. Prosecutors attempted to connect flawed documentation with actual criminal behavior, but they managed to assemble only conjectures that lacked any underlying basis.

Prosecutors then showed another video, this one of my first encounter with the undercover agent—actually, an excerpt that covered only a few moments. The clip showed less than a minute of the entire encounter. I was about to begin the physical exam, while finishing a conversation about a television show I thought the patient might like. I was using small talk to build a healthy doctor-patient relationship. Just as I was about to examine him, the video cut out in point-black fashion, transitioning to fuzzy, inaudible audio and curtailing any video of the physical exam I performed. After a few seconds of inarticulate mumblings, the audio ended.

In selecting that clip, and only showing a segment of it, prosecutors portrayed that initial encounter and all subsequent encounters as lacking appropriate physical examinations, even though the edited video hardly resembled or represented what had taken place during the encounters. The video portrayal left out my discussion with the patient about opioid use and abuse, my request for imaging studies and urine drug screens, and the tapering strategies.

However bizarre all of this may seem, it was not even the most bizarre event. That designation belongs to something that happened immediately before sentencing. Standing at the entrance of the courtroom was my office landlord, accompanied by the DEA agent and speaking at length with the prosecutors before sentencing was to resume at the start of the day. I do not know all that was said, and I was not told about it afterward; but seeing all of them standing together, my mind immediately raced back to the last conversation I'd had with my landlord.

It was a phone call nearly six months before sentencing, and a week after I had to terminate the lease because I could no longer practice. She had called, threatening to make me pay the remainder of what was owed on the lease beyond the termination penalty fee. Or else, she stated, she would ensure that I would suffer. She said she'd been told I was definitely going to prison and that she hoped it would be for a long time. Her threat loomed large in my mind as I watched them from the defense table. The landlord's call had taken only a few minutes, but its impression lingered for months.

Now here she was, present at my sentencing, seemingly to watch her words come to fruition. Silently observing, she sat next to my family, ensuring I saw her every time I looked at them. She did not say anything to me before, during, or after sentencing. She did not have to, as her actions spoke louder than any additional threat.

When it came time to present my defense, we brought the only evidence I thought I would ever need: my patients. We had more than thirty patient letters and six patient affidavits, and three patients appeared as witnesses. I would have had more if not for a recommended limit on the number of patients, who all testified to the quality of care received in the clinic under my guidance. My patients wrote beautifully and spoke from their hearts, and to this day I remain grateful. A physician cannot ask for anything more than the trust and respect of his patients. I received that in abundance.

The prosecutors had nothing to present in response—no patient letters, specific clinical actions, claims, or tangible evidence. Instead, they tried to claim the letters were distortions or fabrications. They had no meaningful, valid retort. But then, the prosecutors had no need for a response, for evidence, or for any type of rebuttal. Interpretations were all they needed.

Every argument began and ended by citing the infamous prescription number—a number prosecutors knew was based on forgeries of the medical assistant and intern. They nevertheless touted these numbers over and over as definitive proof of my criminal behavior. Within these arguments resided circumstantial and anecdotal claims passing as evidence—that if I could make lapses in prescriber partnership agreements, then I must have behaved criminally throughout my entire practice.

That was the core of the case against me, of every argument prosecutors attempted to bring forward. Like the revolving moon changes faces, the changing arguments revealed the inconsistencies in and incoherence of each argument. At times, the salutation "doctor" was used to argue that I should have known better or been more diligent. At other times, the salutation "mister" was used to argue that my trusting patients and believing their symptoms was somehow criminally negligent and medically reckless.

There were times when the prosecutors criticized my medical record-keeping without a real understanding of what was in the records. Without any medical justification, they challenged the presenting symptoms of pain for a paraplegic injured in a motor vehicle accident and a post-operative patient who developed a surgical wound infection. They felt that since they did not need pain medications for their own medical procedures, pain medications were not necessary for other patients, either. "I never needed them," I overheard one of the prosecutors muttering while my defense attorney presented patient testimonials.

Most of the time, it seemed the prosecutors were simply

unaware of the basics in clinical medicine—what it means to care for patients, treat their conditions, and trust what they tell you. They simplified healthcare into contrived interpretations, and clinical decision-making into isolated acts taken out of context, undermining the validity of the law by creating legal arguments that compensated through quantity what was lacking in quality.

However unbelievable this may seem to you, imagine how it appeared to the judge, who alternated between expressing confusion and annoyance. Soon, he gave way to impatience, much like on the first day; after stewing in frustration, he called a recess to the deliberations. He said he had heard enough and would make his final ruling after the recess.

The judge's call for recess was important enough, but his subsequent calls were even more important. He beckoned the DEA agent into his private chamber. The agent transformed yet again, this time into a private confidante, which now completed the metamorphoses of roles into his most lethal form.

As the DEA agent stood up to follow the judge, he and my landlord glanced at each other. The two exchanged nods before the DEA agent walked to the chamber door leading to the judge's private quarters. In mid-stride he looked—through me, past me—to the probation officer sitting behind me. The agent gave another nod, with an added twist of the neck that signaled the probation officer to follow him.

Frozen in suspense, I heard the movements of the chair behind me—every squeak, a paralyzing shriek. I looked from the corner of my right eye, still afraid to betray any head movements, and saw the two men walking in unison toward the chamber door. I sat in stunned silence, feeling the weight of the moment, unable to respond. Yet I understood. Fully aware but helpless, I knew from that sequence of nods that the ruling had been made.

Whatever was to follow—closing arguments, my plea for mercy, the judge's taunts—were mere formalities, pageantries. The closing act of this interpretive rendition was finalized with the shutting of the chamber door, leaving along the way my due process, my liberties, and—in due time—everything else... even my freedom.

INTERLUDE

A prism refracts light into a spectrum of colors, different colors bending at different angles. Each angle reflects an impression along my journey from the physician's office to the federal courthouse—each angle, each word, each piece lost.

When my loss was complete, so was my search; but within nothingness, I soon found meaning. I found meaning in pain, all forms of pain: pain experienced in the moment, pain recollected, pain that comes after the fact, pain of injury, pain from disease, pain exacerbated by stress-inducing activities... Pain is sometimes a cause and other times an effect, but it is always interdependent. Pain is both logical and illogical, appearing uniquely to you or to me.

To find meaning in pain is to distill it all into a single fact—that we all experience pain. Each painful experience is equally valid and truthful, meriting equal standards of care. An undue burden, the burden of pain, is transformed when distributed across a medically appropriate balance.

C. S. Lewis once said, "They wanted to be nouns, but they were…mere adjectives." We perceive pain to be an independent experience, but it cannot exist on its own. Pain can only describe a more fundamental, underlying understanding. When we recognize that distinction, we find the right solutions.

Now let us continue.

PART 2

THE SOLUTION

CHAPTER 12

"You are remembered for the rules you break," General Douglas MacArthur famously said. Once the DEA's investigation of me commenced, their interpretations of the Controlled Substance Act (CSA) came to define me. What began as a series of concocted hunches evolved into a full-scale investigation, culminating in an indictment, a plea agreement, and my being sentenced to imprisonment. Such an evolution reflects how current drug epidemics and figurative public health wars influence healthcare.

Winston Churchill's quip on lies is alarmingly accurate: "A lie is halfway round the world before the truth has got its boots on." Once allowed to spread, misinformation morphs into a blend of fine art and quantitative science, as Malcolm Gladwell describes in his analysis of virality and information dissemination.

Gladwell observed that we wrongly believe information moves person to person, when it actually goes from one source to many people, in a geometric progression in which the speed of spread depends on both the message and the messenger. When my first round of employees forged scripts under my name, the DEA noticed. When the first employee was caught, reported, and fired, she made a desperate attempt to deflect culpability by spinning wild narratives about my patients to local police. Soon, my landlord and neighboring tenants were involved. The intrigue of such claims proved too provocative to ignore; and such conjecture, repeated ad infinitum, became the basis of an investigation.

The federal government, for all its technological sophistication, is surprisingly dependent on individual complaint filings. These can be valuable resources, but only when the source of information and course of investigation are legally and ethically sound. To administer justice fairly, every investigation must be based on valid information. Absent any evidence in my case, the DEA relied on vaguely defined interpretations of a patient encounter as the basis for the investigation, and the high number of scripts to secure an indictment.

Lacking objective data, the interpretations created the legal arguments. DEA agents constructed a narrative of criminal behavior through the thinnest of suspicions, creating a skewed version of reality by omitting certain evidence and reinterpreting other evidence. In the process, the agents revealed their lack of understanding in applying the CSA to healthcare-related situations.

The DEA agent posing as a patient who came to my clinic trained in Quantico, Virginia, at an interdepartmental federal training academy that works with federal agents as well as local and regional law enforcement agents. DEA agents accepted to train at the facility work alongside FBI agents as part of a narcotics training program that includes little to no direct healthcare education. Most of the sparse healthcare training at the facility focuses on financial crimes—such as insurance fraud—correlating criminal healthcare behavior with ill-gotten financial gains instead of discerning whether specific clinical actions or decisions are criminal in nature.

As a result, federal agents repeatedly make mistakes when applying broad, generalized techniques for criminal investigations to healthcare, without regard for the unique characteristics that distinguish healthcare from other fields. The most common transgression is the violation of patient confidentiality statutes known as the Health Insurance Portability and Accountability Act, or HIPAA.

Numerous FBI investigations have been cited for violating patient confidentiality laws, usually because agents are simply unaware that a person's medical records warrant privacy. In my case, the lead DEA agent obtained access to all the patient records by requesting the username and password from a phlebotomist working in my clinic. He, too, violated HIPAA protection laws, apparently unaware that an employee cannot authorize the release of patient records.

The agent who posed as a patient at my clinic used a recording device, called a wire, which was not designed to withstand the physical exams I performed. During his four encounters, his principal goal was to entice specific actions that could be construed as crimes. These included requesting additional pain medications for his girlfriend and asking to be treated without proper documentation. Although I properly addressed these over the course of all four patient encounters, it did not matter. The entire investigation distilled into a distorted analysis of isolated, individual acts absent any clinical context.

A clinical encounter is more than a series of discrete actions. It is an experience through which patients and providers, such as physicians or nurses, discuss medical symptoms and develop treatment plans. Any discussions about clinical care, any mention of opioid deterrence, were ignored and deemed inconsequential in court arguments when compared to a specific or perceived act. Approaching a patient encounter this way distorts clinical care outside of its natural context. This is concerning, since the communication and trust between provider and patient, and the context of the encounter, define the essence of healthcare.

Trust is more important than any specific act and should merit the greatest focus in evaluating a patient encounter. It should be the basis for determining whether a clinical exchange is inherently criminal. An agent trained to solicit illicit drug exchanges sees the entire patient encounter as a crime—and the act of prescribing medication as a criminal transaction. But, as a physician treating a patient, I perceive prescribing medications as one act in a series of actions and decisions in relation to the whole patient encounter.

These differing perceptions of a patient encounter led to different interpretations of each individual act. From the undercover agent's perspective, he tried to solicit a crime by instigating specific criminal acts that would violate standards of clinical care. Absent any outright egregious act on my part, the investigation dissolved into interpretations of individual actions that transpired during the clinical encounter. A clinical decision made in the moment, based on trusting the patient, came to be seen as a criminal act retroactively.

Ironically, and perhaps most tragically, the DEA agents never fully understood the ramifications of their actions. They never explored alternative, more moderate, curative approaches to the investigation. They never questioned what made up the source of or basis for the investigation, only indirectly referring to the physical appearance of my patients as disheveled and therefore suspicious, and the employee who was responsible for the uptick in prescriptions.

From there, the investigation steamrolled. A search warrant was obtained, based on false statements from the original medical assistant—the same employee who wrote all those prescriptions. With nothing more than conjectures, DEA agents took liberties to separate me from my employees and patients while they searched my clinic, detained and interrogated me in a holding cell, and presented documents for me to sign while I was under duress. After the day of the raid, agents perpetuated instability and fear by calling my patients and intimidating my employees into providing confidential medical records.

What DEA agents reinterpreted during the investigation mirrored how prosecutors later reinterpreted the CSA, using misinformation as evidence for a legal argument. An incomplete series of statements and circumstantial arrangements became the basis for a legal argument based on a novel interpretation of the law, derived by selectively choosing certain pieces of evidence and omitting others.

Employee statements were manipulated, nurses were coached to perjure under oath with predetermined responses, and the police report was doctored or discarded. Kafka phrased it best: "There are many fine details in which the court gets lost, but in the end it reaches into some place where originally there was nothing and pulls enormous guilt out of it."

But my criminal case is not a novel on irrationality. It is a case study of an all-too-common phenomenon in legalities surrounding the opioid epidemic: skewing the law to the point where the distorted legal interpretation becomes the argument while disregarding the underlying medical context. As a result, legal arguments succumb to errors of logic that produce inaccurate and inconsistent outcomes. Voltaire observed this centuries ago in *Candide*: "Imagine every possible contradiction and inconsistency—you will find them in all law courts."

In 2020, two individuals posing as patients with pain disorders were found guilty in federal court for feigning injuries and then selling the opioids prescribed by physicians who believed their presenting symptoms to be legitimate. The trust those physicians exhibited in that case was perceived to be in response to a conspiracy on the part of the two patients. Though the two individuals exhibited similar behaviors as the undercover agent who appeared before me, the trust I exhibited toward a purported patient was deemed criminal, unlike the physicians in the other case.

Reinterpreting a law while distorting its underlying context is not an effective legal strategy in most situations. While an otherwise incomplete argument can become stronger through a novel interpretation of the law, concealing a flawed argument under the guise of reinterpretation introduces flawed logic. When federal prosecutors could not find any specific criminal act, they reinterpreted the law to claim that my physical exam was insufficient. They argued that if my physical exam was not comprehensive enough, then the entire patient encounter should be interpreted as criminal. Prosecutors used that line of logic to suggest that my entire patient population was comprised of drug addicts.

As shocking as this may sound, it is nothing new. The CSA has a long history of being widely distorted. Its language provides little to no guidance in interpreting the law in medically appropriate ways. Instead, the law states that providers are liable for "prescribing outside of the scope of medicine."

In response to the opioid epidemic, prosecutors initially

sidestepped the issue of intent and focused on interpreting the above phrase relative to specific actions that transpire during a patient encounter. This tactic allows prosecutors to choose which actions constitute evidence and ignore other actions when reinterpreting clinical care as criminal.

Recently, the Supreme Court stepped in to restore a sense of sanity to the interpretation of the CSA. The high court requires that physicians convicted under the CSA must exhibit criminal intent, known as mens rea; but for many, the ruling came too late. For patients who have suffered throughout the opioid epidemic, the legal victory rings hollow and provides little recourse for their years of agony. Sadly, it will do little in dissuading law enforcement from concocting further interpretations and has not led to a consistent approach to interpreting the CSA across all federal courts.

Throughout its history, the CSA has been interpreted as a reaction to mass public outcries. The CSA was enacted in the early twentieth century and has been amended repeatedly, with many changes altering the law based on whichever drug is anointed as the cause of the then-current epidemic. Over time, the frequency of amendments and convictions stemming from the law's reinterpretations mirrored the intensity of government response to certain forms of drug abuse, like growth rings on a tree.

In the 1960s and 1970s, the law focused on stimulants and antidepressants the same way it more recently has focused on opioids. But for all its faults, the CSA remains the main vehicle for the federal government to convict drug crimes. In the opioid epidemic, it is being used against healthcare providers who government officials perceive as instigators and continued contributors to the epidemic.

This narrative oversimplifies the complexity of opioid overdoses, as seen in the incongruent trends on mortality, or death rate. The Centers for Disease Control's Life Expectancy Report found a general trend over the years of 2018–2020 that, excluding methadone, overdose rates had decreased. Lethal overdose rates for prescription opioids oxycodone and hydrocodone decreased alongside rates for heroin.

Mortality improvements from opioid overdoses were predominant in states previously most affected by the epidemic: Indiana, Kentucky, Ohio, and Pennsylvania. These are the same regions where the mortality of individuals ages twenty-five to sixty-four ranged far higher than the national average, primarily due to illicit drugs, alcohol, and suicide. These causes of death increased over the same period alongside fentanyl mortality, which has risen since 2013, jumping a staggering 10 percent in one year.

It is impossible not to sense some relationship in the numbers and assume the downward trend in certain statistics is responsible for the upward trend in others. Many addiction specialists believe fentanyl is being substituted for other opioids as the primary drug of abuse. But the substitution pattern cannot be defined just by looking at the numbers alone, because the opioid epidemic cannot be understood solely through trends in outcomes data. The epidemic is far too complex. By focusing on such trends, the federal government oversimplifies the epidemic into a convenient cause and effect: equating prescription opioids with overdose mortality, and the number of provider arrests with successfully fighting the epidemic.

The oversimplification is exemplified in former DEA acting administrator Uttam Dhillon's call to action in response to the rising number of heroin overdoses: "We need more convictions." Arrests duly increased, with each reinforcing the DEA's supply-focused approach to combating the epidemic.

As Marie Antoinette can posthumously attest, perception is greater than reality; and the perception that more arrests equal fewer overdoses led to the perception that any arrest is a good arrest. So, when a major international investigation by the US federal government led to a crackdown in China's illicit fentanyl supply chain, it was celebrated as a major victory in the epidemic, spinning the arrest as an indictment not only against the criminals but also against China as the cause of the epidemic. This led to a harsh exchange of words between the two countries.

When public perception shifted toward providers as the cause of the opioid epidemic, the DEA criminalized the entire patient encounter and frightened providers from prescribing even necessary medications, drastically lowering the total volume of opioids prescribed. Restrictions appeared, limiting the number of controlled substances that could be prescribed, and greater scrutiny was placed on specific prescribing practices.

All of this was done under the belief that restricting the number of prescriptions reduces harm inflicted by the epidemic. This belief is reinforced by court rulings that uphold these reinterpretations in legal cases across the country. Soon the risk of diverting prescription opioids became more important than the overall quality of patient care, and prescribing practices in healthcare came to be defined by the DEA's interpretation of the CSA.

This approach has historically run afoul of existing laws and constitutional protections of individual rights. In the past, the DEA has been warned by the Office of Inspector General, a federal oversight agency, about its investigational practices. But prior attempts to rectify or even clarify the CSA led to further misunderstandings, increasing the divide between legal interpretations and the medical context.

As a restrictive law, the CSA limits the exchange of control substances for medical purposes as long as certain requirements are met. What those are and how to meet them have changed over time, creating mass confusion through inconsistent applications of the law. A congressional declaration addressed the matter by stating, "Many of the drugs included [as controlled substances] have a useful and legitimate medical purpose and are necessary to maintain the health and general welfare of the American people."

The definition of an addict was also clarified as "any individual who habitually uses any narcotic drug so as to endanger the public morals, health, safety, or welfare, or who is so far addicted to the use of narcotic drugs as to have lost the power of self-control with reference to his addiction." It was also determined that, "except as authorized by this [law], it shall be unlawful for any person knowingly or intentionally to manufacture, distribute, dispense, possess, or create controlled substances in the course of professional practice."

These explanations did little to clarify matters, and instead increased confusion by introducing new terms that are also subject to wide-ranging interpretations. How does one prove someone is "knowingly and intentionally" prescribing medications to an addict who is not just an addict, but an addict who has lost self-control because of his or her addiction and is a public danger? How does a physician balance the direct harm that might come to individual patients by not prescribing medications with the speculative harm to society if prescribed?

Rather than address this issue directly, the courts added more verbiage as guidelines for future rulings:

"[A] physician is restricted to dispensing or prescribing drugs in the bona fide treatment of a patient's disease, including a moderate amount of drugs to a known addict in a good-faith attempt to treat the addiction or to relieve conditions or suffering incident to addiction. Under the guise of treatment, a physician cannot sell drugs to a dealer nor distribute drugs intended to cater to the cravings of an addict." On request for further clarification, the courts again sidestepped the core issue and simply stated, "What constitutes bona fide medical practice must be determined upon consideration of evidence and attending circumstances." The courts also provided leeway for prosecutors, who are "not required to delineate the precise circumstances that constitute the bounds of permissible practice." This means that, though the law should look at all aspects of clinical care to determine if criminal behavior took place, what is being looked at does not need to be defined consistently or specifically. This makes the law even more dependent on subjective interpretations.

This trend is repeated in court cases that apply the CSA to healthcare providers. Instead of clarifying clinical context, the courts give prosecutors greater leeway to bring forth novel interpretations. Easing standards for a legal argument enables logical fallacies rife with bias to impact the quality of an investigation and prosecution. Most perniciously, it leads to medically harmful outcomes.

Ironically, the one constant found in all legal cases is the inconsistent analysis of the law in either elemental or essential terms. Elemental analysis focuses on specific acts or a set of actions to determine if a law is violated. Essential analysis focuses on broad, generalized definitions or concepts, construed in their entirety. The CSA gravitates toward essential interpretations. But since many of the terms are vaguely defined or poorly understood, application of the law leads to conflating elemental analysis with essential analysis, or to extrapolating specific actions as violations of clinical care.

Prosecutors identify one action, interpret it as a transgression, and use it to portray the entire clinical context as illegal.

Prosecutors in my case first thought the criminal act was my effort to reduce or taper the number of opioids. Then they thought it was my policy of limiting the prescriptions at thirty days. They finally settled on it being the quality of my physical exam. The reactionary way the CSA is interpreted creates a divide between the medical and legal worlds. This discrepancy is an issue across the country, particularly in regions hit hard by the opioid epidemic.

In the Bronx borough of New York City, where the opioid epidemic has been exceptionally devastating, health policy experts and law enforcement agents are at odds on how to manage patient overdoses—as crime scenes or as patient cases to be studied. This has resulted in a Bronx overdose log, an informal but comprehensive account of medical information related to the overdose—information that is not included in police reports. The log illustrates how lack of cooperation leads to documentation differences that result in multiple sources of information, each of which alone fails to capture the full patient story.

This is a grave disservice to patients with addictions. Addicts should be treated like all other patients, as addiction medicine is part of primary care. British psychiatrist Heather Ashton emphasized this in her treatment of patients who develop dependencies on addictive medications. She formalized tapering strategies for patients by acknowledging the need for short-term prescribing of addictive medications—decreasing quantities is a necessary first step in resolving long-term addictions. Organizations like the National Institute on Drug Abuse (NIDA) and the Centers for Disease Control and Prevention (CDC) now advocate for this clinical strategy, calling it harm reduction. But sadly, this approach is nowhere to be found in DEA policies.

As the CSA is structured and currently interpreted, presumption of innocence is effectively negated. Many appeals have resulted in the presiding judges reverting to the initial interpretation of the DEA officer to uphold a conviction. This produces a fortress of tautology that leaves the law susceptible to interpretations of federal agents who lack medical training and do not understand clinical context. These agents try to apply knowledge related to what they are most familiar with and used to seeing: illicit drug deals. But clinical behavior is unique enough to require different investigational techniques.

The clinical encounter is essentially legal, as both the provider and patient typically behave as law-abiding citizens. A drug deal, by contrast, is essentially illegal, with the involved parties complicit in a crime. All laws have an underlying logic, and the application of a law must follow its logical intent. If a specific action during a clinical encounter is truly illegal, then that act—if added, modified, or removed—should impact the overall course of clinical care and the fundamental nature of the patient-physician relationship, altering it from criminal to not criminal or vice versa. Otherwise, the action cited is more an interpretation than an objectively defined criminal act.

In the past, the CSA sanctioned certain acts, such as excessive financial compensation, inappropriate sexual relations, and benchmarking the financial compensation with the number of pills prescribed. But none of these is explicitly defined in the law. Instead, the law leaves itself open to wide-ranging interpretations. The capricious and arbitrary application of the law mirrors the federal government's discordant and reactionary approach to the opioid epidemic.

A report by the Office of the Inspector General revealed

that, in the years preceding the intense scrutiny of providers, the DEA increased production quotas for opioid medications while restricting the available amount of medications that help combat addictions and overdoses. The report suggests that the DEA did not do all it could have to raise awareness among providers and patients regarding the addictive potential of opioids.

Another oversight report found similar derelictions in 2011, when the Food and Drug Administration (FDA) implemented safety training, risk evaluation, and mitigation programs to educate providers on opioid use and abuse. By 2013, only 14 percent of the FDA's goals had been met, and the few physicians who took part in these programs reported "modestly greater" knowledge of prescribing practices.

With the benefit of hindsight, we see that federal agencies knew about opioid risks, but did not properly gauge the magnitude of the epidemic or prepare for the public outcry. Once the severity of the epidemic became apparent and public sentiment turned vitriolic, the federal government ushered in an era of medical McCarthyism.

The perception of fear became the legal interpretation through which the CSA was introduced and upheld in courts. Medications became drugs, opioids became narcotics, and the criminalization of the patient encounter introduced existential fear into every prescription written. With no clear guidelines on how opioid prescriptions should begin, taper, or end, medical societies, federal agencies like the CDC, and state medical boards drew up ad hoc guidelines that revised standards of care seemingly overnight.

Soon, the entire patient encounter centered on the act of prescribing, reflecting the intense government focus and materially changing how physicians and patients interact.

Clinical recommendations became criminal liabilities. Physicians grew afraid to prescribe pain medications, and patients were forced to justify or prove the severity of their medical conditions, antagonizing previously trusting patient-physician relationships. Growing clinical hostilities gave way to even more extreme interpretations of the law, effectively applying a moralistic framework: "You should have known better." Any interpretation of the CSA, no matter how biased, could serve as a legal argument. Unlike healthcare fraud cases, which are understood in terms of ill-gotten financial gains, uncertainty arises when interpreting a complex series of clinical decisions and actions. This places undue burden on the accused to defend actions that may have been in the best interest of the patient but are perceived as criminal by law enforcement who view actions absent of clinical context.

When laws are simplified and applied selectively, they arbitrarily burden those disproportionately vulnerable to biases and novel interpretations. This can be seen in patient encounters across the country. Select providers are targeted and investigated, and then indicted and convicted for specific acts viewed in isolation, set apart from relevant clinical context. This creates the perception that select providers are wholly responsible for the opioid epidemic.

I saw how sensationalized news articles influence legal proceedings. I saw how the opioid epidemic is presented in courts and how federal prosecutors work with DEA agents to concoct crimes out of patient encounters. And I saw how the law can be manipulated and distorted into medically inappropriate interpretations that harm patients.

I learned the opioid epidemic goes beyond patients overdosing. It permeates into the fear patients and providers feel during a healthcare encounter. As a result, the fear of prosecution defines the practice of medicine.

CHAPTER 13

Science and law have been at odds since the beginning of modern science, starting with its founding father, Galileo. While under home confinement, Galileo wrote *Discourses and Mathematical Demonstrations Relating to Two New Sciences*, which includes a satirical allegory of three characters—Simplicio, the common layman; Sagredo, the educated well-to-do man; and Salviati, the wise, scientific mind—who together discuss science and its role in society. Sagredo challenges Salviati and his theories, while encouraging emotional responses and disbelief from Simplicio—an allusion to society's tendencies to reject complex scientific principles for more familiar reactionary thinking, which holds true now as it did then.

"History does not repeat itself," Mark Twain allegedly said, "but it often rhymes." Time after time, legal courts carry out society's reactionary thinking through the pretense of law, compromising our understanding of complex, systemic issues and disproportionately attributing fault to individuals or groups for something far broader in scope. This was the premise of judgment during the Tokyo War Crimes Tribunal following Japan's defeat in World War II. In what some would later call victor's justice, laws were reinterpreted, and new legal terms introduced, to inflict punishment on the Japanese in excess of the war crime statutes developed during the Nuremberg Charter in Germany.

"Crimes against humanity," a concept developed at Nuremberg, allowed Nazi leaders to be convicted individually for atrocities committed during war, namely the Holocaust, but the charges were distinctly different from charges of murder. In contrast, the Tokyo Tribunal used unique phrases, such as "crimes against peace," which created little distinction between conventional war crimes and acts of murder. Any ambiguity in interpreting the revised statutes defaulted to interpreting the acts of war as direct criminal acts with higher punitive consequences. This led to division among the presiding judges, particularly the Asian judges, who viewed the court proceedings as unfair.

Many Japanese saw the tribunal as a charade that characterized patriotism as a crime and any service to the nation as an act of aggression. Soon the Japanese saw the tribunal as nothing more than allied forces seeking retribution rather than justice. The vengeance of victor's justice extended to both sides of the Pacific. Following the war, Japanese Americans imprisoned after failing to swear allegiance received no legal recourse for their unlawful internment and instead faced years of continuing discrimination.

When Japanese Americans sought legal redress, such as in Korematsu v. United States, the Supreme Court ruled that the need to protect the country against presumed Japanese espionage outweighed the rights of individual Japanese Americans. It was a controversial decision at the time; and decades later, it was voided by a California district court on the grounds that the Office of Naval Intelligence had suppressed a report revealing Japanese Americans were not acting as spies.

The polarized political landscape of post-war America led to reactionary court rulings that in hindsight were unfair but interpreted to be justified at the time. This tendency to reinterpret the laws due to public sentiment appeared early in America's history in its original sin of slavery, as courts maintained racially discriminatory policies against African Americans. These rulings often manifested as contrived reinterpretations of laws designed to exact specific punishments or lead to predetermined legal outcomes.

Terms like "separate but equal" were reinterpreted to mean anything *but* equal. In the 1890s, a well-educated Creole named Plessy from Louisiana attempted to board a train car reserved for whites but was promptly removed. Believing he was entitled to fair treatment under the law, he sued for unfair discrimination before learning the courts interpreted social equality to be distinct from legal equality.

This legal interpretation was repeatedly cited to pass racially discriminatory laws that are known today as Jim Crow laws. It wasn't until 1954 that a series of lawsuits, aggregated under one case, Brown v. Board of Education, interpreted "separate but equal" to mean equal in all social and legal settings—a ruling that spearheaded the civil rights movement.

Even today, in bad economic times, regulators ostensibly exact changes to regulate the markets, but really to find specific individuals and groups to blame, using rule of law as pretense for retaliation against financial losses sustained by the public. Landmark statutes such as Cox-Sackley or Dodd-Frank were enacted in these times to restrict perceived high-risk trading. But these laws never address the underlying cause of the financial downturn. They simply transfer financial risk from one investment vehicle to another.

Risk is intrinsic to financial markets, and the allure of converting risk into a risk premium attracts millions to the market daily. But when the markets sour and wealth vanishes, the law spins justice proportional to levels of vindictiveness and simplifies complex financial trades into specific criminal acts. Civil suits become criminal cases, and federal prosecutors unveil cookie-cutter, boilerplate charges and start legal proceedings to indict, and reflexively convict, through plea agreements.

Prosecutors argue that actions of specific individuals are responsible for the market downturn. An inherently systemic risk in the market is distorted to be willful criminal behavior. In conflating systemic risk with individual behavior, regulators disproportionately burden certain individuals or groups to satiate public outcries. A similar pattern defines the opioid epidemic. Legal cases introducing reinterpretations of the law grew more extreme as public outcries grew louder, reducing courts to public spectacles.

High-profile indictments and lawsuits covered prominently in national media influence the masses to believe a narrative that prescription opioids lead to overdoses. Prosecutors tout public demand for prison sentences or present vague legal interpretations, influencing the public to target providers. Media outlets broadcast reports of law enforcement investigating healthcare providers and executives, reinforcing the perception that healthcare providers are to blame for the opioid epidemic and that reducing the quantity of opioid prescriptions is in the public's best interest.

But what exactly is public interest in the opioid epidemic? Physicians, healthcare public policy experts, and now many politicians believe the epidemic was borne from illegally obtained opioids. Numerous studies and reports analyzing the epidemic corroborate as much. We now know more harm than good comes from laws that, due to fear of prosecution, prevent patients with legitimate health conditions from receiving medically necessary opioids. This has led to growing calls for harm reduction policies.

Many federal and state agencies have responded by implementing resources to help patients who have issues with poorly treated pain or substance dependencies. But the calls fall silent in the court of law.

Addiction medicine is a complex, ever-evolving field. We will continue to see more patient-centric policies as we learn more about the relationship between pain and addiction. By reducing medicine's complexity into simplified narratives, courts introduce logical errors that manifest in the legal system as biases against providers and thus hinder clinical progress.

Modern healthcare is effectively becoming a legal entity, in which legal rulings define standards of care. Therefore, the interpretations of law reflect how well these legal standards represent good clinical care. As a result, legal trends in court dictate clinical trends in patient care. The rise in opioid litigation during the epidemic has given commensurate rise to several medically harmful legal interpretations, each case reinforcing a dangerous trend of restricting medically necessary opioids.

Among thousands of civil lawsuits and criminal cases, each has its own spin on opioids' purpose in healthcare, each trying to adjudicate the morality of addiction through legal means, each reinterpreting healthcare laws and statutes that prioritize social concerns over patient rights. In theory, each legal case should be deliberated to the fullest extent required. In reality, the legal system operates through a series of default tendencies, attempting to balance administrative burdens with considerations unique to each case. This often dissolves into a series of default procedural motions, with cases hurried through and addressed as quickly as possible.

Healthcare behavior is a mix of medical knowledge and real-time decision-making with limited information. Healthcare law attempts to standardize this behavior, leading to inevitable simplifications. The original intent of the law and its implementation separate, widening the scope for harmful interpretations. Many courts lack a framework to evaluate complex healthcare behaviors. Absent such a framework, each court determines which clinical information merits review and which aspects of the patient encounter apply to the legal proceedings.

Eventually, different courts establish different interpretations of healthcare law based on the cases presented. These variations predispose and eventually reinforce extreme legal interpretations of healthcare law, since they tend to be the simplest interpretations and therefore the most likely default decisions.

Behavioral economists studying biases that arise from default tendencies find that even subtle differences in default reactions produce wide variability in outcomes. A judge who defaults to studying all aspects of healthcare behavior might have a different perspective than a judge who defaults to passing such work on to law clerks.

Ironically, information overload adversely affects judicial decision-making. This counterintuitive notion has been observed in multiple studies that show judges make more accurate risk assessments to grant bail when they have less information about the defendant. The decision to grant bail is a skill acquired from years of experience seeing the same cases over and over—a skill that no longer applies when judges face unique, specialized cases with unfamiliar, complex variables, as in many healthcare cases. This makes the prevalence of misinformation in the opioid epidemic particularly malicious, as it has overwhelmed the courts with bias.

Many judges are uncomfortable processing all the variables in specialized healthcare cases. As a result, judges delegate decision-making on healthcare matters that require greater subject expertise. This means an evaluation of the medical context also gets delegated—to individuals who forego the nuanced distinctions that define healthcare behavior in favor of default decisions.

Some think of the legal system through the eyes of a judge alone, but the courts are broader in scope than that. Each judicial system features an entire administration of probation officers and law clerks providing guidance and input on legal cases. Despite having more sources of input, most members of a judicial administration lack a proper understanding of healthcare beyond their own personal experiences as patients and simply reiterate generally accepted narratives about a health issue. Sometimes, law clerks will even rely on prosecutors for guidance on healthcare matters, revealing a familiarity bias in the court that prevails despite the obvious conflict of interest.

The legal system abhors uncertainty and will find ways to eliminate it. If it cannot be eliminated, it is glossed over. In many opioid cases in recent years, prosecutors have instilled a simplified narrative as the crux of their arguments, using it as legal precedent to expedite judicial review. Alexander Hamilton once said that the heart of society is the fairness of the courts and their ability to balance power with purpose, with judges serving as symbols of justice. But how can we trust judges to be fair and equitable—to ensure that opioid laws are applied equally—when each court has a wide range of default tendencies?

Prosecutors often rely on earlier rulings that are perceived to be similar, called bellwether cases, to frame legal arguments. These early cases in the opioid epidemic paved the way for simplified interpretations of the law and limited the extent to which clinical context is considered. Reiterated enough times, these rulings formed the template for subsequent prosecutorial arguments in high-profile opioid cases. This phenomenon is like a wave that builds on each ruling, growing stronger by the case. But in reiterating these legal arguments, the biases or default tendencies present in bellwether cases continue to appear in later cases.

Satirist Chuck Klosterman says that "laws are deliberately complicated to allow multiple interpretations," but for all the variations we see in healthcare law, its application is far more uniform and dependent on bellwether cases. If these bellwether cases introduce legal interpretations harmful to patient care, then the application of opioid laws reinforce these harmful clinical standards.

In 2019, Oklahoma's attorney general orchestrated a landmark settlement against Johnson & Johnson for its role in manufacturing opioids, citing public nuisance ordinance laws as basis for the lawsuit. These laws were never intended to be used in such a way, but once the precedent formed to use ordinance laws against opioid manufacturers, this interpretation was repeated in courts across the country.

Ironically, Oklahoma's opioid epidemic is dwarfed by the state's methamphetamine, cocaine, and alcohol epidemics.

State representatives involved in the case plan to use funds from the opioid settlement for rehabilitative services that involve other illicit substances. So, while the Oklahoma courts view this case as a victory against corporate malfeasance, the state's medical community sees it as a financial windfall to address more pressing addiction concerns.

Many high-profile lawsuits appear sound in principle, but in practice these settlements show glaring limitations in the courts' ability to allocate settlement funds in ways that benefit patients. Early efforts to disseminate funds have run into conflicts between state and local authorities, with each claiming to be better suited to manage the money.

In Cuyahoga County, Ohio, an opioid settlement resolved more than two thousand opioid lawsuits, becoming a bellwether case for settlements throughout the country. But once the settlement dollars were obtained, the apparent unified legal stance quickly fell apart. State government officials believe they are better equipped to handle the epidemic-related medical issues through wide-ranging healthcare policies. Local entities complain that the distribution of funds should reflect community-specific addiction needs, something only local officials can understand. These differences, which were glossed over when arguing the broad class-action lawsuit, now form the crux of disagreements between government entities.

The opioid epidemic is far too complex to simplify in one legal mandate, and it affects different parts of the country in different ways. It cannot be solved through traditional legal means or common litigation strategies. Yet the same legal tactics—be it class-action lawsuits or criminal cases—are used in nearly every major opioid settlement case. Take the government's efforts to hold pharmaceutical companies liable.

Prosecutors first target smaller pharmaceutical companies, knowing they are more likely to settle or plea. Prosecutors then use the initial cases to serve as precedent to strengthen the legal case against larger pharmaceutical companies, which also eventually settle. This tried-and-true method has been applied to pharmaceutical manufacturers, retail manufacturers, and even medical supplies distributors. Over time, the magnitude of the settlements overshadows the purpose of each individual case. But once the dollars are collected, few patients see any financial support.

In a civil complaint the federal government filed against Walmart in late 2020, prosecutors used previous opioid cases as precedent to calculate an economic cost for damages. The government used overdose mortality statistics, equating restitution with lives lost.

In making their case, prosecutors presented evidence that relies on a series of behaviors called red flags. The claim was that Walmart is liable for damages caused by the epidemic because the company was not able to properly address vague findings and concerns that appeared when patients came to get their prescriptions filled. On closer examination, these red flags are more circumstantial than definitive, isolated from the clinical context where they occurred; and they demonstrate how much interpretation of the CSA veers from its original intent of preventing overt criminal misuse of opioid prescriptions.

These red flags are insinuations that cannot be interpreted beyond the uncertainty of reasonable doubt. Alone, they carry no merit; but the impact of their use as legal terms—coupled with public hysteria around the epidemic—foster extreme interpretations of healthcare law that run afoul of harm-reduction principles but make for lucrative legal settlements.

When courts reinforce extreme, medically harmful interpretations of the law, the judge's ruling becomes the standard of clinical care and the reference point for future litigation. It becomes a default tendency in the court of law. It's no surprise that the default legal tendencies in class-action lawsuits then mirror the default tendencies in criminal cases against providers. Whenever the CSA is applied to a healthcare provider, the accused physician or pharmacist nearly always accepts a plea deal, further shifting the legal system away from medically appropriate interpretations of the CSA and toward reflexive convictions.

Settling cases without validating the arguments or underlying clinical context accelerates the trend of medically harmful court rulings and reinforces extreme interpretations of the law. Soon, any deviation in clinical practice is met with a skeptical eye and with risk of criminal repercussions.

Legal arguments are no longer required to meet the standards of reasonable doubt, or even to be medically appropriate. Merely presenting an argument, and effectively using court machinations to proceed with it, allows even substandard arguments to become legal victories for prosecutors. But these extreme interpretations of healthcare law create an interpretive tunnel vision that substitutes an analysis of complex medical behavior for default rulings that form legal precedent.

It should come as no surprise that the opioid epidemic worsened during the COVID-19 pandemic. The combination of acute mental health crises with diminished access to care worsened the quality of life for those already struggling with addiction, leading to a slew of overdoses. The class-action lawsuits and criminal proceedings, despite grandiose settlements and headline-making convictions, did nothing to prevent overdoses or protect patients.

The opioid epidemic cannot be solved with the legal system as it is presently constructed. By continuing to rely on the same legal tactics, default tendencies, and contrived legal interpretations, we will only see the epidemic worsen. We need to redefine how we examine healthcare laws in court—and how we implement them in clinical care. We must align healthcare and law in a way that accurately represents the complexity of healthcare as it is experienced by those affected by the law, while advancing medically appropriate interpretations of the law.

In a world where a legal ruling can undo years of clinical study on harm reduction, where a politician yields more clinical influence than a peer-reviewed academic article, we need to be aware of how extreme legal interpretations of healthcare law influence healthcare behavior. "We cannot solve our problems with the same thinking we used when we created them," Albert Einstein said. If we wish to resolve the epidemic, we cannot continue applying the same legal tactics and extreme interpretations that have exacerbated opioid abuse.

Healthcare laws reflect our society's state of health. The two should naturally align, forming a balance between healthcare and law, always in equilibrium and never trending to an extreme.

CHAPTER 14

When pioneering physician John Snow wrote in his chron-
icles on public policy that "the disease was a broadcast," he
was referring to cholera, the bacterial disease that ravaged
London and cities throughout the United States in the nineteenth century.

While most policy experts focused on the rise in incidence
or mortality, Snow noted a commensurate rise in fear that
influenced how people reacted and governments responded
more than the actual disease did. As news spread of cholera,
the behavioral response to the disease far outweighed the
clinical severity of those suffering from it. The ensuing public
response for better hygienic conditions led to the introduction
of government sanitation programs that have since relegated
cholera to the history books, but not before demonstrating the
power of fear in changing collective behavior.

Fear creates a curious anomaly in times of healthcare
crises. It appears more severe than the disease itself, but never
seems to materialize to the extent we predict. Yet the anom-

aly persists, crisis after crisis, giving a fascination to our fears extending beyond the initial emotion. In today's times, if we were to replace cholera with coronavirus, we would have the title for a modern romance novel: *Love in the Time of Corona.*

Fear is almost never an accurate gauge of reality. What we fear in many healthcare crises is almost never valid or fully realized. Following World War II, Japan feared the long-term effects of nuclear radiation would increase cancer rates, particularly among the *nijyu hibakusha,* the double exposed, those who endured the effects of both nuclear bombs. Cancer rates did rise, and by any measure it was an absolute tragedy. But the rise fell well short of initial fears.

When fear is undefined and the risks unknown, people tend to interpret the problem as bigger and more extreme than it really is, and their responses are exaggerated. Eventually, the exaggerations create additional problems or exacerbate the original ones. "Men are very apt to run into extremes," observed George Washington. This political tendency toward extremism has long infiltrated the legal system and now dominates the government's approach to healthcare policy.

A famous example of political extremism is Prohibition, which did embarrassingly little to stop alcohol use and gave rise to the glamour and allure of criminal drug trafficking and recreational use. Substitute El Chapo for Al Capone, and you can see the lingering effects of this culture today. Alcoholism has taken even more lives than the opioid epidemic in recent years, with states like Indiana suffering from an epidemic of early onset liver disease as alcoholism afflicts more young adults.

Many health policy experts believe this trend coincides with the opioid epidemic, as young adults who were abusing opioids switched to alcohol after losing access to their prescriptions. When politicians clamored for something to be done about opioid abuse, they prompted an intense response from local and federal law enforcement eager to restrict opioid prescriptions. This, in turn, changed clinical policies and patient interactions overnight, culminating in new extreme interpretations of healthcare law reiterated as misguided public policy—which has hurt more than helped efforts to address the epidemic.

The same tendencies that lead toward extremism in courts of law also manifest in the court of public opinion—each influencing the other toward ever more extreme, ever more simplified narratives. William Webster, the only man to have led both the FBI and CIA, emphasized "rule of law over politics." Yet many see the Department of Justice as a political weapon as much as a legal institution. Politics and law have always been linked in America. Rather than emphasizing an unrealistic separation, we should identify an appropriate balance that improves the quality of healthcare laws to better reflect healthcare behavior and curtail the tendency to reduce complex problems into political posturing.

Healthcare issues—from restrictive abortion laws to COVID-19 restrictions, from hospital cost data access to Affordable Care Act (ACA) tax penalties—can be resolved by weighing all aspects of each issue to derive an optimal balance between law and behavior, between policy and individual decision-making. Many people implicitly assume that behavior and law relate like crime and punishment. But the wide chasm between healthcare laws and policies, and the corresponding healthcare behavior, produces an array of unintended behaviors and consequences. To understand this, we have to see how unintended errors arise, and once formed, how they subsequently polarize healthcare, starting with arguably the most polarizing issue in America.

The debate over gun control is as old as our country, and in 2018 multiple medical community members first declared it a public health concern. Just as quickly, gun rights lobbyists declared it *not* a public health concern. Inevitably, amid the health policy debate, lawyers intervened.

Constitutional originalists believe the Second Amendment provides the right to bear arms in service of a local militia, balancing individual rights with a civic duty to local government, or balancing an individual right to possess a gun with an obligation to serve in the common defense as a social responsibility. Modern interpretations shy away from this balance and simplify the interpretation to focus on the right to self-protection, while restricting specific behaviors and uses of guns. Laws that balance a civic duty with a legal right are harder to define than laws that simply restrict specific behaviors. But looking at behavior as just something to restrict leads to an endless debate over what to restrict and how much to restrict it.

Healthcare is, by nature, a service to patients; and healthcare laws must balance social responsibility with individual service. Yet most healthcare laws avoid the issue of balance altogether and are fundamentally restrictive. Restricting one specific behavior within a spectrum of complex healthcare behaviors creates unintended consequences that vary depending on the individual and on the interpretation of the law. Abortion, for example, is at times a scientific issue, and at others a religious one, but mostly is seen as a poorly constructed balance of both. Different conceptual combinations produce different interpretations of abortion laws. Should these laws focus on defining inappropriate sexual behaviors, or on the sanctity of human life, or on some combination?

Most abortion laws default to restricting access. But making a clinical behavior more difficult to accomplish does not deter it; it only makes it riskier. The overall number of abortions does not decrease. Instead, the locations where abortions are performed simply switch from one state to another. State-by-state analyses of abortion rates and varying levels of restrictions show that when one state increases restrictions on abortions, abortion rates increase in neighboring states. Women seeking abortions travel farther for medical care as necessary, which has proved to be less safe for patients. A single restriction does not alter all decisions or actions that prompt a patient to consider abortion. Rather, it makes those decisions and actions more burdensome. In legal terms, it places an undue burden.

Modern abortion laws seek to militate against these burdens by attempting to target restrictions more clinically. These laws, called TRAP laws, or targeted restriction on abortion providers, target clinicians or patients by restricting specific clinical behaviors that take place during an abortion procedure. The belief is that addressing a specific clinical behavior will affect the overall intent to seek an abortion. Yet, the more specific the restrictive law, the greater the array of unintended clinical consequences.

In Kentucky, abortion providers must perform a narrated ultrasound for patients considering abortions. The provider describes the fetal heart rate while showing pictures of the ultrasound to the patient. This is now a legally mandated part of obtaining informed consent for abortions in the state. Opponents of the law describe it as unconstitutional, accusing the law of targeting women in their most vulnerable moments and exploiting those moments to deter a potential abortion.

Henry David Thoreau described individuals as "independent entities with rights," a sentiment codified in modern medical ethics, which define a patient as an autonomous individual who has control over his or her body. This implies an individual's informed consent in essential terms, a concept to be viewed in its entirety: either you fully consent, or you do not. But mandating a provision, a specific act of narrating the ultrasound, introduces an elemental framework, which means a specific act must be part of informed consent, and that changes its definition. This alters the decision to sign consent for an abortion into a willingness to tolerate the specific act of participating in a narrated ultrasound, an element that may unduly influence the patient who otherwise would have consented.

Another contested TRAP law out of Louisiana is similarly restrictive and produces similar unintended clinical effects. The law requires abortion providers to have hospital admitting privileges when performing abortions in the state, ostensibly to promote continuity of care should a complication arise. But when applied, the law reduces the number of abortion providers in the state to single digits. Proponents of the law advocate for continuity of care, an important concern for any outpatient procedure. Opponents believe the risk of potential complications from a certain number of abortion procedures does not justify a blanket restriction on nearly all abortions.

In healthcare, the distribution of burdens when implementing a law should account for actual risks and perceived risks, balancing clinical burdens with clinical risks. The Supreme Court upheld this perspective when it ruled Louisiana abortion restrictions were unlawful and that abortion providers do not require hospital admitting privileges. The complexity of healthcare creates a burden for patients that most laws seek to simplify or avoid. This tendency only produces additional burdens on vulnerable patients, as each attempt to address the burden through law merely transfers it to other aspects of clinical behavior.

This problem is inherent to healthcare. It affects everything from polarizing health issues to ownership of medical data. If we believe patients should have access to data to make their own decisions, then we need to explain the data. But that requires having someone explain the data objectively. And in explaining the data objectively, we need to ensure patients understand the data sufficiently enough to make decisions that account for burdens and risks. On it goes, often with the full extent of clinical consequences not manifesting until much later.

This played out in hospitals and courts across the country for one of the most publicized healthcare laws in recent decades, the Affordable Care Act (ACA). The law's original keystone element, the health insurance mandate, was inserted to incentivize patients to acquire healthcare coverage, assuming the threat of financial penalty would motivate them. Yet even after the penalty was nullified in federal court, patients continued to purchase insurance plans through ACA insurance exchanges.

And, contrary to what most lawmakers believed, patient healthcare outcomes—specifically, hospital length of stay following an admission—improved. Removing the mandate likely had little direct impact on length of stay or any one aspect of patient behavior. The relationship is more likely correlative than a simple cause-and-effect relation. But the tendency to simplify complex healthcare issues by ascribing cause and effect prevents a full understanding of the consequences of enacted laws and policies.

Dr. Nora Volkow, head of the National Institute of Drug Abuse, has made a career of studying addictions and has seen this tendency appear over and over in both health policy and patient care. In studying the opioid epidemic, she realized addiction is a complex medical condition that is about more than opioid prescriptions or illicit drugs. Instead, she studies how patients experience addiction. While many public policy advocates now focus on fentanyl, "the most dangerous opioid," Dr. Volkow pays attention to the unique patterns of drug abuse in patients nationwide.

Dr. Volkow acknowledges that methamphetamines are just as lethal, if not more lethal, than fentanyl. She believes funds from opioid settlements should include addiction services for patients addicted to methamphetamines, given the drug's rapid rise in popularity and the tendency of many patients who were abusing opioids to switch to methamphetamines. It should also come as no surprise that the same medications that treat opioid addictions are now approved or being studied to treat methamphetamine addictions.

For patients struggling with addictions, methamphetamines became a substitute when opioids were less available, so it makes sense to try similar treatments for similar patterns of addiction. But law enforcement continues to focus only on blanket restrictions of opioid prescriptions, despite calls from healthcare researchers to study the substitution patterns of behavior: for example, addicts who alternated one drug of abuse for another, depending on the drugs' relative availability.

These patterns show how patients with chronic pain feel forced to consume illicit opioids when they no longer receive opioid medications from their providers. Yet, these insights from the medical community go unnoticed as law enforcement targets patients as addicts. Criminalizing addictive behavior fails because restrictive laws focus on one specific behavior within the continuum of addiction and attempt to address all aspects of a patient's addiction through that one behavior—just like attributing responsibility for the entire epidemic to one aspect of an opioid manufacturer's corporate practice.

When the Oklahoma attorney general who sued Johnson & Johnson through public nuisance laws presented his case, he focused on the company's marketing strategy. He claimed Johnson & Johnson marketed too aggressively, placing undue influence on patients to seek opioids, and that this subsequently led to addictions. The attorney general argued that the company's marketing campaign showed an overall intent to influence patients to abuse opioid medications. This hinges on the assumption that a large pharmaceutical company has prolonged, direct access to patients in a way that can exert such influence.

Pharmaceutical supply chains consist of pharmaceutical manufacturers, distributors, insurance companies, benefits managers, and large pharmacy chains. No studies or legal cases delineate the level of influence any of these stakeholders maintain, or should maintain, on patient decision-making. The entire legal argument assumed a specious relationship between a large corporation's marketing campaign and individual patient addictions, ignoring all other aspects of the pharmaceutical industry and of addiction behavior.

Ignoring medical context is an oft-repeated mistake made throughout the courts when the morality of addiction is judged through legal means. Many landmark lawsuits and convictions, once so keen on identifying culprits to blame, failed to establish a standardized framework to define the dissemination of settlement funds, leading state and municipal governments to bicker over who should administer distribution of the money. But the larger, more significant argument is how to administer the funds among patients and healthcare institutions so as to maximize clinical benefit.

We have no long-term strategy for this. Some believe we should focus only on prescription opioids, while others believe we should invest in addiction treatment for all opioids, prescription or illicit. Many in the medical community advocate for addressing all forms of addiction, seeing more similarities than differences among the various forms of drug abuse.

We also have no particular focus on whom the funds should go to. No study has analyzed whether funds are more effective in educating law enforcement on treatment options for high-risk patients with addictions, or if the emphasis should be on access to addiction treatment with more counselors. The American Medical Association (AMA) has found that states that expand Medicaid coverage to include more benefits have fewer opioid-related deaths. This implies that proactive access to healthcare may improve mortality more so than reactive criminalization from law enforcement. But this has not been tested nationwide.

What would be more ideal than any single approach is a balanced one based on community-specific needs to solve the opioid epidemic. This is possible; such a balance has been achieved in relation to other drug epidemics. "This has turned into a healthcare crisis," Congressman Joseph Kennedy III (D-MA) said in 2019, referring to the then-nascent vaping crisis. Vaping emerged out of an attempt to create a new smoking cessation option, but spawned its own set of addictive behaviors, particularly among adolescents. Or so it was believed.

Vapes, or e-cigarettes, consist of a vaporizer and a cartridge with a liquid nicotine solution. Initially touted as a safe alternative to cigarettes, vapes were evangelized by spunky startups and entrepreneurs eager to market the products. Soon, the cartridges added various flavors to go along with the nicotine. Some contained marijuana. After a few short years on the market, there were more than four hundred flavors of vape liquid. Vaping became so popular among college students that its use doubled from 2017 to 2018. That same year, 20 percent of Americans aged eighteen or younger had used e-cigarettes in some capacity.

By 2019, people were developing mysterious lung injuries severe enough to result in hospitalizations and even deaths. *The New England Journal of Medicine* called teen vaping an epidemic, and the CDC studied the cartridges to find out what was causing these symptoms. Public policy experts and law enforcement went on the offensive, putting restrictions on vape liquid flavors and where vaping could be done. Vaping drug busts made headlines, as highly publicized raids by local and federal law enforcement officers confiscated large amounts of illicit cartridges.

Yet high school students continued vaping in greater numbers. Surveys found that nearly one in four underage Americans were vaping. Schools across the country joined the frontline offensive against the vaping crisis and increased drug testing in schools. Some drug-tested every student over the course of an academic year. Yet despite the increased restrictions, and the publicity of the health risks, more teens continued to vape, resulting in more hospitalizations and more deaths.

Healthcare researchers struggled to make sense of it. Sixty percent of vaping-related deaths involved only nicotine cartridges, but 80 percent of lung injuries requiring hospitalizations involved cartridges with both nicotine and THC, the main psychoactive compound in marijuana. Median age of use was twenty-three, but median age of death was fifty-three. Eighty percent of lung injuries were in users who were thirty-five or younger.

Although the data presented unfamiliar patterns of complications, lawmakers followed a familiar pattern of reacting with heightened restrictions and criminal investigations. High-profile investigations by federal and state prosecutors of vaping companies similarly targeted their marketing tactics. These were reinterpreted to be aggressive and deceptive, as an attempt to create addictions among users. Everyone seemed to forget that the original intention of vaping was to address cigarette addiction.

Vaping companies soon pushed back, demonstrating the value their product provides when used appropriately. When Massachusetts instituted a statewide ban on vaping, the Vaping Technology Association fought the ban and conducted research on the benefits of vaping for patients struggling with nicotine addiction. By changing the conversation from criminal behavior to clinical research, the vaping industry showed that the context around the behavior determines clinical benefits or harms more than just the act of vaping.

Dr. Rachel King, director of addiction psychology at Cornell University, studied vaping as a viable treatment option for nicotine addiction. Dr. King found a complex relationship between vaping and cigarettes that only initially appears simple. In coupling vaping with cigarette smoking, she first noted that by restricting one you promote the other, and vice versa. She then discovered that the vaping epidemic is really two separate epidemics: one affecting older users who use traditional nicotine cartridges, and the other affecting younger users who combine nicotine and THC cartridges. Older users suffered from lung injuries due to lipid-based molecules in the cartridges, while younger users had lung injuries from combining THC and nicotine.

Although the act of vaping may be the same, the health

risks are different. By studying the behavior around vaping—its context of use—Dr. King saw two patterns of behavior and two health risks for two distinct user groups. She concluded that vaping is best used in a balance with traditional cigarette smoking. Instead of aggressively targeting vaping, consequently shifting some users to revert back to traditional cigarettes, she advocates a balance that limits the health risks of vaping while supporting its positive aspects in curtailing cigarette addictions.

This explains why the Department of Health and Human Services opted for a targeted ban on specific flavors of vaping cartridges, permitting traditional flavors like menthol, which are more commonly used among those quitting cigarettes. The targeted restrictions acknowledge the risks in both vaping and cigarettes but also recognize that a balance can encourage patients to use vaping to combat cigarette addiction—vaping's original intended use. Though the inevitable settlements against prominent vaping companies still played out, with the same rhetoric scrutinizing their marketing practices, the size of those settlements has been far less than those in opioid cases.

Primary care physicians and addiction specialists should seek to find a similar balance in juggling opioids, opioid alternatives, and opioid abuse medications like naloxone and buprenorphine. Unlike with vaping, law enforcement has not taken a balanced approach toward the opioid epidemic but recently has lifted additional licensing requirements for prescribing opioid abuse medications. Since providers were restricted by specific licenses to prescribe these medications, access until recently had been limited.

Greater access would help providers not only discuss opioid risks but also more easily provide much-needed treatment for developing dependencies. Access to these opioid abuse medications allows physicians to consider the medical needs of individual patients along with the broader concerns of drug abuse and diversion, which should be the intent of any opioid law or policy. Instead, most healthcare laws interpret specific behaviors as dangerous and reflexively restrict them rather than finding actual solutions. These much-needed solutions come from establishing a medically appropriate balance that weighs all clinical behaviors affected.

This is undoubtedly difficult. Such a balance consists of a fair distribution of medical burdens among all who are affected by a healthcare law. It accounts for the myriad effects and secondary consequences a law or policy may inflict, and it addresses potentially unforeseen burdens that might arise. It balances civic responsibilities with individual rights—not in absolute terms, but relative to patient care—while incorporating the full context of a patient's medical needs and recognizing the interdependence of many medical conditions and broader human behavior.

Such laws might appear on the surface to be more conceptual than practical. But we know what happens with restrictive laws that curtail specific behaviors or patterns. We have seen what does not work. Current healthcare laws target our worst tendencies. They impose punitive measures on clinical actions, thereby restricting it and turning patients and providers into targets. We need laws that address our best tendencies, the aspirational aspects of our behavior that lead us to make good decisions regarding health. Laws that emphasize these aspects effectively balance the various medical and legal burdens in patient care.

Medicine has always been aspirational, but so has law, and the optimal overlap between the two comes from encouraging good behavior, aligning the aspirational elements of each field. This begins by coordinating all interactions and relationships in healthcare with the obligations and burdens of healthcare law, forming a medically appropriate balance.

CHAPTER 15

The first healthcare regulations were not laws but oaths, the most famous being the Hippocratic Oath. Physicians still take this oath today, vowing to uphold principles of good patient care, as a duty that affords them the right to practice clinical medicine.

For as much as we reference the oath, we know little about Greek physician Hippocrates. To understand his medical philosophies, we rely heavily on his students' writings. Hippocrates practiced medicine on the Greek island of Kos, an intellectual center of Hellenistic culture. He challenged many of his contemporary physicians, who advocated for rational and logical approaches to patient care. Hippocrates, in contrast, emphasized intuition and considered direct patient experience the most important factor in curing illness.

Interestingly, the oath was not even written by Hippocrates, but by his students after his death. Ostensibly, this was to formalize his philosophy, but in reality, the oath was drafted to distinguish physicians trained under his methods for the purpose of creating a competitive advantage for his pupils. This transforms a hallowed oath that balances duty with rights into a series of phrases that restricts competition among schools of medicine. This transformation continues in the present, as select phrases from medical oaths are paraphrased into contrived interpretations.

This is exemplified in the phrase "do no harm," which never appeared in the original oath. However, it appears in legal courts today, when lawyers decry the actions of healthcare providers who allegedly violated their professional duties to their patients. But individual responsibilities cannot be discerned through individual actions alone. The clinical context and underlying medical condition define the importance and relevance of any clinical action.

As physician-philosopher Maimonides said, "The greater the contradiction, the deeper the wisdom." Physician oaths describe rights in healthcare as a relationship between broader responsibilities or duties and individual obligations—which can sometimes appear as contradictions but are really two sides in a deep-rooted balance. Linked by the lines in the oaths, relationships in healthcare should be seen as a balance, to be experienced as much as learned, felt as much as deduced. The idea of balance derives from principles of humanism, which serve as the roots of modern medicine and explain why health is characterized through experiences.

All physicians who formed the pantheon of medicine emphasized an experience-based approach to healthcare. Hippocrates characterized medicine as an art to be practiced, saying it consists not of treating a disease but of healing a person.

Famed Roman surgeon Galen began his medical career as a surgeon treating dying gladiators. He became renowned for his experimental approach to medicine, eventually serving as the private physician to the Caesars. Centuries later, Maimonides emulated Galen's career trajectory, becoming the personal physician to legendary Muslim crusader Saladin. Maimonides also took an experimental approach to medicine, but emphasized civic responsibility as well.

These traits later inspired Canadian physician William Osler's humanistic approach to medicine at the turn of the twentieth century. Dr. Osler is best known for turning Johns Hopkins Hospital, based in Baltimore, into a research juggernaut. He also designed a clinical curriculum that became the model for modern medical education in the United States. He prioritized the clinic as much as the textbook, promoting direct patient contact as the bedrock of good medicine.

When looking at medicine through its humanistic origins, we better understand the balance between healthcare and law. Henry David Thoreau described mortality in similar ways, as a balance. He emphasized moral behavior in broad terms, more so than any individual action, as a person's civic duty to society. Thoreau's views on civic duty stemmed from his perspective on individual rights, which he held sacred above all, including above government intervention. He encouraged individuals whose rights were inappropriately compromised to serve as a "counter-friction to a fundamental immorality."

Thoreau believed laws should be in balance with an individual's fundamental rights, and that a law's validity should be measured by its morality. Civil disobedience in response to a transgression of such rights is easy to define for obviously unethical laws, such as those that supported slavery. But for complex healthcare laws, the concept of rights becomes more convoluted. Many have debated about how healthcare fits into the definition of individual rights. Swiss philosopher Henri-

Frédéric Amiel addressed this when he wrote, "In health there is freedom. Health is the first of all liberties."

Legal philosophers today classify rights as either negative or positive. A negative right is not to be subjected to any restrictions by another person or group. A positive right is subjected to oversight by another person or group. Negative and positive rights are incompatible. The former limit or constrain actions, while the latter monitor one person's actions relative to another's. Take the example of two hypothetical individuals named John and Craig. A negative right against stealing would prevent John from stealing from Craig, and vice versa. A positive right against stealing would require John and Craig to protect one another from theft.

American culture values negative rights. The innate desire for liberty has an undeniable streak of rebellion built into it. We value our freedom. But constitutional principles of equity and fairness cannot be upheld in healthcare when healthcare laws are created based on negative rights. This is how healthcare laws become restrictive. Healthcare needs laws based on positive rights, structured to balance the complex and dynamic relationships in healthcare behavior.

"Each man is a sliding scale," wrote Ralph Waldo Emerson, alluding to the fact that patients with the same disease can present with different symptoms, as well as with different degrees of awareness of those symptoms. Emerson was critical of providers who "are materialists, who practice reductionism" by caring for patients based solely on medical data. For Emerson, healthcare was never intended to be distilled down to "just the facts."

Anyone who has ever been sick, or who suffers from a chronic disease, knows it is unfair to pigeonhole a patient to a set of presenting symptoms. Symptoms can change, even as an underlying condition or sickness remains. Healthcare is an experience to be viewed in its entirety. Facts and data only have meaning when viewed relative to the entire experience. Some struggle to understand this. And in those struggles, artificial distinctions form in healthcare that further compound misunderstandings. Italian priest Thomas Aquinas clarified the difference between describing one concept in various terms versus describing two separate concepts. As an example, he posed the idea of virtue. To Aquinas, virtue was an essential concept to be viewed in its entirety, even though people can behave virtuously in different ways. Aquinas distinguished between moral virtue and intellectual virtue, stating that while both are virtues, they appear differently and manifest through a different set of qualities. Yet they are the same concept.

Similarly, healthcare rights are defined through distinct qualities and manifest in different ways, but the fundamental concept of health pervades beyond any clinical or legal distinction. If physicians do not believe they can give adequate advice to a patient or perform a medical procedure, for fear of backlash or litigation, then physicians lose the inclination to share advice or perform procedures, even if it is in the patient's best interest. Physicians might then revert to more defensive tendencies of self-protection, and that affects patient care.

Without virtue, healthcare laws cannot maintain a medically appropriate balance based on positive rights. They deteriorate into restrictive laws defined through negative rights, manifesting as defensive medicine and pitting patients and physicians against one another. When virtue deteriorates in government, cruel, unjust use of power takes over. French philosopher Alexis de Tocqueville warned of this when he discussed "manipulative interpretations" of law by powerful people who lack virtue.

A lack of virtue is exemplified by those who have defaulted to extreme interpretations of healthcare law during the opioid epidemic. Such interpretations place undue burdens on those with chronic pain or substance use dependency, all while fanning the flames of public outcry for vengeance against healthcare providers.

When a law restricts a perceived liberty, the public evaluates the law relative to the rights it restricts, forming yet another balance between public perception and that law. James Madison described this balance as a triangulation, or the best arrangement among all individuals who would minimize legal burdens on any one individual. Madison, a proponent of individual rights, spearheaded efforts to include the Bill of Rights in the United States Constitution.

The constitutional amendments are designed to protect, not restrict, the rights of Americans. Subsequent interpretations of the amendments always balance the protection of these rights with commensurate responsibilities. We have freedom of speech, as long as we do not harm or injure others through our words. We have the right to bear arms, as long as we do not use those arms to intimidate or hurt others.

In contrast, many healthcare laws today are restrictive and impose undue burdens on physicians and their patients. They are designed as if healthcare is a negative right. For healthcare laws to truly represent clinical behavior, they must be designed like the laws in the Bill of Rights. Implementing Madisonian principles of triangulation would establish a medically appropriate balance between law and behavior, as well as between individual liberties and broader social responsibilities.

This requires defining individual rights in healthcare further. Healthcare rights are an essential concept, like virtue, composed of a complex set of actions, beliefs, and behaviors.

Together, they define the individual patient, provider, or pharmacist and the corresponding responsibilities each has for the other. They are positive rights. You cannot reduce an individual to an isolated decision, prescription, or action any more than you can take half a right away from someone. When such laws inhibit one aspect of an individual's behavior, other aspects are affected in unforeseen ways. Each individual experiences a complex mix of actions and decisions, and a single aspect cannot be separated from the whole. The collective mix defines an individual's rights and the full array of behavior contained within those rights.

When the CSA defines the "sufferings of addiction" as distinct from the "cravings of an addict," it assumes the two phrases represent different individuals. In reality, the phrases define characteristics of the same patient, with the variations appearing based on the quality of care received. By identifying and eliminating artificial distinctions, we rectify undue burdens that arise through inappropriately restrictive laws.

When viewed from this perspective, each clinical interaction breaks down into a set of corresponding responsibilities and burdens balanced against one another. Such a balance distributes the *whole* set of responsibilities and burdens. In law, distribution of burdens is perceived in terms of individuals or minority populations disenfranchised in some capacity due to a law, or the interpretation of a law. But in healthcare, distribution of burdens accounts for actual and potential risks when implementing a law into clinical practice.

For example, in deciding if a patient merits a prescription, the physician must weigh the patient's clinical need for the medication with the risk of abuse. This seemingly straightforward legal rubric is woefully inadequate in accounting for potential clinical consequences. The physician must also evaluate whether the patient poses a risk of diversion—the risk that others, such as family and friends, might abuse the medication. This is a risk the physician might not be able to address. Still, it is a risk for which physicians and pharmacists are liable, according to recent interpretations of the CSA. As a result, physicians and pharmacists reduce the number of opioid prescriptions out of speculative fear that comes from the possibility of diversion. In the eyes of law enforcement, this is a victory.

But in reducing medically necessary opioid prescriptions, physicians fail patients with legitimate medical needs. These patients now face an undue burden of not receiving medication for chronic medical conditions. Furthermore, many clinical studies demonstrate little to no correlation between opioid abuse mortality and the total number of opioids prescribed. But for law enforcement, the potential risk of diversion supersedes the risk to patients from poor clinical care.

The perception of the CSA as regulating any act of prescribing is an extreme interpretation of the law. But the law was never intended to be fundamentally restrictive. It was originally interpreted to balance the "sufferings of addiction" relative to the "cravings of an addict," a legal interpretation based on positive rights that coincides more with the approach of relative harm reduction.

This is a flaw in the design of the law. Most healthcare laws, described as statutes, are constructed as a series of definitions. Inconsistencies in weighing individual attributes in a statute's definition lead to legal interpretations that overemphasize a few of those attributes relative to the law's overall intent. Resulting legal interpretations conflate elemental analysis of specific aspects of the law with essential understanding of the law as a whole. This logical error manifests as violations of individual healthcare rights.

Both the US Court of Appeals for the Ninth Circuit and the US Supreme Court have declared that the prosecution of healthcare providers under the CSA must prove that the defendant "acted with intent to distribute the drugs and with intent to distribute them outside the course of professional practice." This suggests that criminal intent, or *mens rea*, must be established regarding the defendant's failure to abide by professional norms. The most important word in the *mens rea* requirement is "intent." It implies that a physician knowingly behaved like a drug dealer. This word was never intended to be taken out of context and characterized through extreme interpretations of individual actions.

This exposes a limitation of the CSA and raises questions about its relevance in healthcare. Pain management and addiction medicine are too complicated to fit the narrow framework of this law. Any attempt to legislate a complex, evolving medical condition through a single legal interpretation always produces incomplete arguments. The law must appreciate the full expanse of clinical medicine—and the full context of all clinical actions—to determine criminality in patient care.

Mens rea is an essential concept defined through different components that present in myriad ways. In different combinations, these components produce different definitions. This is why clinical behavior cannot be deduced from its component actions but must be seen it in its entirety. Accordingly, we cannot define *mens rea* through isolated actions absent the clinical context. Yet many legal interpretations of the CSA argued in courts today do quite the opposite, removing clinical actions from their context.

This raises concerns about the constitutionality of legal

arguments that focus on individual actions, or a series of "should have known" arguments around those actions, to demonstrate criminal intent. These arguments are really insinuations. They cannot be interpreted beyond the uncertainty of reasonable doubt, and they oversimplify the complexity of medical care by reinterpreting the act of prescribing medication outside of its original context of clinical care.

If these interpretations were applied across healthcare, patients would suffer, and widespread harmful clinical behavior would result. Good clinical care thrives on making optimal decisions in the face of uncertainty, as patient care changes with new information, and clinical decisions adjust with additional facts. Through therapy and medication, an addict might easily become a patient with an addiction or substance use disorder. Conversely, through distrust and abrupt discontinuation of prescribed medication, a patient with a nascent addiction might become an addict.

All laws rely on a certain level of intuitiveness in determining their application. US Supreme Court justice Oliver Wendell Holmes remarked, "Even a dog distinguishes between being stumbled over and being kicked." But excessive reliance on poorly informed, nonclinical interpretations alters the original purpose of the CSA to prevent unlawful prescribing of medications akin to what would be seen in drug dealing. The law oversimplifies into nothing more than a subjective interpretation of clinical behavior. This can be overcome only by noting different forms of uncertainty that arise when observing healthcare behavior from a clinical perspective and then reexamining it from a legal perspective.

In the clinical world, one thinks associatively and prospectively, aggregating data in real time to identify the most likely clinical scenario. In the legal world, one thinks linearly and retroactively, piecing together evidence after the fact to construct an argument. Often, information available after the fact is not available in real time. And what is considered important in real time might retroactively appear more or less important.

Many naturally loathe uncertainty; yet it is the most critical concept in healthcare law. To understand healthcare behavior, whether it be patient care or provider decision-making, uncertainty has to be seen as a complex concept, to be viewed first in its entirety and then through its component elements. The medical uncertainty that is so critical in properly interpreting healthcare law appears through this frame of reference. Uncertainty is at the heart of medicine, and analyzing uncertainty is the art of medicine. This is why, until recent decades, the practice of medicine was considered more of an art than a science.

Art is an expression of imagination, appreciated only when viewed in its entirety. A similar dynamic comes with patient care, which appears different depending on the perspective of the person viewing it. This is why Maimonides believed physicians should study uncertainty as a skill to be mastered by pursuing the uncertainty itself—studying what is not known relative to what is known, and analyzing the missing pieces in the constellation of symptoms to ascertain the likely clinical diagnosis by incrementally refining upon what is not known.

In criminal law, this is called reasonable doubt. Attributed in modern law to English jurist William Blackstone, the concept of reasonable doubt dominates our understanding of legal uncertainty to this day. In criminal law, we simplify it into a decision of guilt or innocence, even though legal uncertainty is far more complex. Yet we choose not to look at law this way, and the legal system has established its default tendencies precisely to minimize uncertainty. But the fundamental decision of guilt or innocence, of liability or responsibility, is a matter of relative uncertainty, which we consciously simplify.

In much the same way that physicians refine medical uncertainty, judges analyze legal matters until uncertainty is minimized to the extent that a decision can be made with sufficient confidence. This makes medical uncertainty and legal uncertainty two components of the same fundamental uncertainty.

Earlier, we saw that virtue or aspirational beliefs align healthcare and law. Now we see that uncertainty also aligns the essence of healthcare and law. All complex concepts can be defined through multiple characteristics, and the overlap between healthcare and law is defined through both virtue and uncertainty. Virtue ensures that individual healthcare rights are based on the principles of positive rights. Uncertainty ensures the appropriate medical context is evaluated to the fullest extent possible. Together, they orient the optimal approach to healthcare behavior. When both are fully expressed, they define the responsibilities of each individual in healthcare, in turn defining each individual's rights.

When a factory worker cuts down on his afterhours beer and burger sessions, he does so for the sake of his long-term health and to spend more time with his family. He consciously trades the pleasures of high-fat comfort foods and liquid relaxation for a lifestyle change. He is not sure how much the changes will help him, or if he will reap any long-term health benefits, but he does it anyway.

The factory worker reads online that a healthy diet can reduce the chances of long-term health problems. But then he hears stories of people who ate and drank to their hearts' content and never had a sick day. He hears about others who never drank or smoked, yet died a tragic, young death. As is endemic to our information-laden world today, he is not sure what to believe; but he makes the change, anyway. He believes his decision, which is made out of his sense of virtue, is best for him and his family. Over the first few weeks, despite the uncertainty in seeing any actual changes and not knowing what information to believe, he begins to feel more energetic in the mornings. He attributes the added energy to his lifestyle changes, but he wonders if it is real or just in his head.

Every healthcare decision, and corresponding perception, is mired in a belief (a virtue) and a corresponding doubt or disbelief (an uncertainty) that together define healthcare behavior in patients. Emerson summarized this satirically when he wrote, "I distrust the medical facts." Facts do only so much to expel uncertainty. Often, when we believe we are addressing something unknown in healthcare through facts, we merely transfer what is unknown from one source to another.

In healthcare today, statistical data seemingly drives clinical decisions. We assume statistics to be unquestionable facts, mostly because we ignore the uncertainty underlying the assumptions from which the numbers are derived.

See the three-dimensional figure 1, a drawing of a horizontal cylinder, which depicts a balance among individual healthcare rights, civic duties, and healthcare uncertainty. The three-dimensional axis features healthcare-related civic duties and healthcare-related natural rights on the x-axis and y-axis, respectively. When only those two axes are examined, the figure looks like a rectangle. But when adding the third dimension of uncertainty, the z-axis, the true cylindrical shape comes into full view. Uncertainty shapes our interpretation of healthcare by adding a particular depth to it. It provides a perspective that appears in full view only when we become aware of the concealed uncertainty.

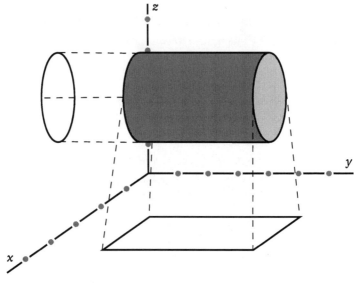

Figure I.

When a provider observes elevated blood pressure in a known hypertensive patient who is being treated through antihypertensive medications, the provider should discern whether the elevated blood pressure is due to a progression in the disease, to acute stress that forms only when blood pressure is monitored (what is called "white coat syndrome"), or to noncompliance with the prescribed medications. The three variables constitute uncertainty in the current clinical presentation. In patient care, each variable should be evaluated as a possible cause of the elevated blood pressure.

If the full scope of uncertainty is not pursued, and a provider reflexively treats the patient with a stronger dose of antihypertensive medications without considering the other options, then the provider is not fulfilling his or her required duty. Simply making default decisions, without considering all options, adversely affects the quality of patient care.

Individual rights and responsibilities in healthcare are all built on underlying uncertainty that can be seen when we balance the uncertainty with virtue. This balance is critical not only in understanding individual patient behavior, but also all facets of healthcare.

CHAPTER 16

"He's on fire!" This is the common refrain among a generation of avid video gamers playing the now-legendary *NBA Jam*. Most credit the game's unbridled popularity to its emphasis on the "hot hand." After a basketball player makes three shots in a row, the player inevitably believes the next shot will go in the basket. When a poker player wins several hands in a row, the player feels more confident in winning the subsequent hand. It is a feeling we have all experienced, whether during family game night or on a successful financial trading day.

The only problem is that the feeling may be an illusion, as now a growing body of data suggests. Regression models from the field of sports analytics show the probability of a subsequent event does not change based on previous events. Each event is independent, although we see them as related. Many prominent athletes, including NBA player LeBron James, strongly disagree. James does little to hide his disdain for the perception that the "hot hand" is an illusion. Those who believe otherwise, he asserts, lack firsthand experience to understand what it feels like. "Those guys never played the game," he says.

In his book *Sacred Hoops*, legendary NBA coach Phil Jackson weighs in on the issue as he cites examples of coaching players to develop a "state of inner harmony." Jackson trained players to block out unnecessary negative thoughts and focus on the present game situation, separating emotions around what has transpired from awareness of what needs to be done. Jackson writes extensively about his philosophy of in-game mindfulness and visualization techniques, concepts that sound eerily similar to what athletes call a "hot hand."

Hot hand and inner harmony may very well be the same thing, and any perceived difference might be based on whether the state of mind is induced consciously or appears to happen spontaneously. Perceptions, the combinations of thoughts that converge to create conscious understanding, define how we interpret something. We create perceptions to make sense of uncertainty related to something we may be attempting to understand. While the process might seem straightforward, it is anything but that, and it is often done incorrectly. Most biases arise from poorly formed perceptions of things we do not fully understand, so we devise shortcuts.

When watching a drama, we see actors who portray characters and act out a sequence of events. But we are able to pay attention at any given time to only one of these three elements: ourselves, the actors, or their characters. This makes the phrase "pay attention" more literal than one would imagine. It connotes that attention comes at a cost. Attention directed at one thing distracts attention from another. In watching stage actors perform, once immersed in the performance, we pay attention to and identify with the characters, following along in their trials and tribulations, despite knowing each character is an actor's performance.

These are incomplete perceptions. They cannot capture the full scope of uncertainty and, when applied to real world scenarios, often lead to poorly formed solutions to a problem. Yet they possess an illusory aspect that persists even when we are fully aware of the illusion, as with Müller-Lyer lines, an optical illusion in which two lines of the same length appear to be of different lengths. We know the lines are the same length, but the angles of the diagonals create the illusion that they are not.

In healthcare, though the uncertainties are more complex, the illusory perceptions are similarly persistent. Each interpretive error compounds with each interaction in healthcare, forming what Ralph Waldo Emerson called an "optical illusion about every person we meet." Even the most mundane clinical decisions are rife with perceptions that mask underlying uncertainties.

When trying to solve a difficult clinical problem, some clinicians simplify the issue into something easier to solve, but they end up addressing only the simplified version—thereby conflating the simplified solution with what would be the solution to the original problem. Many are theoretically aware of this; but they instinctively simplify with hardly a second thought. The mind gravitates toward simple relationships, such as straightforward, linear cause and effect. This results in erroneous leaps in logic. Behavioral economists refer to this as fundamental attribution error, where we attribute a specific cause or reason to a specific effect for relationships that are not directly connected.

We, as clinicians, like studies such as the Framingham Heart Study—which observes the risk factors for cardiovascular disease—because they show neat, tidy links between clinical conditions and diseases. We do not like studies that are more abstract, such as one that shows the relationship between cognitive behavioral therapy and the severity of menopause symptoms. Such studies require us to integrate abstract information within the framework of clinical care—no easy task. Does behavioral therapy work alongside medication-based therapy for menopause, or in place of it? Is there a particular level of severity of symptoms at which behavioral therapy should be considered instead of, or in tandem with, medication?

For patients with severe cognitive impairment or outright dementia, medications have proved to be of limited effectiveness. A study found that 35 percent of dementia cases can be prevented with physical exercise and structured cognitive exercises. As a result, AARP now recommends a "whole package of behaviors" as therapy to reduce incidence of dementia. Behavior as therapy is a longstanding belief in medicine—take exercise as an example—but it seems to be disregarded in favor of straightforward relationships because we cannot define the clinical effects of behavior through cause and effect.

We know behavioral therapy reduces dementia. But when we acknowledge this, we create additional uncertainty around *how* such therapy can reduce dementia. Does it matter if the therapy is self-guided, or should it be done with a guided instructor? If there are time and resource constraints, should specific behaviors be targeted more so than others? The more we focus on implementing behavioral therapy, the more uncertainties arise. As a result, we create rule-of-thumb guidelines to simplify the uncertainties. These form manageable protocols that guide behavioral therapy, assuming they address all the underlying uncertainties that correlate behavior with dementia.

Providers hardly ever consider whether the guidelines are effective when treating dementia patients, since they cannot focus on implementing them while simultaneously questioning the assumptions from which they formed. Providers simply accept the guidelines without question when caring for patients.

Greek stoic philosopher Epictetus cautioned, "Do not be kidnapped by your impressions." Yet this is what we do in this country's economic ethos as defined by Wall Street. It teems with different investment philosophies and strategies, each a different perception on market uncertainties, and each with its own set of errors. Incremental errors in each individual interpretation aggregate into larger errors, perpetuating volatile market cycles by which economists coin such lively catchphrases as "market exuberance" or "animal spirit."

An entire industry has grown around predicting market behavior based on complex formulas and algorithms, as though that additional information might stave off future errors. But we continue to see market cycles. Needless to say, stock market behavior is complex, as hordes of traders place financial bets by blending knowledge in a dynamic environment of constantly changing variables. Familiar patterns appear repeatedly, despite close monitoring of market behavior. This is because the errors do not form out of a lack of information, but instead out of perceptions that persist over multiple market cycles, regardless of any additional knowledge gained.

This dynamic applies to healthcare as much as to finance. The two graphs show a comparison of trading skill developed over time and vaping hospitalizations in the fall of 2019. In both graphs, an acute increase is followed by an acute decrease with an extended, flattened line. The authors who studied trading skill argued that the upward curve is the learning curve all traders must go through, and the downward curve reflects a combination of learned skill and attrition rates—those who quit before their skills developed.

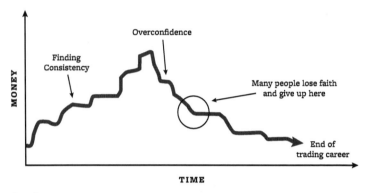

Figure 2.

Similarly, in the graph that shows vaping hospitalizations, the upward curve is the rapid growth in popularity of e-cigarettes, and the downward curve reflects the combination of people who tragically died from vaping-related complications, those who quit after a few uses, and users who learned how to vape without succumbing to life-threatening consequences.

It makes sense that similar patterns emerge. Both behaviors have addictive properties, both require learning a skill, and both have uncertain outcomes. These two behaviors—vaping and stock trading—despite appearing to be different, are similar when studied from the perspective of uncertainty. Uncertainty plays a far more important role in our lives than most imagine, and this is pervasive throughout history.

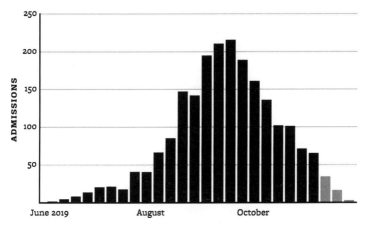

Hospital Admissions for Patients with
Vaping-Related Illnessess in the US

Figure 3.

Military historians have a name for the influence of uncertainty: they call it the hinge factor, which has proved to be the deciding factor in some of history's most famous battles. The Battle of Waterloo was decided as much by poor communication and bouts of diarrhea as by any strategic maneuvering from the British or Prussians. More recent analyses of how colonialism led to a Eurocentric world order theorize that the geographic landscape had an enormous influence we failed to see. Many cultures met their Waterloo moments due more to the latitudes and longitudes of their native lands than any perceived European cultural superiority.

It comes as no surprise, then, that Prussian military strategist Clausewitz called uncertainty "the most common and most important element" in military history. It played an outsized role in determining military outcomes and plays an equally common and important role in healthcare. We tend to rely on clinical perceptions to make decisions, but by studying the uncertainty beneath them, we see the complexity that defines healthcare behavior.

Healthcare is a story with changing narratives. Broad clinical practices and individual patient management guidelines have both changed with new information or data, either reinforcing or revising existing narratives. But to see the uncertainty in healthcare, we must see through these narratives. Uncertainty is like magma swirling turbulently under an encrusted outer layer of perceptions, not readily apparent unless actively searched for. When we do not see it, we fall prey to perceptions that may lead to biased thinking.

Falsely attributing cause and effect has led to a simplified understanding of the opioid epidemic. It has produced incomplete solutions that cannot address the complexities that caused the epidemic—and created conflicting perceptions that gloss over the true problems. Lawmakers try to solve the opioid epidemic legally by defining terms, like "cravings of an addict" or "sufferings of addiction," to characterize medically appropriate clinical behaviors. They believe these definitions standardize clinical care and help treat patients, but they are merely incomplete, simplified perceptions.

Using poorly defined terms as the pretense for legal arguments reduces complex patterns of clinical behavior to an illogical sequence of cause and effect. Those same legal arguments are then used to define criminal motivations—in effect avoiding any complicated resolution to an immensely difficult problem by substituting for simpler solutions in the form of convenient legal jargon.

This might be seen more clearly were we not inundated with news about opioid-related lawsuits and arrests. The pervasive, repeated headlines affect our beliefs by reinforcing the same narrative. Behavioral economists call this familiarity bias.

We know about this and hear it happening all the time, but we still fall for it—just like increasing access to a song makes it more popular, regardless of whether it is good.

Trends have a powerful effect on behavior. They explain why misguided interpretations of the law mirror the public's mistaken perceptions of opioid use. The narrative that says providers illicitly prescribe medications to the public, and thereby have spurred the opioid epidemic, is too tantalizing and just plausible enough to meet all the Gladwellian characteristics of virality.

Belief soon became law, and extreme interpretations of the law rose in concert with the stigma of opioid use among patients. Any opioid prescription was scrutinized as a potential drug of abuse, despite its clinical benefits. Journalist Derek Thompson epitomized the error in this extreme approach when he wrote, "Taking care to avoid being wrong is not the same as being right." This summarizes how policy makers, who advocated for extreme approaches to the opioid epidemic, sought so hard to deter any potential prescription mistakes that they compromised patient care in the process.

With beliefs backed by such pervasive narratives, the DEA needs little more than vague hunches to investigate provider practices for opioid misuse. They then use these hunches to justify investigations and indictments, effectively placing the Sword of Damocles over the head of every provider who treats a patient for pain.

We see this pattern repeated by federal regulators who reduce the complexities of healthcare through guidelines that initially appear simple and beneficial but result in interpretive biases that create lasting damage. In 1961, the FDA removed the drug thalidomide from the market after multiple cases found it to be associated with horrific fetal abnormalities in the offspring of women who had taken the drug to treat morning sickness during pregnancy. But the FDA went further. It not only removed the drug, but it also vowed never to let another such tragedy unfold. The FDA developed an elaborate drug approval process through which it now costs upward of billions of dollars for drugs to obtain regulatory clearance.

Such a process made sense as a reaction to the thalidomide tragedy, but it loses all sensibility when applied to future drugs seeking approval. Many new antibiotics for drug-resistant bacteria are currently unavailable for patients because the cost of market approval adds up to more than the market size and sales potential. The lack of new antibiotics allows multi-drug resistant bacterial infections to proliferate. Policy experts now call it an epidemic. It is an epidemic formed out of a reflexive tendency to provide an antibiotic for any constellation of symptoms that appear to be infectious, regardless of whether the antibiotics were needed.

In the early days of the COVID-19 pandemic, providers prescribed medications with questionable efficacy, regardless of whether patients were symptomatic. Frightened patients purchased non-FDA-approved test kits in large numbers online, flagrantly bypassing all regulatory oversight designed to avoid such clinically harmful behavior. In those moments, the public's fear of the virus overtook any regard for the regulatory process—which, ironically, became mostly ineffective in the most critical of times.

Instead, we saw a rapid series of interpretations and reactions to facts as they surfaced. Healthcare professionals attributed cause and effect without knowing the full cause of the pandemic, struggling to make sense of what was transpiring, even when all the relevant facts had not yet appeared.

The COVID-19 pandemic unveiled in real time what manifested more slowly during the country's many drug epidemics. The rise of freebase cocaine in the 1980s, particularly among the African American community, ushered in the crack epidemic. Drug use had a devastating effect in urban communities, exacerbated by an imprudent, aggressive response from law enforcement. This resulted in heavy-handed criminalization of even minor drug offenses and the unwinding of the fabric of urban communities.

Families fell apart as they lost loved ones in the criminal justice system or to cycles of addiction. When law enforcement's initial efforts were perceived to be ineffective, or not as effective as they would have liked, they responded by increasing the intensity of the same aggressive approach. Law enforcement officials defined success by the number of drug dealers arrested and imprisoned, and by the reduced supply of drugs available in the illicit market.

By all measured metrics, the crack epidemic was improving. But the metrics offered a distorted perception of success. What law enforcement believed to be an improvement in the crack epidemic was simply a substitution—using metrics that were easily obtainable, but only indirectly related to the actual cause of the epidemic. Crack use actually increased during the early years of the heightened emphasis on criminalization, before eventually decreasing. Why it later decreased is a widely debated subject. Most law enforcement agents will tell you their efforts led to the decline.

But recent analysis has shown multiple reasons for the decline, including a demographic shift from older users who used crack cocaine with heroin to younger users who preferred marijuana over more malignant substances. This is a startling rebuke to law enforcement's traditional approach to addiction, supporting the theory that crime, particularly drug-related crime, occurs in cycles—rising and falling based on a complex array of factors often independent of law enforcement.

Similar cyclic patterns appear in the opioid epidemic. Law enforcement officials believed reducing the supply of prescription opioids in the community would reduce mortality, so they arrested providers and pharmacists in droves, assuming any arrest would net a positive impact. But studies have repeatedly shown no relationship between the number of opioid prescriptions and opioid-related mortality.

After realizing such an aggressive approach is harmful to the patient, healthcare policy experts created prescribing guidelines to balance government oversight with proper medical care. They were known as the CDC Guideline for Prescribing Opioids for Chronic Pain, enacted in 2016 and revised in 2022. This guideline, along with variations of similar guidelines created by state medical licensing boards and medical associations, were implemented by insurance companies and state regulatory organizations to help providers make prescribing decisions.

Soon, the guidelines designed to improve patient care came to define how opioid prescribing decisions were made. As a result, the limitations in the guidelines came also to define patient care in general for those treated with opioid medications. Policy experts responded by revising the guidelines. It began with a few addendums, then some caveats and disclaimers. Eventually, revision after revision came out, each purporting to be better than the last. But each was nothing more than a reinterpretation of what policy experts perceived to be safe prescriber practices.

They believed that gathering more data would improve our understanding of the epidemic and consequently bring about better guidelines. Emergency departments were among the first to compile data on opioid-related overdoses, so many of the guidelines are largely influenced by patient outcomes in acute care settings. This led to an overemphasis on acute metrics as markers of overall success in the opioid epidemic, and it exemplifies how reporting bias influences perceptions in healthcare. While mortality and overdoses are considered the main metrics to measure, most opioids are prescribed by primary care physicians in chronic care settings.

The lack of data on prescribing protocols in long-term care settings and patient outcomes caused healthcare policy experts to misapply acute care metrics outside of their intended clinical context. Studying prescribing practices in chronic care settings requires metrics that study opioid abuse when patients first develop dependencies, instead of monitoring for overdose events that appear long after an addiction has developed. But many remain fixated on correlating opioid prescribing with opioid abuse, despite overwhelming data that suggests otherwise. This shows how biases formed from our perceptions have more impact on policy than the data does.

Attribution error blinds us to what appears obvious in hindsight. We know Americans are prescribed more opioids than most patients in other parts of the world. We know hundreds of thousands of Americans have overdosed on or are addicted to opioids. What's not obvious is how the numbers—mortality, overdose rates, and job productivity losses—initially came about. The rise of the epidemic is loosely attributed to a single, broad upswing in overall opioid use. But the upswing is really a long-term trend accentuated by a short-term trend, both combining to create the appearance of an increase in opioid use, but for different reasons.

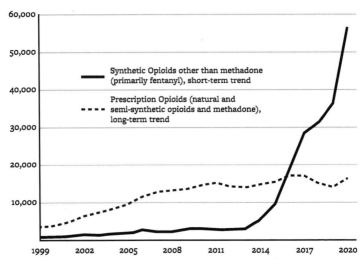

National Drug-Involved Overdose Deaths
Number Among All Ages, 1999–2020

Figure 4.

The long-term trend represents patients who have chronic pain due to chronic medical conditions—a trend that increases along with broader demographic trends in the patient population. As Americans grow older and live longer on average, overall medical needs expand. The most cost-effective and widely available treatment for chronic pain is prescribing medications like opioids. Accordingly, the population growth among patients treated for chronic pain accounts for the long-term rise in opioid prescriptions.

The short-term trend represents younger individuals who abuse opioids and develop addictions, predominantly from opioids obtained illegally—either medications diverted from family or friends, or synthetic opioids purchased from street dealers.

Before the opioid epidemic reached peak levels of outrage and stigmatization, opioid medications were prescribed at the discretion of the provider, who would ask patients to quantify pain as a number. Providers would ask patients to characterize their pain on a scale from one to ten, with ten being the worst pain the patient could possibly experience. If a provider felt opioid medications were necessary to reduce pain from a 10/10 to a 4/10, but not to a 2/10, then that provider prescribed less than did a provider who felt more comfortable placing the patient at a 2/10 pain level. The decision-making was subjective, as was the patient's perception of the pain.

Unlike other chronic conditions that have an objective metric to compare with, pain has two subjective points of interpretation: the provider and the patient. Consequently, clinical practice styles have varied significantly. Despite the variance, trends show an overall growing patient population that documented pain as a medical condition. This explains why the DEA permitted more opioids to be manufactured as recently as 2013. The federal government, providers, pharmaceutical companies, and insurance companies all agreed opioids are an acceptable treatment for chronic pain. But none of them expected the short-term trend of opioid abuse to have the effect it did, both statistically and socially.

The lax efforts of the FDA and DEA in the early part of the 2010s reflect their initial perceptions of opioid abuse and diversion. The later draconian measures of suspicion and intimidation reflect government reactions due to changing perceptions of opioids. Going from increased quotas of opioids to medical McCarthyism is a drastic jump. It happened because the federal government conflated the two trends and deemed those in the initial, long-term trend responsible for those in the second, acute trend. By interpreting two trends as one, the government reinterpreted the entire healthcare system.

Healthcare supply chains were looked at as veritable drug

cartels. Patients with chronic pain were treated like patients with substance use disorders. Providers treating leg pains were at the same legal risk as providers extorting cash for pain pills. Arrest after arrest took place, and poorly conceived policies on opioids proliferated, all originating from a core misconception.

Reactions reverberated faster than the healthcare industry could adapt. Medical insurance companies, accustomed to opioids and other generic medications being the primary treatment option for pain, had limited coverage for more expensive alternative medications or procedures. Providers and patients were suddenly forced to navigate Byzantine layers of prior authorizations to secure coverage for more expensive treatment options. Attempts to do so often proved fruitless, leaving patients to suffer or to identify illicit alternatives to manage their pain. The rapid drop in opioid prescriptions, widely touted as a success, simply increased the relative percentage of people who obtained illicit opioids—precisely because law enforcement's aggressive response disproportionately targeted the very patients who most needed opioids.

Those in the short-term trend, users whose original intent was to abuse opioids, went on to abuse other drugs. But those in the long-term trend, patients with legitimate chronic pain, now struggled to receive the same medical care to which they were accustomed. They endured heightened scrutiny for the continued treatment of conditions already diagnosed years before, and this left many patients unable to keep pace and feeling ultimately abandoned by healthcare. Many patients felt, and continue to feel, unfairly targeted. With little recourse, they blame providers, pharmaceutical companies, or other patients who are 'ruining it for everybody,' perpetuating the cycle of attribution errors.

Providers, insurance companies, and pharmaceutical companies disagree about who is responsible and what can be done. Providers, forced to identify alternative medications, face unclear and ever-changing criminal risks. Many providers who attempted to wean patients off opioids turned to other types of pain medications, including drugs like gabapentin, which typically treats neurological conditions such as seizures but has some benefit in pain management.

But then the FDA issued a warning about an increase in inappropriate prescribing practices for opioid alternative medications, leaving providers again at risk for treating patients who have pain. With the risk of criminalization growing, many providers stopped prescribing opioids or treating chronic pain altogether, abandoning their patients.

Figure 5 depicts the effects of changing government intervention. While overall quantities of opioids decreased, the decrease disproportionately affected those with chronic pain more than it did those who abused opioids. The result was a greater percentage of opioids being abused than being appropriately used for medically legitimate health reasons.

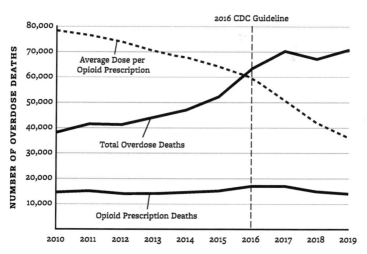

Figure 5.

Patients in the long-term trend needed opioids to manage their pain, but suddenly found themselves with little to no recourse. Patients in the short-term trend, more focused on satisfying their addictions, transitioned to other illicit drugs to seek a high. At first it may seem difficult to discern one group from the other. But a closer look at the trends reveals subtle patterns of behavior that distinguish the two.

Start by looking at broad trends in drug abuse. If patients abusing opioids were receiving them only through the healthcare system, we would see a direct increase in heroin and fentanyl mortality commensurate with a decrease in mortality from prescription opioids. Instead, we see a substantial decrease in mortality from prescription opioids, little to no increase in heroin mortality, and stark increases in mortality from methamphetamines, fentanyl, and alcohol, with slight regional variations in the popularity of opioids versus methamphetamines.

The changing mortality patterns correlate with individuals from trend two, in which the type of high matters less than the act of getting high. With drugs going in and out of style, behavior is predicated on drug choice and potency more than anything else.

The two graphs show horizontal curves with the vertex on the left. The top graph (fig. 6) is commonly seen in finance, known as the Sharpe ratio, which compares the return an investor can generate relative to the assumed risk. The bottom graph (fig. 7) compares the potency of an illicit drug relative to the risk of taking that drug. The similarities in the curves illustrate parallels in fundamental human behavior when comparing uncertainty, risk, and addictive behaviors.

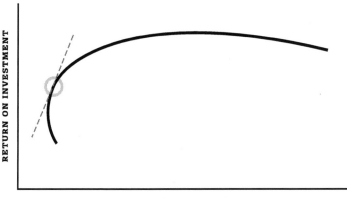

Figure 6.

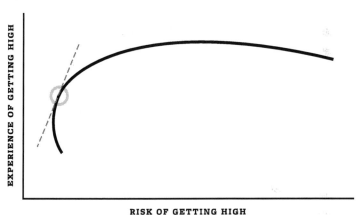

Figure 7.

We all stratify risks relative to rewards. This applies to drug abuse as much as to finance. The potency-to-risk ratio determines which drugs become popular or fashionable. Addicts often select drugs that maximize potency and minimize risk—which, for those addicted, is often the amount of money needed to purchase the drugs. Once fentanyl, a highly potent opioid, became cheaper than heroin, it gained popularity because its potency-to-risk ratio became greater than that of heroin.

This ratio can be used to predict which illicit drugs will become popular, because addiction is a cycle that sways like fashion trends. Laver's Law, a formula that suggests fashion trends are cyclical, states that because all new fashion contains aspects of both new and old styles, the combination of the two predicts incoming styles. In a similar way, trends in drug popularity combine old and new forms of the high a drug produces. The declining popularity of heroin gave way to fentanyl, a much more potent opioid, and to methamphetamine, which produces an opposite type of high.

Today, methamphetamines are creating the same issues in many communities that heroin and prescription opioids did in recent years. Many addiction specialists now seek to extend opioid treatment protocols to include those struggling with both fentanyl and methamphetamine addictions.

It can be argued that trends in prescription opioids and mortality are not truly independent, as the popularity of opioids could have increased with increasing access, much like increased access to marijuana increases its popularity. We would then assume opioid abuse increases with increased access to healthcare systems and prescribers. Intuitively, this makes sense; but if the relationship between opioid prescriptions and mortality were predicated on access alone, multiple opioid epidemics would have already played out. Prescribing trends among providers exhibit their own cycles, with the total number of opioids prescribed increasing and then decreasing over past decades.

The greatest increases occurred when pain was interpreted as a vital sign in the 1990s, and medical guidelines thereafter strongly advocated for eliminating pain through aggressive pain management therapies. But when analyzed year over year, mortality trends do not correlate with changes in prescribing trends. In fact, most correlations between mortality and opioid overdoses come from data averaged over multiple years. Still, decisions continue to be made in reaction to short-term changes based on conclusions drawn from long-term trends. During the COVID-19 pandemic, we all watched as our favorite restaurants shut down, small businesses closed or went under, and mortality inched upward. By focusing attention on the growing incidence and mortality, we gave rise to a pandemic of fear that emerged alongside the actual COVID-19 pandemic. Our self-induced pandemic of fear turned a public health crisis into an existential crisis, affecting every aspect of life.

This same fear appeared in the opioid epidemic and continues to shape its narrative. It should be no surprise that patterns of behavior during the pandemic are similar to those during the opioid epidemic. In both cases, we looked for something or someone to blame. With COVID-19, some blamed the delayed response and insufficient resources, while others blamed the novelty of the virus and its unforeseen intensity.

Then the financial markets took a hit, and people started counting lives lost. The more they counted, the more they feared, and soon the fear overtook behavior. People demanded tests, not realizing that, regardless of test results, the treatment would be the same: quarantine. People demanded tests even as they knew the results could be wrong. Fear was treated like another symptom of COVID-19, along with cough and fever. By curing fears, we subconsciously believed we were treating the virus.

The irrationality of fear led physicians to forgo prescribing ethics to self-prescribe 55,000 scripts of hydroxychloroquine. Fear turned worst-case scenarios into likely scenarios, leading local government officials to demand higher numbers of medical supplies and ventilators than models projecting infection and hospitalization rates suggested they would need. No one can say whether the request was appropriate or an overreaction. It was a subjective assessment that came down to perceptions held by those in positions of power.

This is the nature of complexity in healthcare. Healthcare professionals knew in the fall of 2019 that a severe flu season was expected in spring 2020, because Australia—a nation after which the United States models its seasonal viral responses—had an abnormally severe influenza season. But few epidemiologists believe the coronavirus outbreak predictions should have been based on the influenza virus's patterns.

Several unique viral outbreaks have occurred in past decades, including a mild coronavirus outbreak called severe acute respiratory syndrome (SARS) in 2002. It seems medical professionals should have been aware of the risks. But every time it seems we should have predicted a health crisis, it ends up being unique enough that the uncertainties overwhelm what we might have anticipated. This is because uncertainties in healthcare appear differently in the moment than they do after the fact.

If a patient takes one medication, as clinicians we manage adherence to the medication, the disease's progression, and the medication's potential side effects. If a patient takes five medications, we have to worry about adherence to and side effects of each medication, as well as the progression of each disease that corresponds to each medication. When fully accounting for all factors that affect patient care and the presentation of symptoms, healthcare becomes complicated fairly quickly.

A recent study on co-prescribing opioids with a class of anxiety medication called benzodiazepines found that one-third of providers prescribed anxiety medications for back pain. Physicians were either prescribing anxiety medications outside the medications' intended scope, or they were using benzodiazepines to wean patients off opioids, recognizing that pain and anxiety are, for some patients, different presentations of the same underlying condition.

The reasons for prescribing the anxiety medications vary among the providers in the study—and are probably some combination of the two stated reasons—but the perception of each individual prescription generates a different response. Providers perceived to be prescribing benzodiazepines outside the scope of their intended use would warrant legal action. But providers attempting to wean patients off opioids, by treating the anxiety that stems from back pain, could be seen as providing medically appropriate care, assuming we see benzodiazepines as a less harmful alternative to opioids. The same behavior elicits contrasting perceptions and reactions.

Healthcare uncertainty is a complex concept that should be understood broadly at first, and then distilled into its components. To understand its full context, we need to create a framework that balances the broad view with all the granular components to reveal the uncertainty in its entirety. When discussing the vaping epidemic, we analyzed the uncertainty in the data to make sense of confusing and incongruent information and discovered that, although vaping was at first perceived to be a complex, mysterious epidemic, it was really two unique trends superimposed. We followed that by showing the vaping mortality curve is basically a learning curve.

Does that imply that lives could have been saved by preemptively educating the public on safe vaping practices? The answer hinges on a trio of perceptions: 1) whether you see vaping as a tool for smoking cessation or for drug abuse, 2) whether you believe in harm reduction, and 3) whether you see drug education as an implicit moral hazard against drug addiction. The number of perspectives through which this question can be viewed is larger than we would have initially thought.

But these issues are often distilled down to one perception, which is given all the attention while all other perspectives are buried. Along the way, clinical complexity is simplified in favor of a prevailing narrative. These mistakes affect how we think about healthcare—not just for policy issues, but for even basic clinical diagnoses.

Lung cancer has long been attributed to cigarette smoking. But a recent study found an increasing incidence of lung cancer among women was higher than the rate of increase among women who smoke. The study found that 15 percent of lung cancer occurs in nonsmokers, but 24 percent occurs in nonsmokers who are women. Another study of nearly 12,000 lung cancer patients found that nonsmoker patients made up 8 percent of total lung cancer patients from 1990 to 1995, but 14.9 percent from 2011 to 2013. This indicates that the direct relationship between smoking and lung cancer might not fully explain lung cancer incidence.

Statistics that attempt to correlate a complex set of behaviors and risk factors on outcomes alone are inevitably incomplete. This is the same problem noted when poorly constructed healthcare laws appear in clinical care. They do little more than distill complex medical behavior into guidelines and measurements.

We see this demonstrated with healthcare insurance, which began with the idea that cost sharing reduces unnecessary care. But insurance plans constructed with mandatory deductibles often result in more harm than good, because the deductibles influence when patients choose to receive their medical care. Every decision to utilize the insurance policy and receive care becomes a patient's personal calculation on whether the care is worth the deductible payment.

This was a sticking point when legislators unveiled a slew of high-deductible insurance policies under the Affordable Care Act, which made it prohibitively expensive to use insurance coverage. Many chose not to use it despite having to purchase it, which defeats the purpose of health insurance. Deductibles are designed to curb unnecessary use of medical care, hinging on the belief that patients would default to using their insurance when clinically necessary. But if the deductible incentivizes the opposite behavior, then the purpose of insurance changes.

An ACA plan from Illinois sidestepped this problem by implementing a default enrollment policy through which uninsured patients were automatically signed up for an insurance plan regardless of whether they intended to select it. The default altered the decision from whether to use insurance to deciding when and how to use the prohibitively expensive insurance plan. This changed how patients perceived their health plan. The ACA plan assumed the automatic default enrollment would simplify obtaining and using an insurance plan, but it only changed patients' behaviors toward using their insurance—an unintended effect of oversimplifying a complex behavior through a default decision.

This mistake was repeated in Arkansas when the state attempted to implement work requirements for patients eligible for the state's Medicaid plans. The well-intentioned plan created two layers of hurdles. The first was the job requirement, and the second was the proper reporting of the job requirement. Curiously, the second hurdle became a bigger deterrent for many applying for enrollment. Many gainfully employed people were denied Medicaid coverage because they did not properly complete the reporting process.

Like laws, healthcare policies are effective only if the intended purpose accurately represents the full breadth of the behavior it addresses—as experienced by those affected. Insurance policies, while essential for many patients, are effective only when the structure of the plan matches the intended behavior of the patient using it.

Policies are formalized rules that direct intended behavior, but the unintended consequences of simplifying complex behavior lead to perceptions that run contrary to the original intent of the policies. These are often more consequential in the actual behavior observed. We call this the principle of dual effect—any healthcare decision has both a positive and a negative effect, an opportunity cost. But the two effects are not mutually exclusive. In fact, the relationship between the two is as important as the effects themselves. Any relationship between a policy, guideline, or law and its underlying clinical behavior creates an inherent paradox in the sense that the predominant perceptions determine intended behavior, but uncertainty in those perceptions determines actual behavior.

When perceptions change, so does uncertainty, creating contradictions in the behavior acted out and the behavior intended. Figure 8 depicts how these paradoxes form. It shows a normal bell curve, which represents patient behavior, with vertical lines that characterize the behavior incentivized by a policy or guideline. Patients to the right of the curve are actively compliant with their health. Patients to the left of the curve are grossly noncompliant. Patients in the middle, forming the bulk of the curve, are at times actively compliant and at times noncompliant.

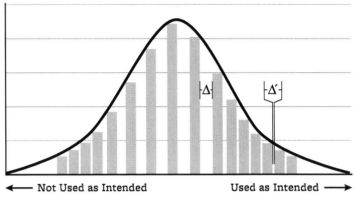

◄——— Not Used as Intended   Used as Intended ———►

Figure 8.

The width between the lines is called a delta. The wider the lines, the larger the deltas, and the more uncertainty in the behavior. Ideally, the deltas should be zero. Realistically, the goal is to minimize the size of the deltas to minimize the unintended effects that characterize the patient's behavior relative to the policy's intended effect. Patients in the middle of the curve have wider deltas because there is greater uncertainty in their behavior. With more uncertainty comes a greater likelihood of moral hazards where the behavior seen runs contrary to the intended policy.

Association healthcare plans—insurance plans that lack consumer protection rights—are cheaper alternatives to traditional healthcare plans; but they require patients to be more active in understanding what their plan covers. Often preferred by small businesses, association plans require members to be more engaged and bear greater responsibilities in managing their plans, but they offer lower premiums for the policy holder. They provide a financial incentive for patients who are more active in the management of their health. Conceivably, those who are more compliant can maximize the benefits of such an insurance plan while minimizing unnecessary costs that come from deductible or premium changes that might incur when using it.

Figure 8 shows the interaction between the policy holder, the patient, and the association healthcare plan. The bell curve defines patient behavior, and the vertical lines show the various cost points resulting from the plan. At any point along the bell curve, a patient decides whether to engage with the insurance plan—the intended behavior—or seek medical care outside of the insurance coverage. Vertical lines along the curve that have wider deltas allude to patients that waver in using the policy correctly.

Optimally designed insurance plans reward appropriate patient behavior by balancing medical coverage with the associated costs. But inevitably, disparities arise between the intended structure of the insurance plan and the patient's decisions. The likelihood of these disparities leading to adverse patient decisions depends on the uncertainty within the deltas.

This depicts the complex balance between the level of patient engagement and a policy's intended purpose, and it exemplifies the relationship between uncertainty and complexity in healthcare.

CHAPTER 17

"Eureka!" exclaimed Archimedes when he discovered how the principle of specific gravity differentiates pure from impure gold. The Greek physicist was working on a project commissioned by the king of his native Syracuse. While the purpose of the project may be lost to myth, the word lives on in our everyday lives. Its Greek origin is *heuriskein*, the word root for heuristic, which is the method by which our minds create simplified, automated ways of thinking and find solutions to otherwise complex problems.

Studied by behavioral economists for decades, heuristics explain how our thought patterns form. We now apply heuristic techniques in healthcare, to study thought patterns that occur in fleeting moments of a quick medical decision or brief patient interaction. Heuristics reveal inherent limitations—flaws in how we think through problems or in the thoughts that define what we presume to be true.

A study of amateur Scrabble players exemplifies this. Players were asked to decide whether a commonly used letter appears more often as the first or third letter in a set of words. Most players said the first, because players are trained to look for the first letters of words. Their minds defaulted to an assumption that the most common letters overall appear most often as the first letters—a false association based on limited information.

Healthcare is filled with such biases, whether these are attribution errors, substitution errors, or default tendencies that confuse incomplete but consistent information as representing the full set of knowledge. All of these are heuristics, all hiding in plain sight, appearing in the medical decisions we make and in the words through which we communicate. They may appear to be harmless, but over time they lead to biased perceptions that become clinically significant and harmful to patients.

The patient encounter, the heart of healthcare, is unique in its speed and complexity, unlike in any other setting found in society. Patients discuss the most vulnerable and intimate aspects of their lives, and providers analyze these experiences while extracting clinical knowledge, together forming the patient narrative. This is the essence of patient care. Indeed, our entire perception of healthcare is understood through the process of storytelling. Clinical experiences dictate the stories we tell ourselves and others about health.

When two people speak normally, thought patterns driving both verbal and nonverbal forms of communication are balanced, or symmetrical. Whether two friends meeting for lunch, a couple of coworkers chitchatting at the office, or any other traditional setting for one-on-one conversation, it is assumed most conversations will be on equal footing.

In contrast, the clinical encounter is asymmetrical from the onset, as every interaction is between someone who is a perceived expert and someone else who is not. The word "perceived" is important. An expert, says behavioral economist Daniel Kahneman, is someone who has studied something in depth and developed more associations, or a greater number of intersecting thought patterns, than a nonexpert.

The expert in healthcare—the clinical provider who has studied medicine—understands the relationship between symptoms, physical findings, and clinical data in greater depth than the patient does. But learning something in detail also influences how someone thinks; and this then creates a thought pattern unique to the provider that in turn forms its own heuristic.

As a result, a dichotomy forms between provider and patient. The provider perceives the presenting symptoms of the patient in the context of previously obtained clinical knowledge. The patient perceives the presenting symptoms as a direct personal experience. The exchange of information is asymmetrical—because the frame of reference is different. Though the expert may have a better understanding of clinical medicine, it does not equate to an absolute understanding of every presenting clinical condition.

Recognizing something in greater detail does not mean a person automatically recognizes it with greater accuracy. Yet many are drawn in by expert views and often accept them without question, largely because more knowledge is mistaken for more accurate knowledge. But just because you are closer to the target does not mean you hit it. Conflating the heightened marksmanship of an expert with absolute expertise simplifies an otherwise complex conversation about a person's health into a one-sided lecture.

If your blood sugar is high, it is much easier to hear that a medication once a day can control your blood sugar than to delve into a discussion about the relationships among stress, behavioral changes, and family histories. Patients and providers alike struggle to understand how all these factors relate—and the relative influence of each. But these very uncertainties dictate the patient's response to the medication recommendation.

Figure 9 shows the relationship between information given and the response taken, with two curves to represent a known response and an unknown response. The known response is our conscious reaction. The unknown response is the more subtle, unconscious manifestation we are not aware of but that we are impacted by—the "I did that?" moment. Notice how the perceived expert, with greater associations of facts and data, still struggles with uncertainty (albeit less uncertainty) than the perceived nonexpert.

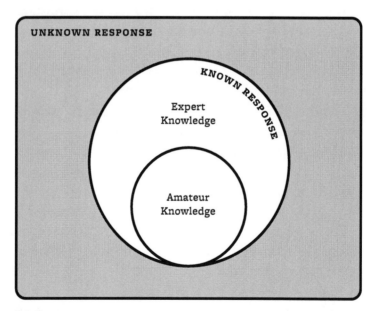

Figure 9.

Providers and patients both see the same uncertainty during a patient encounter, but the response to the uncertainty separates the provider from the patient. A provider relies on more clinical information—greater association patterns—to address a larger portion of the uncertainty. But neither the provider nor the patient can address it all.

A presumption that one knows all there is to know ignores the underlying uncertainty present in every patient encounter. This bias, common in healthcare, is called the narrative heuristic. Since clinicians abhor uncertainty, some tend to simplify and modify any complex concept into a comfortable, convenient narrative, however incorrect: disease and pill, problem and solution.

As a result, many providers would rather adhere to guidelines and protocols that define standards of clinical care. Because providers are formally educated in clinical medicine, they train their minds to revert to what they know and have studied. It simplifies the patient encounter but introduces biases in the process. Medicine is an oasis of knowledge in a desert of uncertainty, and a clinical encounter is nothing more than an excerpt from an ongoing story we don't have full view of and might learn more about only after it is well underway.

It is no surprise that reactions to three recent healthcare crises—the COVID-19 pandemic, the vaping epidemic, and the opioid epidemic—all began with false starts, which led critics to lament delayed responses and decry an apparently inexcusable lack of awareness. While these three epidemics are different, the similarities in behavioral responses reflect similar underlying uncertainties that characterize each one. Initial perceptions form, attempting to explain the epidemics, which then give way to an opposite set of perceptions attempting to explain why the initial explanations were false. On it goes, an ebb and flow of incomplete perceptions jockeying to simplify underlying uncertainties.

These perceptions and subsequent reactions are heuristics, thought patterns based on limited information that respond to subjective biases instead of objective facts and observed data. During the turbulence of an acute healthcare crisis, like the COVID-19 pandemic, heuristics appear and collapse in rapid succession. The changing thought patterns also appear in slower-moving epidemics, albeit with much more subtlety, and can have prolonged effects over the course of multiple patient encounters, as patients with chronic pain or substance dependencies know quite well.

During a patient visit, heuristics define the encounter between patient and provider, leading to familiar patterns of thinking that collectively influence healthcare policy. This pattern explains the tendency to rely on guidelines when treating patients who present with familiar sets of symptoms. Therefore, what is considered to be the standard of care is really an opportunity cost of attention, defined by the predominant heuristic.

Clinical care is standardized through guidelines that streamline the clinical workup for a patient presenting with a set of symptoms and reinforce clinicians' decision-making patterns. These standards are defined through evidence-based medicine, emphasizing concrete data and known facts over more qualitative symptoms. This approach may provide a solid foundation for patient care, but it will not address patient care comprehensively. In a rush to quantify medicine, patient care is simplified by distilling clinical information into data and guidelines that effectively make decisions for clinicians. Along the way, healthcare professionals lose track of the uncertainty residing in qualitative aspects of medicine.

Uncertainty is too pervasive and dynamic to be glossed over in clinical guidelines. Like energy as defined in the field of thermodynamics, uncertainty cannot be created or destroyed, but only transferred. Trying to eliminate the underlying uncertainty in one part of patient care creates additional perceptions rife with uncertainty elsewhere. The more granularly we seek to explain something, the more opportunities we produce for additional uncertainties to form. It becomes far too complex for any provider or any patient encounter; and instead of dealing with it all, providers substitute one bias for another. As Einstein said, "As our circle of knowledge expands, so does the circumference of darkness surrounding it."

We forget this when practicing clinical medicine, but we retain it somewhat in clinical research. Clinical researchers know that studies are only as good as the study design, and study outcomes are influenced by what is studied as much as by how it is studied. Most clinical study outcomes are called statistically significant outcomes, defined by how much uncertainty was acknowledged and properly accounted for. But in practice, clinical data transforms into absolute certainties, and guidelines become the standards by which decisions are made. This is a fundamental mistake, because data alone do not address the clinical condition. It only provides a perspective from which an interpretation of the clinical condition can be developed.

If a patient has a persistently elevated blood sugar level, then the initial instinct is to treat the patient with medication and normalize levels to within recommended guidelines. But what is considered appropriate blood sugar level changes for patients who have poorly controlled diabetes. The actual treatment of diabetes depends on taking the medication not to reach a sugar level within a set range, but to avoid both excessively low and high blood sugar values. The goal is to achieve a dynamic balance between the presenting clinical symptoms and the fluctuating blood sugars.

The standard for normal blood sugar levels changes relative to the changing severity of the diabetes. It cannot be defined through standard guidelines for patients with prediabetes compared to those with poorly controlled diabetes. We incorrectly believe we are reducing uncertainty in healthcare when we are merely transferring it to the guidelines—both to the underlying assumptions and to our own interpretations of them.

Data creates as many unknowns as knowns, transferring what is unknown from clinical decisions to the uncertainty of applying data from a broad statistical model to one specific patient. In the fast-paced world of clinical care, this is hardly ever considered. But uncertainties influence the ways clinicians think and the decisions they make, leading to interpretive errors, since many would rather choose a bias than take a head-on approach to the uncertainty.

Figure 10 provides a way to look schematically at uncertainty. We start by focusing on the thought patterns that arise at the intersection of certainty and uncertainty in any patient encounter. The overlapping shaded region represents anything that was learned or recently understood. The unshaded, uncovered portion on the right side of the uncertainty circle represents what remains unknown. Inconsistencies in patient behavior or decision-making arise when it is mistakenly assumed that the overlapping section of uncertainty encompasses all aspects of the uncertainty in patient behavior.

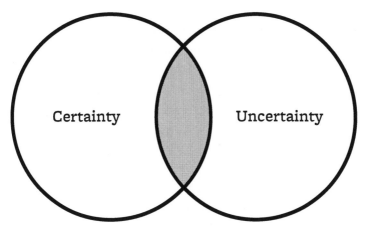

Figure 10.

To make matters more complex, over the course of multiple encounters, the intersection of the two circles changes dynamically as the patient-provider relationship evolves. By mistaking the shifting overlap of what is known and not known for a fixed, comprehensive understanding of everything there is to know, the provider initiates a wide range of thought patterns filled with incomplete interpretive errors that rise and collapse over the changing uncertainty.

It is difficult to comprehend uncertainty as a dynamic element. Even the best-known models of uncertainty are simplified versions of the original premise. This includes the Pareto principle, the famed 80/20 rule developed by the Italian economist to describe distribution of costs and services. Applied today in healthcare, it describes the distribution of efforts and outcomes. In adolescent psychiatry, it has become of a rule of thumb to describe the balance between available clinical resources and additional needs for children with mental health conditions: 80 percent of adolescent psychiatry care focuses on 20 percent of the adolescent psychiatric population.

This may be true sometimes, but it is certainly not true all the time. Pareto never intended this ratio to be static. Rather, he saw it as a dynamic relationship changing through that fixed ratio. A minor difference in wording makes a major difference in how this principle is applied, and likewise how clinical data should be perceived and implemented in patient care. Many studies have alluded to the relationship between anxiety and social media among adolescents, and one such study found that one-third of all teens have anxiety, identifying social media as the principal cause. If the simplified, static version of Pareto's rule were applied to this study, clinicians might consider reducing social media for the adolescent population at higher risk for anxiety. But some therapists now advocate for social media use in specific contexts to *ease* anxiety. The answer, then, is not found in any one approach to social media as right or wrong, but in whether changing approaches to social media reduces or increases anxiety in individual adolescents over time.

Focus should be on the change in perception and how that change occurs. This does not occur in rational, predictable ways—because thoughts and behaviors are anything but rational. Take, for example, racial disparities in patient outcomes, originating out of perceptions that form in response to uncertainties in a patient encounter. Sociologist and civil rights activist W. E. B. Dubois wrote, "Racism at a certain point goes beyond rational thought." Racism in healthcare goes beyond overt discrimination, as most healthcare providers are not outright racists. Yet a persistent disparity in clinical decision-making and patient outcomes exists in relation to African American patients.

Repeated studies have found that Black patients receive fewer pain medications at lesser frequencies than white patients in acute care settings. Hardly any provider would say they decide what medications to prescribe based on a patient's race, but the data conclusively proves a difference. Perhaps many providers are not honest about their racial tendencies. More likely, racial behavior is inherently complex and manifests both consciously and subconsciously.

Historically, the medical community believed Black patients had higher pain tolerances due to perceived physiological differences, including thicker skin and different lung capacities. The latter misconception continues to permeate clinical medicine and affects any patient who has ever had lung capacity evaluated with a spirometer. This instrument was first used in the Antebellum South to measure slaves' lung capacity.

While use of the spirometer in such a manner is abhorrent and long since discontinued, the data continues to be populated in such a manner, as many spirometers designed today still have separate settings based on race. The spirometer is an example of healthcare data that gives rise to unforeseen perceptions that go beyond the original intention of the data—that, if not properly observed, reappears in medically harmful ways.

A study analyzing pulse oximeters, devices that measure blood oxygen, found that Black patients had undetected episodes of decreased oxygen concentration, or hypoxemia, three times as frequently as white patients. The study did not attribute this to any one cause but noted that variations in the data between Black and white patients create their own risk, since the interpretation of the data is different for Black patients compared to white patients. Those interpretations, largely based on subjective perceptions of data, adversely affect Black patients.

Past attempts to correct for racial disparities in healthcare tried to develop guidelines that standardized clinical decision-making. These attempts inevitably failed, as trying to regulate healthcare through guidelines is like placing a buoy in the middle of a turbulent ocean and expecting all passing ships to heed its warning. The turbulence in the ocean affects the ship more than the marker set by the buoy.

In the infamous Tuskegee syphilis experiments, government researchers knowingly infected Black military men with syphilis for four decades to study the disease's long-term effects without informing the patients in the study. Though the government has since apologized, the Black community's distrust toward clinical research and the healthcare industry still reverberates today and plays a significant role in ongoing health disparities, by influencing the heuristics that appear among Black patients.

Perceptions affect not only race, but also gender. Studies have shown that women in acute care settings wait longer than men on average to receive pain medications. Many of these studies attribute the reported discrepancy to sexist tendencies subtly displayed among providers. This could be true in select cases, but behavior is cultural. Some women may be more passive than men in healthcare settings or less willing to complain.

By emphasizing the belief that women wait longer in acute care settings because of sexism, women may reactively feel slighted or respond with uncharacteristic suspicion during an encounter with a clinician. Any questionable behavior on the part of a provider toward a female patient during an acute care encounter—be it longer wait times, another patient emergency, or additional charting requirements—could potentially be perceived as discrimination. That could be the right perception, but not necessarily correct all the time. This tendency to draw absolutes, or extreme reactionary beliefs in the presence of uncertainty, perpetuates a cascade of biased, erroneous interpretations.

All patients have developed unique thought patterns that impact their perspectives on healthcare, drawn from specific past interactions with providers that influence future interactions. Though many perceptions form across multiple interactions of patients and providers, they both react with similar patterns of thinking. These are the heuristics they depend on instead of addressing clinical uncertainty directly. Since both patients and providers would rather succumb to familiar biases, they revert to the same patterns and exhibit the same behavior across different clinical scenarios.

History may be a thousand narratives, but belief in one silences the others. In healthcare, the predominant perspective tends to become the only perception. Other thought patterns quickly coalesce, either reinforcing what we already believe or being discarded from conscious thought. This is typical of heuristics. The mind automatically simplifies all available information and uncertainty for one singular mode of thought, one prevailing perception.

When a patient presents with right lower quadrant pain, vomiting, and an elevated white blood cell count, most providers might assume the patient has appendicitis. In a typical scenario, this is treated by surgically removing the inflamed appendix—a procedure known as an appendectomy. But the three presenting symptoms do not have equal weight in determining whether to proceed with surgery. When only two of the three are present, those two presenting symptoms affect the relative likelihood of the surgeon performing an appendectomy or not. If pain and vomiting are present, a surgeon may be more cautious in deciding to perform surgery, compared to if only pain and an elevated white blood cell count are present.

Since white blood cell count is a lab value and not a subjective expression, surgeons consider it to be more reliable. But this reliance is just a heuristic that depends on the accuracy of a lab value in determining whether surgery is the appropriate course of clinical care. The decision is only as good as the lab value's accuracy.

Healthcare's emphasis on standardized, data-driven decision-making has only limited value in improving patient care. To further improve patient outcomes, our understanding of healthcare must extend to include patient perceptions. Perceptions form the heart of the patient narrative, or what is gleaned through observations of and conversations with patients. It is the essence of the patient-provider relationship. "Patients have always told stories to doctors," said British neurologist Oliver Sacks.

A single patient story can reveal more than an entire set of clinical data. The face of a patient who overdoses on heroin after being abandoned by the healthcare system rings far louder than any statistic. Personal stories of families affected by the opioid epidemic affect policy changes far more than even the best-designed clinical studies.

Narratives provide critical insights, as radio broadcaster Studs Terkel showed decades ago in chronicling the lives of hardworking Americans and sharing in their daily humiliations. By putting a face to a job title, and shedding light on the inner angst each person felt, Terkel revealed through audio recordings aspects of people's lives academics found mostly mundane but were of immense importance to regular individuals.

Patient-provider interactions are made up of a stream of narratives, built over time, encounter by encounter. The thought patterns that form between provider and patient determine future conversations and the quality of care. In aggregate, they have far more influence than medicine's more quantitative aspects. How we think about something influences what we think. While clinical data can suggest a range of diagnoses and therapies, only through the right perspectives do we arrive at the best decisions, since the perception of the data leads to the decision-making.

The COVID-19 pandemic showed firsthand how data alone cannot predict patient behavior. We saw entire populations choosing to either obey or disregard social distancing guidelines—not based on mortality or positivity rates, but on their subjective views of the pandemic. Soon, rifts formed between those who feared the public was not taking the pandemic seriously enough and those who thought the pandemic was a hoax or severely exaggerated.

The pandemic was both an outbreak of a contagious virus and a subjective phenomenon. But, as with complex concepts in healthcare, the two components were perceived as separate and distinct. Like the relationship that forms between an author and the reader, the data illustrating the number of COVID-19 cases and deaths, and the perception of the data, are intimately related and cannot be understood separately.

Similarly, how we speak reflects our thoughts. In each clinical encounter, patients and providers communicate and convey the thoughts they wish to share. Depending on immediate patient needs or changing concerns, the tenor of the conversation changes with the changing thoughts. The words a patient chooses influence development of the provider's perception, and the words the provider uses influence the patient's thoughts and responses.

Aristotle wrote, "Audiences are made." He understood that an exchange of thoughts and words can be moderated.

With the right choice of words, an awkward conversation turns humorous. With the wrong choice of words, a pleasant conversation quickly sours. Actively controlling how we think and speak dictates the course of a conversation. This is especially true for the patient encounter, in which a rapid series of decisions with long-lasting effects extend well beyond the conversation. Thoughts and words take on heightened meaning because fewer thoughts and words are exchanged.

Multiple studies that examine the importance of expressing gratitude during the patient encounter have verified a sort of reciprocity of perceptions, in words spoken and emotions conveyed. Providers who express gratitude are perceived to be of higher quality, and they experience higher patient compliance with treatment protocols than providers who come off as less grateful. The importance of this goes beyond optimizing the quality of communication and, when properly applied, can lead to improved patient outcomes.

In a case in which belief becomes biology, clinical researchers proved positive emotions can reduce pain. Specific emotions, such as trust and gratitude, not only reduce pain, but also redefine pain into a positive emotion, changing the long-term perception of pain by shifting it during the patient encounter. Such change is needed in the opioid epidemic.

Pain has developed a distinct stigma in which any presentation of pain tends to automatically engender a perception of fear, overwhelming the thoughts that arise during a patient encounter and influencing the actions and decisions of both patient and provider. Paranoia is often fear's initial manifestation, and when discussing pain, providers become cautious and distrustful. The paranoia is expressed in thoughts that become the words providers speak; and those words, in kind, influence what patients think—so a corresponding aura of suspicion reverberates. Soon, thoughts become full-fledged perceptions that shape the entire patient encounter, as the provider and patient transform into caricatures—the patient disintegrates into an addict and the provider into an uncaring physician. This introduces an added dimension of stress into what should be a trusting, open environment.

Researcher Bruce McEwen has shown that this stress has an adverse effect on the brain and the ways patients behave. McEwen analyzed stress in different situations, tracing the progression of stress both acutely and long term. He showed how even mundane stress experienced daily produces hormones that mediate brain activity and influence behavior. He found that patient encounters, though lasting only a few minutes, can produce intense bursts of stress if traumatic enough—similar to the patterns of stress experienced by combat soldiers that often lead to post-traumatic stress disorder (PTSD).

This makes for an interesting comparison and perhaps explains the subconscious origins of war analogies in healthcare. Former surgeon general Dr. Jerome Adams, who was part of the task force that led the federal COVID-19 relief efforts, described early efforts to minimize peak effects of the virus as "our Pearl Harbor moment." But healthcare is not warfare, and the wartime terminology artificially conflates two vastly different missions.

Healthcare requires and thrives on trust and compassion, not paranoia and fear. Trust is crucial for clinical care, and arguably the most important aspect of the patient encounter. Trust, or a lack of it, affects how we speak, the words we use, how we feel when we listen, and our thought patterns.

During the COVID-19 pandemic, the public experienced wave after wave of misinformation, preliminary reports that were too preliminary, and miracle solutions that turned into terminated studies. Many grew weary of trying to figure out what and whom to trust. Soon that lack of trust defined the entire outlook on the pandemic. This created a war of two fronts—the virus and public perception of the virus—that was fought via media outlets around the world.

This is not very different from the battles many patients with acute and chronic pain have experienced in recent years against providers who have succumbed to the existential fear of prescribing opioids—the pain, and the public perception of the pain. Providers, once willing to diagnose and treat chronic pain patients, now often refuse to treat them, even when presented with medical records and imaging results. Concerned with avoiding any risk of litigation, providers more often view patient care from a legal perspective than from a medical perspective, compromising patient care and trust.

Soon, that becomes the dominant perception. But when providers focus on avoiding legal risk, thoughts of trusting and treating the patient eventually disintegrate. Neuroscientists who study trust have verified that the active projection of trust leads others to reciprocate it. Trust begets trust. The lack of trust from one person destroys it in the other. Trust creates a mental framework that balances various perspectives of patient care and emphasizes medically appropriate decisions. Without this framework, the patient encounter becomes an empty exchange of competing interpretations.

Some may argue trust is a bias that creates thought patterns like any heuristic. But trust uniquely predisposes people to structure multiple perspectives into their thinking. As a result, trust allows a provider to feel comfortable making medical decisions that most might otherwise consider risky. If a provider trusts a patient to take medication as directed, then the provider feels comfortable prescribing it. If not, the provider may decide against prescribing the medication despite it being medically necessary.

More important, trust gives structure to healthcare's uncertainty. When a patient presents with a constellation of symptoms and signs, trusting the patient to explain the symptoms allows the provider to confidently treat the patient. The patient, sensing the trust, reciprocates with honesty and integrity. When the patient and provider both exude trust, they approach uncertainty the same way and produce similar patterns of thought. Trust makes for better, more balanced patient care.

Initially, it may appear that trusting a patient puts the provider at greater risk than not trusting at all. But without trust, virtue is lost in clinical care. A certain amount of risk is necessary for good patient care. Trust balanced with risk should be considered as two components of the same complex concept, held in balance, like virtue and uncertainty. Providers should not focus on whether to trust, but instead on how to optimize trust while accepting risk as an integral part of healthcare.

The most famous physicians in history were natural-born risk-takers. "The risk of a wrong decision is preferable to the terror of indecision," Maimonides wrote, encouraging the medical community to willingly be wrong as long as the error comes in the name of medical advancement. Hippocrates challenged many conventionally held medical practices of his day by emphasizing the patient experience as the most important part of clinical care. Galen built his reputation by attempting high-risk surgical experiments on wounded Roman gladiators.

But in today's litigious world of healthcare, the art of medicine is replaced by an industry of litigation, and the individual physician by a system of guidelines, policies, and laws. Healthcare has always been more science than law, and science requires experimentation. Medicine is practically founded on calculated risk. We celebrate risk when it produces positive outcomes, as when Dr. Jonas Salk developed the polio vaccine. But when risk produces negative outcomes, it leads down a rabbit hole of litigation and regulation.

While today, Dr. Jonas Salk is seen almost as a folk hero, and the polio vaccine as a testament to American ingenuity, the many issues that came after he introduced his vaccine are long forgotten: We forget the batches of vaccines that led to numerous deaths. We forget the Cold War competition between Dr. Salk's vaccine, which consisted of multiple injections, and the alternative oral vaccine researcher Dr. Albert Sabin developed. We forget that Dr. Salk's injection vaccine was initially opted for because it was developed faster, but the oral vaccine was later adopted because it was easier to administer and proved to be safer.

Dr. Salk's success is emphasized because the polio vaccine was an important milestone in medicine. By highlighting the successes over the failures, we remember only the successes. But in today's healthcare, we emphasize the risks and legal liabilities in patient care—particularly, the risk of medication abuse. So, by emphasizing the risks and liabilities, we think only about the negative aspects.

The cost of errors in healthcare, even well-intentioned ones, is high. The stakes are high enough that many healthcare institutions actively avoid any possible clinical risk. Risk is now controlled to the point that even legally sanctioned medical experiments, clinical research, are wound up in a tight web of regulatory oversight and institutional review, resulting in additional costs and years of delay. Statistician Milton Friedman warned decades ago of the financial costs from excessive regulatory oversight in healthcare when he said, "The cure is worse than the disease."

In response, there are additional costs incurred from risk-averse clinical decision-making. Many physicians order extra studies, tests, and drug screens far beyond what is medically necessary, because of the legal risks associated with not ordering them. Providers need to be comfortable trusting patients, but if the threat of legal repercussion becomes too great, providers will change their behavior, compromising patient care and driving up its costs. This shows the influence law has on healthcare; if unchecked, it leads to poor outcomes. Healthcare should be regulated by law, not directed by it.

We know trust is essential to good patient care. But some clinicians tend only to implicitly acknowledge it and rarely apply trust as part of the decision-making process in healthcare. Like the structure of an atom, trust is the space around the nucleus—largely ignored to focus on the nucleus of data and clinical evidence. But we now know the figurative space around the nucleus determines the behavior of the atom, just as thought patterns determine how providers and patients respond to clinical data and facts. If trust is lacking, providers might make decisions based on its lack, regardless of the data. Worse, when the perceived risk of a clinical decision becomes too great, providers wrestle with indecisiveness.

Malcolm Gladwell describes a human tendency to default to trust, which predisposes us to initially trust people. In fact, our minds are better equipped to perceive truths than to detect lies, so unless we have an overt reason not to, we tend to trust. While providers know trust is the basis for good medicine, legal pressures change a provider's default tendency to that of distrust, affecting the essence of healthcare.

As discussed, virtue and uncertainty are important to healthcare law. Together, they define healthcare responsibilities and the distribution of burdens. At a more individual level, a similar balance exists between trust and risk in a clinical decision. Trust should be the predominant perception in any patient encounter, balanced with an awareness of any corresponding risk.

Risk and uncertainty are the same concept; but one appears as a consequence of individual decision-making, and the other as an effect of broad strokes in healthcare policymaking. Though the scales may be different, the thought patterns that form in response to risk and uncertainty are the same and should be understood in the same way. This is why the same default tendencies are seen in health policy as in individual patient behavior, and why so many recurring patterns appear on large and small scales. Fortunately, the solution is found in trust.

For patients who present with pain or substance use dependencies, trust comes from recognizing the thought patterns that form their perceptions of pain, layer by layer.

CHAPTER 18

In 1628, an English physician who served as the personal physician for two kings wrote a book that nearly destroyed his clinical practice. His name was Dr. William Harvey, and his book, *An Anatomical Study of the Motion of the Heart and Blood in Animals*, controversially refuted many of the widely held theories on blood flow originally developed by Galen nearly one and a half millennia earlier.

Despite the prominent and illustrious career he had enjoyed to that point, Harvey's new theories, surrounded by controversy, created a negative impression on the public. Many patients left his practice shortly thereafter. Eventually, though, Harvey's ideas became the standard approach continued today in studying cardiac anatomy and physiology. It is not clear whether patients who left Harvey's practice ever came back, but the initial negative impressions were proved false soon enough through the test of time.

Healthcare has a longstanding tendency of swaying from perception to perception—each perception a reaction to an earlier one. However different perceptions may be, they all share a common characteristic in that they are inherently incomplete. This very characteristic determines how subsequent reactions will form.

The topic of vaccination has always been a fiercely contested one. Each argument, no matter how eloquent, revolves largely around individual rights versus collective benefits. Those who champion individual rights focus on the risk of receiving a vaccine injection; those who stress collective safety focus on the risk of being infected by a disease the vaccine intends to protect against. At face value, arguments on both sides are justifiable. Each vaccine injection carries an individual risk, and vaccines in aggregate provide a collective benefit. But the collective benefit is determined by the aggregate behavior, which is the sum of all decisions and actions that lead individuals to receive the vaccine. The more who receive it, the greater the overarching benefit, which varies based on percentage of the population that gets vaccinated, while the risk per vaccine is fixed per individual.

The issue comes down to a balance between the varying benefits to the community against the fixed individual risks of vaccines. This can be visualized as a ratio that increases or decreases based on the percentage of a population that receives the vaccine. Those who are against vaccines focus on the fixed risk, while those who are for vaccines focus on the collective benefits of widespread immunization. Soon, the argument becomes the only focus, leading both sides to debate over inherently incomplete stances that instead should be contextualized as a balance between two perspectives.

This explains why the argument is debated so heavily. Each side simply focuses on their own perception, without considering the broader context of the argument. Behavioral economists call this denominator neglect—situations in which people focus only on the most overt aspects of any argument but cannot consider the full context of the issue. Denominator neglect is largely a problem of perception. It can be corrected if the argument is reinterpreted as a balance among multiple perspectives.

More often than not, simplified interpretations dominate healthcare policies and decisions. Remember, people look for what is familiar in what is new, and that tendency leads healthcare policymakers to repeat mistakes. This familiarity bias also leads to incomplete interpretations that prompt reactions based on limited information. When the COVID-19 pandemic began, medical supplies were produced and stockpiled based on models that predicted the virus's geographic spread and infectivity. But no preparations were made for the fear that ensued, the uncertainty that manifested most conspicuously when cities and states complained of shortages in supplies as the pandemic ravaged their hospitals and communities.

Fear created a discrepancy between what was anticipated ahead of time and what was requested in real time. People made predictions based on what was known, but did not anticipate for the unknown. Though our focus gravitates toward what we know, our reactions are consistently in response to what we do not know. This explains the responses to the pervasive fear early in the pandemic.

When the World Health Organization first labeled COVID-19 a pandemic in March 2020, WHO Director-General Dr. Tedros Adhanom Ghebreyesus warned that the label would create two perceptions. The first would reveal the grim truth about the virus's severity, and the second would unleash waves of fear among people attempting to cope with a poorly understood, poorly defined health crisis. He was right on both accounts. People understood that the label conveyed the severity of the virus's spread, and they reacted with fear to the uncertainty of its effects.

The attitudes that followed—irrational demands for tests even after the tests lost value, xenophobia against Chinese culture—were responses to fears that formed within the void of uncertainty. As the uncertainty underlying the pandemic changed, so too did our dominant perceptions. This trend is repeated in all healthcare epidemics, as what is unknown is substituted for simple narratives, negating the need to understand the uncertainty at the heart of the matter.

This mistake is compounded when it is repeated until it becomes familiar. The familiar soon becomes true, and it becomes the predominant perception through which an event or situation is understood. And just as quickly as perceptions are formed, they change as new unknowns appear.

Dr. Deborah Birx has been in the public eye for decades as the voice for healthcare public policy. She guided public policy initiatives for the HIV/AIDS epidemic beginning in the 1980s and continued to lend her support to the COVID-19 task force under the Trump administration. Much of her effort during both the HIV/AIDS epidemic and the COVID-19 pandemic centered on effective communication. Dr. Birx is one of the first to recognize the importance of communication in managing healthcare behavior.

"Can we communicate effectively enough so that the American people take these guidelines seriously?" she said early on. "Because that is the only thing that's going to change the course of this pandemic." Communication is a form of treatment, because it treats the most significant aspect of health: people's perceptions. If a patient has poorly controlled diabetes, no medication treats its complications as effectively as the patient's awareness of the importance in managing blood sugar levels.

Communication depends on trust to moderate the patient's approach to uncertainty and balance known clinical information with the unfamiliar. Effective communication acknowledges uncertainty and maintains a heightened awareness of it.

When the public heard that COVID-19 vaccines were being developed, confidence in and willingness to receive the vaccine were high. However, when the vaccines became available, public confidence and willingness dropped, many citing the speed of vaccine development as a source of concern. Public confidence gradually rose only after initial doses were administered.

These changing public perceptions reflect changing uncertainty relative to the vaccine. At first, the public was confident, perceiving the vaccine as a solution to COVID-19 in a generalized sense. When this shifted to an individual decision, perception changed because the uncertainty changed. Now, instead of looking at the vaccine as a general form of treatment, people viewed it relative to personal benefit and risk. But when people saw others take the vaccine, be it family or friends in their community, the risk of the vaccine appeared to decrease, and it seemed safe.

Changing levels of trust came in reaction to the evolving nature of uncertainty as the perception of COVID-19 vaccines evolved over the course of the pandemic. This shift in perception is typical to healthcare scenarios steeped in uncertainty. This includes clinical encounters with military veterans who suffer from PTSD stemming from traumatic brain injuries (TBIs). Many veterans struggle to explain their symptoms when discussing TBI with senior officers and nonmilitary colleagues, particularly since symptoms and the perceptions of those symptoms continually change.

To raise awareness of TBI and its changing, ambiguous symptoms, the Defense and Veterans Brain Injury Center, along with American Veterans (AMVETS), conducted multiple studies analyzing the presentation of symptoms over TBI's progression. The studies found that most early symptoms and signs are often misinterpreted, at times even disregarded, by senior officers or health providers. This perpetuates further disease progression due to the added stress of poor communication.

In response, veteran aid organizations educated the public about the invisible injuries of war—particularly, the initial symptoms. Those who have not served in military combat likely lack the understanding necessary to appreciate the disease, and this creates an undue burden on TBI patients to justify the significance of their disease.

A similar burden is sometimes placed on pain patients, who now struggle with new legal realities and stigmas that add stress to exacerbate already severe and complex health issues. For pain, in particular, the social and clinical aspects affect its overall progression and influence patient perceptions as much as the disease does. These two aspects should be seen as two components of the same disease.

The burden of pain magnifies its intensity. The social and economic impact of pain cannot be separated from its clinical presentation. Patients' perceptions of their medical conditions impact their clinical behavior—and, consequently, their clinical outcomes—data and the interpretation of data, forever intertwined.

During the pandemic, many prisons were at risk of outbreaks due to the close quarters of prison cells and large populations of inmates. The Federal Bureau of Prisons implemented a policy that identified inmates at the highest risk of COVID-related complications and recommended they be transferred elsewhere or allowed to serve the duration of their sentences in home confinement, thereby reducing the risk of spread among inmates.

That was the intent, but its implementation engendered significant distrust among inmates and prison administrators. Rather than screen inmates based on medical conditions, administrators evaluated inmates based on recidivism and health risks, with the former outweighing the latter. For administrators, the perception of a short-term medical risk from COVID-19 was conflated with long-term criminal recidivism risk. As a result, the inmates selected were not the most at-risk medically. The inmates immediately noticed this bent.

Many inmates had family and friends call the prison system, obtain medical records from outside institutions, or file complaints citing the inconsistent selection criteria. Once inmates lost trust in prison administrators' abilities to properly screen for medical risk, they responded in ways to improve their chances of being selected, gleaning any advantage they could.

Inmates questioned the lack of clinical training among prison administrators making the selection criteria, seeking outside medical advice to justify the significance of their clinical care. Some even filed legal motions asking for medical reprieve from federal judges when none was given through the prison system. The ensuing legal battles between inmates and administrators were a result of conflicting perceptions that appear when trust is lost. This epitomizes conflicts throughout healthcare that appear when distrust becomes the dominant perception.

"There is very little new information in this world," wrote Emerson. "Most of it is old information repackaged." Similarly, many trends in healthcare are repeated thoughts applied in different clinical contexts. Familiar thought patterns emerge from the same uncertainty underlying clinical scenarios that only appear to be different. But the reactions reveal the similarities. These thought patterns have predictable variations. They vacillate like waves on a beach, responding to the same uncertainty in slightly different ways. The differences become significant when certain perceptions are strong enough to reinforce the differences across multiple actions and decisions.

These differences explain how certain providers end up serving specific patient populations. A provider who sees a lot of elderly patients gets more referrals for more elderly patients. A hospital that sees patients who mostly have state-based insurance attracts more patients with that insurance coverage. These trends emerge through thought patterns that form when treating those patients as much as from the clinical actions and decisions that reinforce the thought patterns.

A cough and rash in urban Baltimore would lead to a different clinical workup than the same symptoms presenting in southern Indiana near the Ohio River valley. The differences come from diverging incidences of diseases seen in one area versus another, reinforced in the thought patterns that appear in the perceptions of the differential characteristics of the diagnoses.

The figures show two graphs. The first graph (fig. 11) is a wave drawn in a solid line curving upward and then downward. Imagine the points at which the wave intersect the horizontal line as a single patient encounter, with the origin of the curve as the first encounter and each subsequent intersection a subsequent patient encounter. The solid line represents the provider's thought patterns, as seen in both the first and the second graph.

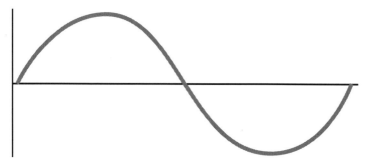

Figure 11.

In the second graph (fig. 12) are three waves: one solid, one dotted, and one dashed. The latter two represent a patient's thought patterns, each from a different patient encounter. The encounter depicted by the dotted line went well, with effective communication taking place between provider and patient. The encounter depicted by the dashed line went poorly, with a mostly distracted provider rushing the encounter, which made the patient feel more like a chore than a patient.

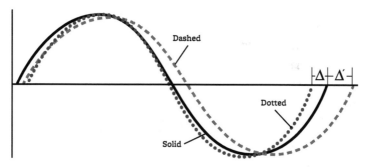

Figure 12.

The separation between the dashed and dotted waves relative to the solid wave represents differences in thought patterns that formed during the two encounters. When effective communication takes place during the encounter, thought patterns mirror each other more closely than when communication is poor. The separations in the curves, when observed over the course of multiple encounters, create specific patterns unique to each provider and patient, explaining the origin of the phrase *thought patterns*.

Changes in these patterns reveal changes in the patient-provider relationship. The patient and provider reciprocate emotions and thoughts in relation to each other, either cultivating or destroying the trust in a clinical encounter. Both biological and consciously created, the level of trust reflects one's approach to new information in healthcare.

"The information was confusing at the beginning," said Dr. Birx after her tenure coordinating the White House COVID-19 Response Team had ended. "I think because we did not talk about the spectrum of the disease, everyone interpreted what they knew." Dr. Birx was noting how the lack of trust and effective communication led to vastly different thoughts and approaches to the pandemic, creating a range of perceptions that conflicted with one another. It is no surprise, then, that the federal response to COVID-19 was similarly disjointed. If communication is ineffective, the follow-up behavior will be equally ineffective.

What is true at the highest levels of healthcare policy typically rings true among daily patient encounters. Thoughts and words reflect likely behaviors. The more the thoughts, words, and actions are aligned between provider and patient, the greater the trust that forms. Trust reinforces positive healthcare behaviors, reveals hidden stresses and angst within the lives of patients, and identifies patients' perceptions of their health.

The COVID-19 pandemic proved that even small viral

pathogens can appear in complex ways. Indeed, all diseases in healthcare are complex and have a spectrum of presentations. Until the uncertainty is the focus, we will repeatedly revert to default tendencies and rely on dominant perceptions to form understandings of what we see. When this happens in the legal world, we get inappropriate interpretations of healthcare law. When this happens during the patient encounter, we get reflexive medical decisions based on incomplete perceptions.

When we train our minds to shift focus toward the unknowns we subconsciously react to, we begin to recognize the underlying uncertainty that influences our behavior. We stop responding to our fluttering perceptions and balance the various perspectives that support or refute our beliefs. Such a balance is needed to overcome the extreme beliefs that define laws and policies around the opioid epidemic. More important than treating pain or preventing overdoses is a balancing of the symptoms and perceptions of pain and addiction.

Addiction medicine is a complex field that expands across primary care, behavioral health, and psychiatry. Due to that expansive range, the healthcare field struggles to develop consistent treatment protocols for patients suffering from substance use dependencies. If a patient with diabetic nerve pain develops a dependency on pain medications, does that person remain a diabetic patient, become a pain patient, or now receive treatment solely as a patient with substance abuse issues?

Addiction medicine is complex, and what is thought of as three different medical conditions is really three character-istics of the same disease. Artificial distinctions in addiction medicine separate different presentations of the same clinical condition. This does nothing to help the patient and instead hinders the overall quality of care.

If a patient develops high blood pressure and remains hypertensive even after taking appropriate medications, the provider and patient then work to adjust the medication to the appropriate dose to control the patient's blood pressure to within normal parameters. A patient is not stigmatized for missing a dose or requesting additional medications. Those perceptions simply do not exist for other medical conditions.

But patients presenting with either pain or substance dependency receive different medical treatments, components of their diseases dissected to create two separate fields. Pain management is separated from addiction medicine, even though the two are closely related. Most pain patients develop some form of dependency—be it physical or mental—to their pain medications and require a slow adjustment when changing the dose or frequency, particularly with opioids. Not long ago most patients and providers felt comfortable acknowledging this. Now many providers disingenuously deny even the slightest dependency in patients who present with pain, even though dependency is a known side effect of opioids.

Decades ago, if a patient developed a dependency, it was perceived to be a side effect and managed carefully through close communication between provider and patient. Perceptions of pain management were quite different back then, when pain was considered a fifth vital sign and providers were trained to aggressively treat pain whenever it was present. Providers were more concerned with the effects of chronic inflammation secondary to the pain, believing the inflammation was more harmful to patients than the risk of overtreatment.

Standards of care at that time considered the potential risk of a dependency acceptable, as long as the patient did not endure a prolonged inflammatory response. Clinical studies closely monitored the progression of inflammation in patients with pain, and medical societies created protocols focused on reducing pain-related inflammation.

In hindsight, it was not the correct approach to pain management. But instead of finding a balance, there was a jump from one perception to another. Emphasizing treatment of inflammation in pain is as extreme a response to pain management as what is seen today. The interpretive pendulum has swung from one end to the other. Now, the perceived risk of dependency is so great that providers let patients suffer through pain and bear the stigma of their disease. Ironically enough, this creates additional stress that worsens a patient's inflammatory response.

Both approaches are incomplete, filled with biases that distort medical data to fit the most dominant perception held at the time. Before, studies focused on chronic inflammation in patients with poorly treated pain. Now, studies focus on dependencies of patients treated with opioids.

For all its research and political scrutiny, pain management has few practical treatment options. Types of treatment include physical therapy, spinal fluid injections, and pain-moderating devices, such as pain pumps and nerve stimulators—but mostly, pain medications. Most treatment protocols for pain management incorporate more than one treatment option, so patients are often treated through a combination of medications and alternative therapies or procedures. This is why the rise of opioid prescriptions in recent years mirrors the rise in the number of procedures performed to address pain.

Opioid medications have always been, and continue to be, the most cost-effective treatment for pain. This means insurance companies prioritize coverage for medications and guide providers to treat patients with pain medications. Often, a trial of opioid medications is required before insurance coverage is provided for pain management procedures.

The clinical benefits of most pain procedures are studied *alongside* opioid medications, not as a *replacement* for opioid medications. The increase in prescription opioids reflects a broader upward growth in pain management. With the increase in pain patients, the entire field grew, including the number of opioids prescribed, pain procedures performed, and new pain treatment devices entering the medical device market.

The federal government was well aware of and actively supported this growth, until it was reinterpreted as something completely different. The government then conflated chronic pain treatment with the rise in illicit opioid abuse.

"Many ideas become false when taken to extremes," said George Washington. The government's extreme reinterpretations proved to be as biased as the misconceptions of pain that came out of the medical community years before. This extremism prompted the all-too-familiar cascade: opioids were now narcotics, clinical care was now criminal enterprise, and trust gave way to policy changes and legal scrutiny that were reinterpretations masquerading as solutions.

Opioid guidelines that try to predict patient behavior fail as many predictions about the future fail—by foreseeing the future in terms of the present. Addiction medicine, like pain management, is evolving, and its growth trajectory is anything but straightforward or predictable. The medical community is still learning how to treat addiction as a disease, and whether it should be treated acutely or as a chronic condition is still not formalized.

Guidelines cannot serve as the sole basis for how to treat patients in pain or with addictions. The perspectives of addiction medicine change depending on how the patient's presenting symptoms are seen relative to the patient's overall medical history, how the patient presents, and whether the provider perceives addiction as something to treat or a chronic condition to manage long term. How current perceptions will shift with future clinical knowledge about addiction medicine is unpredictable. It will change in ways that are decidedly irrational.

"Any upgrade can be justified on the pretense of healing," writes historian Yuval Noah Harari. Many patients with nascent dependencies or addictions justify continued use of pain medication in order to work to provide for their families, or simply to live without the constant nagging of physical pain. Their behavior reflects their perceptions of their pain more than even their symptoms.

Guidelines that regulate the prescribing of opioid medications do not address these convoluted perspectives. Healthcare behaviors are reinterpreted through convenient guidelines that simplify difficult clinical decisions. This creates the familiar paradox of interpretations when complex behavior interacts with inherently limited guidelines that do not encompass the full scope of the situation. No guideline will stop a drug-seeking addict from posing as a patient to secure prescription opioids.

Drug-seekers know how to manipulate the healthcare system to obtain opioids. Yet we still think we can prevent this type of behavior. In foolhardy attempts to curtail diversion and inappropriate use of opioids, the average patient encounter is overwhelmed with a tangle of guidelines and red tape. Well-intentioned patients and drug-seeking addicts alike must jump through hoops to obtain an opioid prescription. Drug-seeking addicts are able to do this more skillfully than patients with chronic pain.

If guidelines call for a restriction on the number of opioids prescribed, an addict visits the provider more often. If guidelines call for urine drug screens, an addict finds a way to pass the test. Attempting to restrict a specific behavior in healthcare might set up hurdles, but it does not necessarily stop that behavior.

"May I never see in the patient anything but a fellow creature in pain" is a line in the Oath of Maimonides, a pledge recited by medical students throughout the world. But pain is anything but one simple perspective—and, over the years, the perception of pain has become more complicated.

Opioids have been used throughout history, beginning with Sumerians, who referred to the opium poppy as a "joy plant." Despite medical advancements achieved since then, healthcare professionals never seem to advance beyond linking pleasure and pain as opposing perceptions. This balance defines the treatment of pain as much as its presenting clinical symptoms. Since pain treatment depends on the provider's perception of both the presenting pain and the patient, any study of pain and addiction—and its application toward an individual patient—is incomplete without the accompanying historical and emotional context through which pain is understood.

Pain is a clinical symptom and subjective phenomenon, two components of a complex disease, as the underlying cause of pain is seen through the perception of that pain. Multiple perspectives are formed, many of which are far removed from modern perceptions of healthcare—including balances between good and evil, suffering and pleasure, and fundamental right versus wrong. Theologian C. S. Lewis described this convoluted layer of thoughts as "misery and misery's shadow." Pain is understood through these layers and equated with a visceral sense of doing wrong or of being evil.

English poet John Milton probably influenced the narrative of pain as much as any modern clinician when he wrote, "Pain is perfect misery, the worst of evils." He even correlated pain as punishment in the name of justice: "Of worse deeds, worse suffering must ensue." Milton's interpretation of pain heavily influenced nineteenth-century views of medicine through literature, which lays the foundations for modern healthcare perceptions.

Victorian poet Robert Browning wrote a poem romanticizing a blood disorder, defining the disease and the patient as having a relationship that proved to be "pure and good," mostly because the disease caused the patient in the poem no pain. Diseases have been and always will be understood by their most apparent symptom, even in the age of medical research. For patients with diseases that include the symptom of pain, its presentation is usually the most apparent symptom and therefore creates the dominant perception.

By the middle of the nineteenth century, tuberculosis was an epidemic in Europe and America. Much of what was learned about the disease—how it spreads and its mechanism of action—occurred at this time. But rather than focusing on the germs that caused the disease, the public focused on the presentation of the "romantic disease." The appearance of the thinning, pale faces of the afflicted spurred an infatuation that transformed into a style trend still seen on fashion runways around the world today.

The relationship between pain and the patient is an ongoing narrative told through the experiences of each symptom. Even with modern clinical knowledge and its technological sophistication, many rely on literature and philosophy to comprehend pain. Tolstoy, arguably the paramount philosopher-author of recent centuries, equated pain with morality. In *The Death of*

Ivan Ilyich, the protagonist expresses a sense of shame in taking opium for his pain, feeling his lack of willingness to endure pain is a sin.

The belief that the ability to endure pain is a moral virtue has prevailed throughout history among religious philosophers such as Augustine, Thomas Aquinas, and C. S. Lewis. For these philosophers, to bear pain is to bear a righteous suffering. Pain is not a medical symptom, but a virtue to display. "A load so heavy, only humility can carry it," in the words of Lewis.

Pain has not always been wrapped in such moralistic terms. Stoic philosophers from ancient Greece advised accepting pain without reaction, and instead seeing pain as a modifiable perception, which can change based on how you approach it. The philosopher Epicurus advised that "avoiding pain is not the same as pleasure seeking." This embodies the rational, balanced perspective of pain that many Stoic philosophers expressed. Marcus Aurelius wrote, "Whenever you suffer pain, keep in mind that it is nothing to be ashamed of."

Today we attach additional layers to these differing interpretations of pain as we continue to shape our perspectives on it. Nothing has been more influential to the interpretation of pain than humanism, which promotes an individualized, subjective perspective. "What I feel is good, is good, and what I feel is bad, is bad," wrote philosopher Jean-Jacque Rousseau, who internalized his perception of pain with his direct experiences of it.

This is largely how pain is interpreted today—through experience. But experience is more than an account of what is felt in the moment. It is a complex combination of current and past perceptions, imbued with objective memories and subjective emotions surrounding those memories.

Neuroscientist V. S. Ramachandran believes pain is an opinion. Much like how opinions change, so does the perception of pain, relative to present and past experiences. Changing perspectives of pain, based on time, make it appear as two different elements from the past and present, as a duality. This is why both C. S. Lewis and Emerson described pain in terms of the pain itself and the shadow it casts.

Pain is not just a reflection of an underlying injury or disease; it is a figurative conversation encompassing all physiological and emotional layers of a patient. Studies have shown that people who are in love feel less pain, and people in the grip of fear feel it more.

Pain research has shown that the relationship with a provider affects the level of pain a patient experiences, demonstrating pain as a real physical condition but also a state of mind. Experiences form the predominant perception of pain, simplifying all thoughts into that one belief and forming an Occam's Razor, in which the most overt belief becomes the only one worth acknowledging while all other thoughts are discarded as extraneous.

A study comparing similar injuries between war veterans and civilians found that only 32 percent of the veterans, versus 83 percent of the civilians, requested pain medications for their respective injuries. The authors concluded that their past experiences of war gave the veterans a higher pain tolerance. A belief that they should endure pain is indoctrinated into war veterans. This shows that tolerance is a subjective belief more so than an objective biological response.

The experience of pain consists of layer upon layer of different perceptions that in the moment may appear vividly real. This makes the modern quest to cure pain just another reaction in an ongoing series of changing perceptions, and the search to find the perfect pain medication just another layer of scientific veneer added on top of the more abstract notions of pain.

Pain will always be relative to many factors. Study of pain in biochemical terms will, therefore, always be incomplete without also studying pain's dynamic perceptions, which are simultaneously independent of, and related to, its biochemistry.

For patients who endure pain daily, their perceptions are an eclectic mix of many perspectives, drawn over time and superimposed onto their existential angst. Some see pain as a challenge to overcome, basing their self-worth on the ability to persevere. Others see pain as an unfair burden placed on them, claiming relief from pain as a right to which they are entitled. These varying interpretations lead to diverging patient behaviors that create further distinctions in healthcare concerning perceptions of pain and its treatment.

A patient's resilience is praised when that patient overcomes a debilitating injury. In neurologist Oliver Sacks's book *The Man Who Mistook His Wife for a Hat*, readers admire the patient's ability to overcome complex neurological diseases, whether by playing an instrument or continuing to work despite worsening symptoms. But resilience is quickly reinterpreted as shame, depending on the medical condition, the medications taken, or even the perceptions of the patient.

In author Jhumpa Lahiri's short story "The Treatment of Bibi Haldar," readers observe how the characteristics of resilience are met with scorn, as Bibi seeks her own treatment methods for her neurological condition and infertility. She presses on—despite enduring ridicule from neighbors who try to impose antiquated views of marriage and pregnancy, and having to overcome social disgrace in order to be healed.

A Faustian bargain of self-justification emerges when

patients get caught in a conflict that places individual needs against the broader social perceptions of their medical conditions. Many patients shoulder an overbearing stigma due to current perceptions of pain. The burden leads many down a path of isolation and overt depression.

"No man [is] an island unto himself," wrote English scholar John Donne. Patients with pain or substance dependencies need the support of a trusting healthcare system. But once isolated due to the COVID-19 pandemic, without the medical resources necessary to address their conditions, their perceptions of pain and addiction became figurative burdens that proved too much for many to handle. The ramifications were seen in the rapid rise of overdoses and deaths of despair during pandemic lockdown.

Holocaust survivor Victor Frankl acknowledged that adversity is not evenly dispersed, but that facing adversity with the right frame of mind creates opportunities to respond positively.

When former NBA player Chris Herron openly discusses his dependencies, he creates the impression that discussing opioid abuse is permissible. When Dr. Rana Awdish shares her experiences with opioid dependencies post-surgery, and the cognitive dissonance it created, she empowers other healthcare professionals to understand rather than to judge addictions.

New York State Senator, and former drug addict, Peter Harckham has emphasized nonjudgment since he was elected to the state assembly. Through his unique experiences as both lawmaker and lawbreaker, Harckham knows firsthand the importance of trust and communication. He knows their role in shifting the minds of the public away from criminalizing addiction medicine and toward identifying medically appropriate solutions—offering addiction therapy for patients instead of making criminals out of untreated addicts.

The right perspective creates the awareness needed to recognize that pain and addiction are characteristics of the same underlying medical condition. Addiction is an experience as much as pain is an experience. The transition from one to the other should be studied as much as pain and addiction are studied independently.

"Pain is to be understood analytically and conceptually," psychologist Dr. Ronald Melzack wrote in advising how providers should evaluate patients with pain. Dr. Melzack, nicknamed the "cartographer of pain," established the foundation for modern pain management and did more than any individual in the last century to standardize its treatment.

His work centered on two concepts: quantifying the interpretation of pain through a numerical system, and building a repository of vocabulary words to help patients express their pain. He believed the ability to describe pain in different ways helps patients express their experience of pain and consequently helps providers discern its source.

Most are asked about pain level based on a scale from one to ten. Hardly any are asked to describe symptoms in as many words as possible. But to Dr. Melzack, both sources of information are equally important. He understood pain is a symptom and a perception to which he ascribed words that served as a linguistic label to comprehend pain. By better understanding pain, patients more effectively manage it.

Words matter, affecting clinical outcomes in ways yet to be fully understood. The patient narrative is an interpretive journey through which symptoms and experiences are transformed into a coherent story. How that story is perceived is as important as the story that is told.

CHAPTER 19

"Study the monochord." These were the famous dying words of Pythagoras, who was arguably the most famous mathematician in Greek antiquity. He was not referring to an ancient stringed instrument, but to the string itself, specifically the intervals, or frequencies, generated when plucked at different points along the string.

Pythagoras is depicted doing just this while hunched over in a sculpture at the Chartres Cathedral near Paris. While the sculpture has received worldwide acclaim, Pythagoras was not exactly venerated during his lifetime. The island-born Greek completed much of his education and work while imprisoned inland in the famed city of Babylon, as a war hostage of Persian conquest, far from his home of Samos in the Aegean Sea.

Pythagoras is most famous today for his work on triangles, but his work extended to all dimensions of mathematics and of life. He believed relationships in nature can be studied as ratios, that they are related to one another through an underlying mathematical function he called harmony.

Harmony is found beneath the swirling perceptions of healthcare, within the uncertainty. To see it, one must become aware of the uncertainty. Absent awareness, we simply move from perception to perception, creating the cognitive equivalent of a blending of languages. Language experts call this a *sprachbund*: a region where the local population speaks multiple languages that swirl among residents, with each person selectively choosing words and grammatical structures, all in an apparently disorderly manner. But out of the chaotic blend of languages spoken, written, and heard comes order.

In a similar process, clinical perceptions combine to create order out of the uncertainty in our minds, though we often remain ignorant of this process. Healthcare is considered an analytical, data-driven field, but how we perceive the analytics and data determines how we behave—the figurative atomic space around the nucleus. Perception plays a much greater role in healthcare than one might imagine. Gregor Mendel, ascetic monk and founder of modern genetics, which is a famously data-driven field of science, intuitively sensed the ratios of autosomal dominance and recessive phenotypes from observable characteristics in peapods. Afterward, he verified his assumptions through data.

Many struggle to acknowledge this, readily inserting presumed facts and data to justify something intuitive or perception-driven. When you see an attractive face, you intuitively perceive it to be attractive. You do not measure the angles and dimensions to see how well they fit together. Yet when asked why a face is attractive, to justify your intuition you might cite specific features, or even the golden ratio (1.618), which defines the ideal facial dimensions of beauty. But intuition, at its core, is a perception, a series of perspectives and biases aggregated. What appears to be one coherent belief is really a synthesis of different thought patterns layered on one another.

Each belief consciously expressed derives from a perception, which itself is a composite of many perspectives and biases. Thought patterns flutter in our minds, selectively coalescing to create and recreate perceptions waiting to be consciously expressed. This is seen in the trends that define the opioid and vaping epidemics. In healthcare, a curve is never a simple curve, but is instead a complex series of complementing and contradicting trends perceived to be one pattern.

Studies that mine data from social media platforms observe that in patient chat rooms that host discussions about various medical conditions, most patients emphasize their personal experiences and emotional sentiment in dealing with their diseases, even for complex autoimmune conditions or rare cancers. Patients perceive their health through emotions, which are derived from their perceptions, no matter how complex the disease.

During the COVID-19 pandemic, researchers utilized government funding to study different medications for treating symptoms produced by the virus. This mostly consisted of retrofitting existing medications used for other clinical conditions into the treatment for symptomatic patients with COVID-19. Each drug addressed a specific aspect of the inflammatory process caused by the body's reaction to the virus; but the body's inflammatory process is vastly complicated and not yet properly understood. It is no surprise these drugs proved mildly beneficial at best, and mostly ineffective over large populations. To attempt to solve a complex problem by addressing only one aspect of inflammation leads to an incomplete solution with varying reactions. This applies to health policy as well.

Malcolm Gladwell wrote about a study that found forty cents on every medical dollar goes toward waste or fraud. But in that statistic, he equates two very different inefficiencies in fraud and waste. Fraud is willful misuse for financial gain, and waste is inadvertent spending on clinical services found to be unnecessary only in hindsight. The outcomes may be the same, but the series of decisions that lead to each outcome are different. In healthcare, it is excruciatingly difficult to ascertain the motivations underlying a sequence of decisions by the outcome alone.

The differences appear in patterns of behavior observed over time, not through isolated statistics. And when relying solely on outcomes data, we are left with incomplete solutions and usually proved wrong. Author Chuck Klosterman describes the concept of wrongness in both subjective and objective terms, noting that together, incorrect perceptions and actual mistakes define the full breadth of what it means to be wrong.

Engineers use a process called the risk minimization framework to standardize decision-making and to avoid being wrong. They start with the premise that they are wrong and then strive to minimize their wrongness. But being wrong in engineering is far different from being wrong in healthcare, where the complexities of human behavior add more variables—and more irrationality—than in technical fields like engineering.

Complex patterns define the interactions of healthcare and form our understandings of a disease or treatment. But these patterns are hopelessly transient, falling apart and reforming as new perceptions are created in healthcare.

During the early days of the opioid epidemic, considerable emphasis was placed on urine drug screens and imaging studies, which were then organized and codified through newly minted guidelines providers were expected to use when treating patients. The guidelines promoted standardized care, but they shifted the provider's perceptions away from direct patient communication.

As providers grew to rely on the guidelines to verify the need for opioid medications, they made decisions based primarily on the guidelines. If a urine drug screen was positive for prescribed opioids, then the provider prescribed opioids. If negative, then the provider would abruptly stop prescribing opioids, even if the underlying medical condition had not changed. This one thought pattern reduced all patient care to a relationship between medication adherence and urine screens, while failing to appreciate the complexity of managing patients who are treated with opioids.

A patient who passes every urine drug test can easily fall into patterns of addiction. And a patient who struggles with legitimate pain exacerbations may not exhibit any signs of inappropriate addictive behavior—despite not having enough pain medications to last between appointments—and consequently fail to produce the opioid in a urine drug screen. The shift from urine drug screens as one of many factors in evaluating patient care, to the pivotal factor in deciding whether to prescribe medications, damages the quality of patient care and reveals inherent limitations in the test.

Urine drug screens can have false positive and false negative test results for a host of reasons, including the total amount of urine sampled, additional medications the patient is taking, and varying rates of detection levels. When all sources of error are configured into a test result, each sample becomes an interpretive puzzle, with clinical implications that materially affect quality of care. This is conveniently overlooked and distilled into a single positive or negative test result, without further consideration.

When providers make decisions only from urine drug screen results, the quality of each decision is limited to the quality of each test result. Patient care is effectively confined to urine test results, which are rated by the CDC to be of low quality when evaluating compliance with opioid medications. Most evidence in support of urine drug screens comes from expert opinion or small case studies that reiterate the tests' importance merely because they appear to be important. The purported data are merely anecdotes that pass as evidence that is then repeated until a perception becomes standard clinical practice.

Indoctrinating perceptions as clinical standards of patient care leads to clinical decisions based on flimsy pretenses that fall apart on closer examination. Early in the pandemic, when patients clamored for COVID-19 tests, many of the tests were not administered properly and included major errors in the results. This rendered the tests questionable at best. Yet the demand for tests rose, despite public awareness of their limited value—almost as though the comfort of getting tested mattered more than the actual test results.

Similarly, evaluating patients who take opioids by repeatedly drug testing their urine gives providers a sense of comfort through the pretense of clinical oversight. This sense of comfort morphed into an existential reality when legal scrutiny intensified during the opioid epidemic. In overemphasizing the importance of urine drug screens, providers over-tested patients, fearful of prescribing opioids without a test result to justify the decision.

Instead of focusing on a single right or wrong decision, clinicians should develop the right understanding of what is known and unknown—create the proper context to evaluate opioid dependencies—and structure their approach to patient care through that framework, thereby minimizing errors when making prescribing decisions.

Theologian Soren Kierkegaard described two forms of error that can apply to such decisions. The first is to believe what is not true, and the second is to not believe what is true. This framework is already used to evaluate the validity of test results in large clinical studies. To believe what is not true is what comes from a false positive result, and to not believe what is true is what comes from a false negative result.

But the faulty logic arising from these errors is not accounted for when evaluating individual clinical decisions. On that level, perceptions are far more influential than data in contributing to the likelihood of an error, because they carry greater sway in clinical decisions. This makes behavioral economics and philosophy more useful when studying errors in healthcare on the individual level.

Philosophers who have studied how we become aware of our thoughts have traditionally focused on their formation and manifestation. They first studied uncertainty—what they do not know. Then they pieced together, thought by thought, how they know what they know. They then aggregated these thoughts into a system of patterns. This is how awareness is created from uncertainty.

This process is described in two steps. The first step is schematization—how we take observations in real time and attempt to understand them. The second step is heuristics—how we take our preliminary understandings and create perceptions that form our conscious awareness. These are the cognitive biases discussed previously. Every experience is a two-step process that begins with trying to understand the initial uncertainty, and then moves on to form perceptions out of those understandings. In aggregate, this generates a perpetual state of cognitive flux that philosopher Immanuel Kant called the mind's "free play."

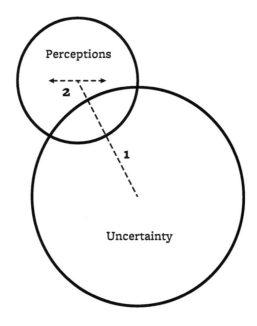

Figure 13.

When news of COVID-19 dominated every headline on television, online, and in print, people interpreted any symptom as a potential symptom of the virus. This prompted people to seek clarification from their providers or to search online to make sense of their perceptions. Providers had to interpret a broad array of symptoms, like cough and fever, just as much as they had to educate patients on how to distinguish their perceptions of vague symptoms.

Similarly, patients with chronic pain present with wide-ranging symptoms that require equally nuanced analysis.

Initial uncertainty during a patient encounter arises from the presenting symptoms and the perception of those symptoms, as shown in figure 14. In the diagram, the larger circle on the bottom represents uncertainty. The two smaller circles overlapping each other, along with the larger circle below, are examples of two perceptions that form out of the uncertainty in treating a patient who is prescribed opioids.

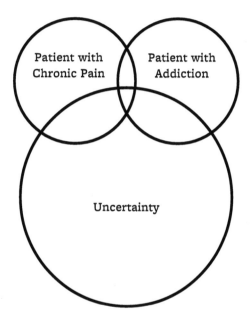

Figure 14.

The larger circle on the bottom of the figure is labeled "Uncertainty," which is where initial understandings are developed. The smaller circle on the left is marked "Patient with Chronic Pain," and the smaller circle on the right labeled "Patient with Addiction."

The diagram is modeled after a Euler-Venn Diagram, or EV diagram, to portray thought patterns that form conscious perceptions. The diagram's three circles show how uncertainty forms the basis of thoughts later expressed. The part where the two smaller circles overlap is the blending of perceptions—a conscious uncertainty of what to believe. This is different from unconscious uncertainty, depicted where the smaller circles overlap with the larger circle—the moment before we have a coherent perception and are still attempting to make sense of the uncertainty in the observations.

Uncertainty is hard to grasp without a structured way of looking at it. Uncertainty is best understood by establishing a frame of reference to organize an approach to it. When encountering something unknown, we create thoughts that try to make sense of what we see. These thoughts come from existing information, past experiences, and current observations. This is depicted as the solid arrow coming from the center of the uncertainty sphere into a sphere that depicts a perception. The solid arrow entering the perception circle signifies thoughts that emanate from that initial perspective and form conscious beliefs that are then acted upon.

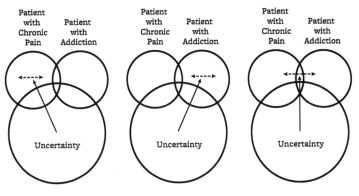

Figure 15.

The diagram has three different representations of a patient encounter from the perspective of a provider seeing a patient who presents with pain. The solid arrows originating from each of the larger uncertainty circles point toward one of three areas in the perception spheres. In the first diagram, the arrow points left, meaning the provider interprets the patient to have genuine symptoms of pain. In the second diagram, the arrow points right, meaning the provider interprets the patient to exhibit characteristics of addiction—this patient is possibly malingering to receive pain medications.

If the frame of reference points into the overlapping section, as in the third diagram, then it means the provider is consciously uncertain of how to interpret the patient's symptoms. Most of the time, however, the frame of reference points to one sphere outside of the overlapping regions, since most providers usually have some predisposition for what they interpret.

Notice the smaller, dashed arrows that point sideways off the tip of the larger, solid arrow. These represent the range of perceptions we carry with us at all times. They point in opposite directions because, when we think, we hardly ever think in just one way. In fact, we naturally carry opposing views on most things. We may outwardly carry a firm opinion about something, but we subconsciously think about the opposite of that opinion, as well. But we prioritize the thoughts we already believe to be true and consciously express one dominant perception, disregarding the contrary thoughts.

Although these diagrams are conceptual, they represent real decision-making processes for providers and underscore the influence of uncertainty in healthcare. This was largely taken for granted until the pandemic ravaged the world and showed how much uncertainty affects patient behavior and provider decisions. "No one realized a pandemic was going on," an anonymous Chinese patient was reported as saying in early 2020. That patient spoke for all who were caught off guard.

The tendency to be continually surprised by new trends in healthcare is a well-known familiarity bias. When presented with a new set of symptoms or a new disease presentation, clinicians initially try to understand it in familiar terms. Clinical biases almost always prioritize the familiar, as perceptions instinctively create a frame of reference that assumes we have seen this before. We rely on these initial perceptions to interpret new information and anchor how we further comprehend it.

Only when we have added enough unique perspectives—enough figurative arrows in the EV diagram pointing toward uncertainty—do we adjust our frame of reference with beliefs that acknowledge the uncertainty. Every new perspective, be it a direct observation or new information received, adds another arrow to the frame of reference. This accumulates into a collection of perspectives that together determine the range of perceptions through which something new or unfamiliar is interpreted.

When we first heard of the COVID-19 variants, we were not sure how to understand them. For many still coming to terms with the pandemic as a disease, it takes yet another shift in perception to become aware of and understand the heightened risks the variants pose. This occurs differently in different people. For those familiar with virus mutations and epidemics, it might not take much to shift their perception. For those struggling to understand whether the pandemic is real, this shift may require more information and more time. It depends on how the person integrates new information, and what existing perceptions the person holds.

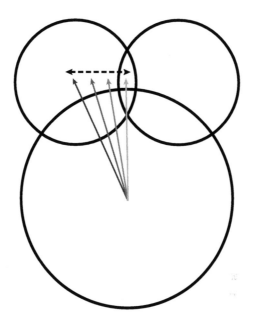

Figure 16.

To observe something new, and recognize it as such, one needs to first understand what makes it new. This begins by understanding the uncertainty through which thoughts are derived. We naturally perceive something new as relative to things we already know or are familiar with. Only after actively shifting our frame of reference do we entertain the possibility that we are observing something new. This is a new perception consciously introduced by focusing on the uncertainty in the originally held belief.

We can do this by refocusing attention on thoughts opposite to a dominant perception. If I believe I should order a test, I should also consider why I should *not* order a test. Whenever a perception prompts a decision, emphasize the opposite. Once considering both the predominant belief and its opposite, the uncertainty can be seen in both perceptions: what makes one decision a better option compared to its opposite? This consideration, and subsequent determination, is how awareness is expanded. When emphasizing the unknown, a better understanding emerges of what is known.

This changes how clinical decisions are made. Instead of deciding on something and reflexively acting, different options are balanced against one another. Healthcare decisions become the clinical equivalents of opportunity cost decisions. The decision to order a lab is no longer an instinctive order, but a balanced consideration to order or not, integrating all factors that go into it—cost, medical need, and unnecessary punctures to the patient—and weighing each accordingly.

When great chess players look at a chessboard, they see the pieces and the empty spaces. Great clinical decision-makers look at any decision in terms of what is known and unknown, and of relative benefit and risk, fully aware of what goes into any decision. Without structured clinical decisions, perceptions are generated reflexively. Even when a protocol is available to structure an approach to clinical care, some clinicians struggle to consistently make sound decisions.

Protocols try to standardize decision-making—but, ultimately, perceptions dictate our responses to protocols and the eventual decisions. For example, a provider who missed diagnosing a patient's anemia will thereafter order hemoglobin blood tests on more patients and with greater frequency. No protocol can account for that reaction. But awareness of such tendencies when establishing a structured way of thinking allows providers to interpret new information without reacting to previous perceptions. It starts by recognizing the uncertainty and leads to better decision-making.

Dr. William Osler advocated for this way of thinking when

he emphasized bedside teaching for medical students learning how to evaluate patients. He believed maximizing direct experiences with patients leads to better quality of care—not because it gleans new data or uncovers something previously hidden, but because direct experiences help providers better understand the patient, develop a more accurate assessment of how the patient thinks, and more clearly perceive how the patient internalizes the care received.

Many argue that it is unnecessary to think like this on a consistent basis, since most of medicine is recognizing a familiar constellation of symptoms and then diagnosing and treating patients accordingly. But this reflective approach eventually becomes a thought pattern mechanically observed and repeated, working as long as nothing new is encountered. When that happens, the provider notices only things that are familiar, gradually becoming aware later on of any apparent differences. When minds think this way, decisions are made in this way. It makes for bad medicine and leads to misdiagnoses for new symptoms or unfamiliar diseases.

This is why most of the care for cancer patients focuses less on optimizing early detection of initial symptoms, and more on treatment protocols after the cancer has grown and become symptomatic. Early detection requires a shift in awareness to correctly interpret early symptoms. It requires optimizing the approach to uncertainty around a set of vague symptoms. Cancer researchers who study early detection find that perceptions of symptoms are as important as the symptoms themselves. As symptoms change with the progressing cancer, shifting perceptions determine when and how patients seek care.

These thought patterns will always come and go in dynamic, chaotic ways, dodging conscious awareness. But without structure to balance thoughts and create some level of awareness, we haplessly move from thought to thought, and then from decision to decision.

Philosopher Georg Hegel describes this dynamic process of fluctuating perceptions and reactions as dialectic thinking. Most providers, when first learning how to practice medicine, try to structure these perceptions. For any new patient presenting with a set of symptoms, newly minted providers closely observe the symptoms to determine potential diagnoses. This is done by analyzing each symptom based on what it represents and does not represent. This skill is taught at all levels of academic medicine. But once taught, it is abandoned. The skill to analyze unfamiliar symptoms is replaced by reflexive thought patterns that correlate patient presentations with the most likely diagnosis.

The problem is worsened by integrating healthcare technologies into patient care. Rather than making healthcare more efficient, technology makes healthcare reliant on perception-driven biases. In using tools like artificial intelligence and machine learning models, clinical decision-making leans away from the provider's ability to make decisions and toward the capabilities of the technology to make decisions, creating a dependency on those capabilities.

Technology-based solutions rely heavily on algorithms to approximate clinical decisions and treatment protocols. These are the computational equivalent of heuristics. They might work for routine decisions with fixed parameters, but when making clinical decisions with dynamic uncertainties, these computations quickly fall prey to familiarity biases. Regardless of healthcare's technological advances, it always comes down to understanding how perceptions form out of uncertainty. Instead of addressing how these thoughts formulate, there is a rush to reiterate the same thought patterns through technology that simply produces the same errors.

Some health policy experts have advocated introducing genetic testing or other types of quantitative analysis into routine patient care, believing the additional data will help with treatment. But more data does not lead to better decisions; nor does it lead to improved patient compliance with treatment. The data analyses only transfer the uncertainty in traditional patient care across an entire expanse of new information, giving rise to new perceptions with their own sets of reactions and unforeseen consequences.

If such testing or analysis is to be introduced into clinical care, then certain factors should be studied—including the value of the additional data relative to the behavior it modifies, and the decisions that data prompts. Otherwise, providers may risk reacting to errors in the tests caused by the uncertainty in the data sets. This would not lead to better clinical decisions, but merely introduce different forms of errors.

We saw this in 1967, when surgeon general Dr. William Stewart declared the first of many figurative wars in healthcare by inciting a war against infectious diseases. He mounted a campaign to eradicate all infectious diseases through the aggressive use of antibiotics. A half century later, these are the lingering effects of that war: 700,000 deaths in 2019 due to antibiotic-resistant infections (pre-COVID-19); eighty-eight million antibiotics prescribed without a patient encounter between 2004 to 2013; and drug development for novel antibiotics being basically nonexistent. The only companies willing to develop antibiotics are startups, since large pharmaceutical companies have refocused their drug development efforts toward medications that treat clinical conditions with higher financial upsides.

Did we win the war? The question is nonsensical because healthcare is not a war to win, but a balance to attain—accepting what we do not know and embracing uncertainty. That balance is found in nearly all clinical conditions and diseases. It is believed sickle cell disease arose as a response to malaria exposure, offering those with the specific sickle-cell blood type protection against malaria at the cost of suffering from the blood disorder.

A lesser-known relationship exists between inflammatory bowel diseases and exposure to parasites—the parasite trichinella in particular. When examining many diseases and the corresponding immunological responses, we often find an innate balance governing the interaction. Biologists believe this balance was disrupted when we eliminated exposure to natural bacteria and parasites—to which our bodies had grown accustomed—in the quest for hygienic living conditions, giving rise to previously uncommon autoimmune conditions.

But the relationship is more complex than simply equating pathogen exposure with immune responses. Most studies that attempt to attribute one specific trigger as the cause of an inappropriate immune response demonstrate no meaningful cause-and-effect relationship. Patient symptoms arise from all immune triggers and should be weighed together in a balance. Absent the full awareness of this complex balance, we are left with incomplete interpretations that struggle to make sense of relationships rife with uncertainty, and we find ourselves oscillating from perception to reaction.

There is more we do not know than what we do know in regard to immune responses. Even the traditionally held belief that viral pathogens are bad for us is proving to be not entirely true. It is estimated that up to 8 percent of our genes come from viruses, and many proteins in the body behave like some of the deadliest viruses in the world. This makes the study of uncertainty about our immune systems critical in understanding the balance of factors that guide its behavior. Anything that disrupts this balance, whether it is eradicating germs with antibiotics or eliminating natural bacteria through excessive hygiene, leads to effects that run counter to original intentions. This is because healthcare behaves dialectically, shifting from one response to its opposite, whether in the world of inflammation, infectious diseases, or clinical perceptions. In the latter, our fluctuating thoughts regulate and shape the way we communicate. It may feel unique because it is more cognitive, but the patterns are the same, whether in our minds or in our cells—or in health policy.

Dialectic principles explain the cascade of reactions observed in law and policy around the opioid epidemic. First, there was the emphasis on the treatment of pain, until pain management became the focus of care.

Then, narratives surfaced of lives lost and families destroyed by opioid abuse. This was followed by the onslaught of aggressive government intervention and reaction, which then led to another set of narratives. All sides attributed blame to others, prompting ever more extreme reactions. On it went, cascading in a dialectic progression in which mythos, or emotion, became valued over logos, or reason—until mythos *became* logos. Extreme emotions became the basis for our perceptions and, eventually, our assumed reality.

When consciously acting on perceptions, we reinforce only the beliefs we currently hold. We rarely come across a situation in healthcare by which we change our beliefs through our own volition. To challenge a current view, new perceptions are always required. But increasingly, new perceptions are discarded in favor of thoughts that reinforce what we already believe, further tilting the balance. When encountering others who hold beliefs similar to ours, we become more extreme in our own beliefs. This is because we gravitate toward beliefs that reinforce our own views, instead of incorporating beliefs that both reinforce and refute what we believe. We create selective echo chambers in our minds. The more we reinforce a belief, the more extreme it becomes.

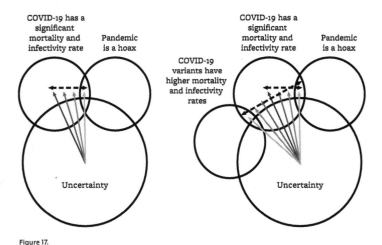

Figure 17.

The figures show that when exposure to health news increases, the veracity of existing perceptions is reinforced. With each additional input of information, overall perceptions become more extreme, because only those that align with pre-existing beliefs are integrated. Notice how firmly entrenched the original perception that COVID-19 has significant mortality and infectivity becomes once additional information about COVID-19 variants becomes available.

As the views around opioids polarized, federal regulators became more rigid, and providers became more reliant on

2016 CDC guidelines to make decisions and determine clinical care. Since the way we think affects the way we communicate, the guidelines referenced when prescribing opioids defined providers' interactions with patients. Uncertainty transferred from provider and patient to the guidelines. But it was not seen that way until the uncertainty in the guidelines led to errors in clinical decision-making, which worsened patient outcomes for many throughout the country.

The 2022 CDC guidelines now try to balance the need for opioid medications with the underlying risk of opioid abuse. But uncertainty is still present, and lingering questions remain in applying these guidelines to specific patients, continuing the cascade of perceptions and reactions from providers and patients. The back-and-forth dynamic creates a dialectic of thought patterns among providers—who are uncertain as to whether to continue prescribing opioids—and patients, who respond with fear and angst to the uncertainty of not knowing if they can continue to receive medically necessary pain medications.

The EV diagram (fig. 18) shows the following perception shifts among providers and the ensuing shifts evoked in patients. In the scenario on the top, the provider trusts the patient. The patient recognizes the trust and maintains compliance with opioid medications. In the scenario on the bottom, the provider distrusts the patient, and the patient recognizes the distrust. The diverging thought patterns mirror changes in perception as trust erodes between provider and patient, leading to further shifts with additional consequences.

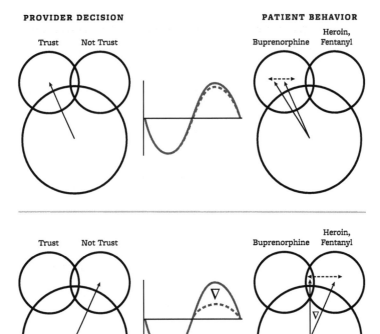

Figure 18.

Suppose the provider distrusts the patient, believing the patient is developing dependencies on opioid medications. If the provider does not trust the patient, the provider may not consider opioid abuse medications and instead simply discontinue seeing the patient. This would influence whether the patient transitions from opioids to heroin or fentanyl, instead of to medications such as buprenorphine, which has proved to help patients manage substance use dependencies. The provider's perception of trust impacts the patient's behavior and has the potential of turning patients with nascent addictions into outright addicts.

The perceptions derived in a patient encounter influence patient behavior, corroborating the notion that quality of communication affects quality of care. This is seen in emergency rooms across the country in treatment of acute care patients. In some hospitals, prior to initiating the encounter, patients are asked to define their preferred style of communication: whether they prefer providers to speak in technical terms or in a personable way, and whether they prefer providers to speak concisely or take the time to delve into clinical details. This simple gesture paves the way for effective communication and fosters trust at the onset. By identifying how the patient best communicates, providers communicate more effectively and make better decisions that lead to better care. In establishing an initial framework for communication, the dialectic progression of communication in the acute care encounter resonates toward optimal patient outcomes.

This pattern can be used to define more than just clinical communication in one encounter. All of healthcare can be observed through this dialectic trend. Perceptions form reactions, only for another set of reactions to form in response. The fluctuations create complex systems seen through the balance that holds all the perceptions together.

Take, for example, a diabetic patient who appears for a follow-up visit with his primary care physician. He has been taking his medications regularly but has been noncompliant with the recommended diet to avoid high-carbohydrate foods. In the months between visits, his blood sugar has escalated. When the provider asks about his medications, the patient states that he takes his medications as prescribed but does not mention his lack of dietary compliance.

The provider discusses only the patient's medications and believes the diabetes is progressively worsening, forgetting to address the patient's eating habits in detail. After the clinical visit, the provider believes the patient's diabetes has worsened. The patient's perception is different. He believes his diabetes is controlled, and that he can easily lower his blood sugar through dietary changes despite not having yet done so.

The perceptions that emerge are different for the provider and the patient. Each attributes a different cause to the elevated blood sugar, and each directs attention toward that one cause, leading to diverging beliefs about an appropriate treatment. Different beliefs lead to different clinical decisions that, once reinforced over time, create diverging ideas on how to diagnose and treat diabetes.

Simply put, this patient will not receive optimal care for his diabetes because he perceives his disease differently than his provider does. The provider believes the patient is compliant, while the patient knows he is not. The patient believes he can eventually control the diabetes with diet, while the provider assumes more medication is needed. Both sides have fundamental misunderstandings that will worsen as each responds differently to their unique, initial beliefs.

"If you wish to understand the universe, think in terms of energy, frequency, and vibration," physicist Nikola Tesla said. He may have been talking about the universe at large, but he could just as well have been talking specifically about healthcare. For all its technological sophistication, healthcare is beholden to the perceptions held. The thought patterns that create these perceptions must be examined to truly understand patient behavior—beginning with an awareness of the complex balance holding the thought patterns together.

In mathematical terms, a balance is a ratio. This was what Pythagoras was studying all those centuries ago. To him, the vibration of chords represents the interaction of all things in the universe—with the ratio of the vibrations characterizing the nature of the interactions—an analogy that perfectly defines all relationships in healthcare.

CHAPTER 20

"Young man, I invented the modern age," Henry Ford once said, late in his career, to a child who questioned his continued relevance. Ford's derisive remark was characteristically short, but over the years the child's questioning proved prescient. The personal attributes that had made Ford a successful entrepreneur—enterprise and boldness—curdled into arrogance and obstinacy as he clashed with others in his company over his misguided policy decisions.

One was the elderly Ford's decision to enlist his young employee Robert McNamara to lead an initiative encouraging drivers to wear seat belts. Ford and McNamara insisted on a paternalistic, commanding approach, despite overwhelming opposition from other executives in the company. In short order, the two were proved incalculably wrong, with disastrous effects lingering even today as drivers of all ages throughout the country routinely refuse to wear seat belts. Ford and McNamara's attempted tactic is what behavioral economists call a nudge, an act intended to encourage or guide a specific behavior. But this nudge was in fact a nuisance. By promoting that behavior, they encouraged its opposite.

Fundamentally, a nudge raises awareness of a perception that then prompts an action. Analyzing perceptions in healthcare in this way helps correlate specific thoughts with decisions made by providers and patients. When nudges are designed to prompt specific clinical perceptions that lead to specific actions, conceptual frameworks turn into meaningful solutions.

A few decades ago, the University of Michigan Health System introduced a policy of apologizing whenever a medical error happened. The organization soon noticed a reduction in its number and overall size of malpractice lawsuits. That one action, a nudge prompting an apology after a mistake, created a perception among patients and their families of genuine remorse on the part of providers, and reduced the likelihood of a prolonged legal battle in court.

Like perceptions, nudges elicit specific behaviors and produce intended effects, but they also produce a host of secondary effects as reactions to the initial nudge. Many of the secondary effects are beneficial, though unforeseen. Just as common are nudges passing as nuisances, with secondary effects that oppose the intended effect, giving rise to unintended behaviors.

Take how we talk as an example. The way we communicate affects the thoughts we form, and the thoughts we form affect the way we communicate. Basic communication between a provider and patient is a veritable circuit of nudges between the spoken word and perceived thought. When word and thought are not properly aligned, it leads to frustration and angst. Some patients complain about a lack of communication with their providers, feeling a sense of helplessness or lack of importance.

Healthcare's solution has been to improve the patient

experience—more convenience, better access, and an abundance of satisfaction metrics. While some of these factors have improved quality of care for patients, the improvements are limited, as they do not address the full set of perceptions underlying poor communication.

We attribute a specific effect, such as improved satisfaction, to a specific cause, like convenience, and concoct some form of cause and effect. While such thinking can lead to improvements, they are limited and inconsistent, because the efforts are oversimplified. When trying to force particular outcomes out of a complex process by altering a particular cause we think leads to a desired effect, we produce a slew of unintended consequences.

Instead, we should observe the layers of perceptions that go into patient behavior and study those relationships. We can then structure nudges to address the perceptions rather than a single task. The better a nudge represents the full array of perceptions, the better it prompts the desired effect. But most perceptions appear in the fleeting moments when a nudge appears. Some perceptions manifest later as behaviors or decisions, appearing as late as weeks after the perceptions first form. Nudges, therefore, should address both long-term and short-term perceptions in healthcare, and appear close to when the perceptions form.

This does not follow the principle of cause and effect. There is no simple, linear relationship between nudges and perceptions. Instead, seemingly unrelated factors correlate in unpredictable ways that change based on frames of reference. This is why intuition plays an immense part in healthcare. It is the sum of our perceptions, extracted from past experiences and current observations. Intuition determines our thought patterns and influences our decisions.

Most of what we consider intuition in healthcare is the amalgam of implicit thoughts and feelings. Intuition affects how we perceive clinical data and the more quantifiable aspects of healthcare. Underneath the data and guidelines, healthcare distills down to subjective beliefs, derived from intuition, and is decidedly qualitative. Yet we prioritize what is quantitative. This creates a contradiction between what we react to and what we perceive, and it explains why most nudges are largely ineffective.

We overcome this by quantifying thought patterns that lead to conscious perceptions into nudges, effectively quantifying intuition. This incentivizes our intuition to consider all perceptions in a clinical decision, and it turns subjective thoughts and feelings into nudges that appear more recognizable because they look more quantitative. This type of nudge adjusts the frame of reference by prompting particular perceptions that lead to intended actions.

However, most healthcare systems currently use nudges as reminders, in reference to rules or guidelines. These types of nudges are unsuccessful in the same way that guidelines are limited. Properly structured nudges influence perceptions of which we are and are not aware. Nudges based on guidelines address only the most overt behavior, not accounting for the associated, secondary behaviors that form in response.

When used to their full extent, nudges prompt an understanding as much as an action. For example, such a nudge can provide a reason for patients to consider long-term health risks that might not appear significant at the moment by converting implicitly assumed risks into explicit prompts. It comes down to what perceptions a nudge elicits and when that nudge appears.

During a patient encounter, the conversation that takes

place between a provider and a patient is more than an exchange of words. It is an exchange of beliefs and decisions that take place through the medium of conversation. In any clinical encounter, the conversation reflects the changing perceptions of both provider and patient. To optimize that change, the appropriate thought patterns must be nudged during the encounter or immediately afterward.

Suppose a patient, who has a history of chronic pain managed with opioids, is requesting additional medications to manage his worsening pain. The provider is skeptical about increasing the medication, in part due to the legal ramifications, and also because she is unsure whether she should trust the patient without additional oversight. Once the provider orders urine screens and checks the prescriber database, and the patient presents with no concerns, the provider feels more comfortable raising the quantity of opioid medications—but not completely comfortable.

The provider anticipates the conversation continuing during the next patient encounter, with the patient more assertively requesting additional medications. The provider must now weigh the decision to raise the medications against the urine drug screen results and prescriber database, and determine whether to trust the patient, based on two sources of information. Absent any trust on the part of the provider, this reduces the patient evaluation to two points of reference.

When trust is lacking, providers decide in rapid succession whether patients are in pain, have nascent dependencies, or are malingering out of ulterior motives—a dynamic spectrum of behaviors that have overlapping presentations. Providers distill these perceptions into one decision, ultimately based on intuition. This entails organizing all the aggregate, subjective perceptions into one decision. A timely, well-structured nudge appearing in such a moment can create the right frame of reference to help providers appreciate the full complexity in making this clinical decision.

This requires understanding patient behavior in ways that go beyond test results and databases. It hinges on fostering trust during the patient encounter. For patients who struggle to validate their pain, and for providers scared to prescribe medications out of fear of legal ramifications, that trust, once elicited through structured nudges, facilitates the communication necessary to help providers make medically appropriate decisions.

No single nudge, no matter how well developed, can accomplish this. But a series of nudges appropriately structured and timed relative to the patient encounter reinforces the thought patterns needed to optimize patient and provider perceptions—and cultivate the necessary trust. Each nudge should evoke thoughts that appear when considering a clinical decision.

Instead of crafting a nudge that asks, "Did you avoid foods high in saturated fats today?" ask instead for the patient's thoughts relative to the act of avoiding high saturated fat foods: "How much effort did it require to avoid foods high in saturated fats today?" The nudge questions the required effort to engage in or abstain from an action, focusing on the thoughts that went into the perception that either led to or did not lead to an action. Structuring nudges as a balance of thought to action contextualizes the nudge to elicit perceptions that would optimize a decision. It implicitly assumes the patient is aware that such foods are bad for his or her health. Then it contextualizes the question to analyze how that awareness, once triggered, affects a patient's decision-making.

Awareness, problematically, fluctuates as quickly as

thoughts come and go. Evoking the right perceptions is effective only if done at the right time. For nudges to be effective, they need to be timed relative to the patient encounter or to the clinical behavior it intends to modify, both prospectively and retrospectively. Prospective nudges prime the person to think a certain way prior to a patient encounter, or prior to engaging in a clinically significant behavior. Retrospective nudges reflect on the recent encounter or behavior to understand the perceptions that have formed. Timings for these nudges depend on the context of their use, and of the perceptions the nudges intend to produce or react to.

A detailed example of nudges designed to address provider and patient trust in opioid prescribing is shown in the section at the end of this book titled "Optimizing Opioid Prescribing and Dosing Through Nudges." They show how to create nudges by modeling questions as ratios and timing the two types of nudges to maximize intended awareness relative to patient behavior.

Prospective nudges frame questions as thoughts that appear relative to future actions that will transpire during the encounter, balancing a subjective perception with a clinical action that may happen. These nudges are presented as a survey to both the provider and patient prior to the clinical encounter. For the provider, questions would analyze the role of trust in decision-making. For the patient, questions would analyze the impact the provider's decision to prescribe additional medications might have on the patient's willingness to reciprocate trust.

Retrospective nudges monitor the nascent perceptions that formed after the patient encounter, in reaction to the clinical actions and decisions that took place. The provider chooses to trust the patient and provides additional medications, as per the patient's request. Such an action should increase trust between provider and patient. Optimally designed nudges would study the change in trust relative to a clinical action—in this case, the act of prescribing additional medications. If the provider felt compelled to prescribe additional medications, and did so only under perceived duress, then the coercive nature of the conversation would reduce trust in subsequent encounters.

These nudges do not have to be structured relative to a formal interaction in healthcare. They can also center on individual behaviors that have health implications. For patients struggling with obesity, that specific behavior is food consumption. Patients know healthy eating habits are important, but they often succumb to poor dietary choices in moments of overwhelming stress. Nudges help patients who struggle with stress-related eating by reinforcing the right perceptions at the right time in the appropriate context.

Prospective nudges evaluate the mental exertion required to avoid bouts of overeating and balance competing perceptions—such as willpower—against acute mental stressors, to anticipate future negative perceptions the patient may later struggle with. Retrospective nudges evaluate the reaction of patients who have stress eaten recently, monitoring for the patient's reaction to the unhealthy behavior. Changes in emotional responses between prospective and retrospective nudges reflect the changes in perceptions that come from stress eating. Observing these changes helps patients recognize potential future actions by predicting perceptions that lead to and come in response to certain behaviors.

This also gives rise to a contradiction: how can we evaluate perceptions, if we must quantify them in order to observe them?

The answer is more intuitive than rational, related more to the art of medicine than to its science. Tolstoy said art is the transmission of feelings—a maxim conspicuously similar to the one Osler used to describe his experiences with patients. Like Hippocrates before him, Osler saw medicine as an experience that develops over time, encounter by encounter. Thoughts and words exchanged build a relationship, or a type of mental association, making effective communication and the perception of high-quality patient care a form of treatment.

When we align our perceptions to optimize healthy behavior, we naturally see how our thoughts prompt our actions. That awareness can be implicitly or explicitly derived—either we intuitively think to behave in a healthy way, or we are prompted to think that way. But the end result is the same: the perception aligns with an intended action.

Regardless of how well designed a nudge may be, its value comes from the authenticity of its responses. Authenticity is yet another perception that changes based on clinical context, and it is incredibly difficult to maintain. Often, when trying to be authentic, patients fall short of their intended perceptions. Studies have shown that patients are far less compliant with treatment protocols than most would acknowledge, since the total cost of noncompliance in healthcare far outweighs the percentage of patients who admit to being noncompliant.

What we consider to be our ideal selves might be an unrealistically high standard to reach. This is why we should focus on relative perceptions that build over time and emphasize trust, a perception that develops relative to another person. Nudges that evoke perceptions of trust optimize the quality of patient communication by aligning the interplay of perceptions between providers and patients. At its foundation, it is a play of intuition.

The phrase "shaping out" provides the most accurate way to characterize how trust forms over time across multiple patient encounters. To study trust between providers and patients, observe the mutual perceptions. This is accomplished through a modified version of an implicit association test. Psychologists use the test to glean a person's perspective on how two or more issues relate. It can be modified to glean the perceptions of a provider and patient relative to each other.

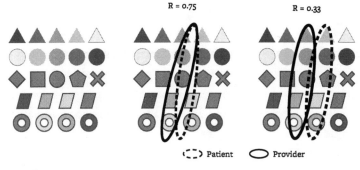

Figure 19.

We would ask provider and patient each to list their preferences of forms and images over a series of multiple-choice questions, and then observe the patterns of preference selected by the two, relative to each other. The questions appear in rapid succession, asking providers and patients to select certain shapes and colors. This test would be administered shortly after a patient encounter—once enough perceptions have formed between the provider and patient—and scored based on how strongly the patterns correlate. The closer the two patterns of responses, the stronger the association between the provider and patient. Strong associations imply a strong degree of trust.

The superimposed responses are displayed in a scatter plot to compare the degrees of overlap through a statistical process known as regression analysis. Patterns that completely overlap have a score of 1.0, while patterns with no overlap have a score of 0.0. Mapping perceptions as patterns might appear to be an odd way to study a patient encounter—almost like turning it into an interpretive Rorschach test. But patterns elucidate nonverbal, intuitive aspects of expression, which represent more than half of all communication between any two individuals. Nonverbal cues evolve and change over time. When studying the patient encounter as a pattern, we observe the changes as they develop. These changes distinguish motivations in behavior that might otherwise appear ambiguous, such as malingering false conditions or disingenuously presenting medical symptoms, or when a patient is too ashamed to admit she can no longer afford her medications. Disparities in patient perceptions manifest in patient communication, which precede clinically significant disparities in patient outcomes. Perceptions change as patient encounters change, and disparities that appear over time begin through changes in perception.

The traditional patient encounter has undergone unprecedented upheaval in recent years, changing in ways anticipated and unanticipated. Telemedicine slowly gained traction for years, but it was never adopted so readily as when the need arose during the COVID-19 pandemic. When patients could no longer see their providers in person, they resorted to telemedicine. Fluctuating perceptions that flash in and out through the new medium, appearing and disappearing, can provide insight into how the changes toward a digital interface affect patient care.

It was assumed to be a natural transition from an in-person

patient encounter to a digital one, with much of the encounter remaining the same. But perceptions that arose during these encounters were far more different than initially predicted. In changing the mode of communication, perceptions change as well. The shift is unpredictable because none can anticipate what thoughts will arise through the different forms of communication.

Eventually, the perceptions that form will prove more clinically useful than the various gadgets and guidelines that flood the telemedicine market. These glorified widgets try to replace the traditional patient encounter through digital means. Often, it means more convenience and accessible care, which is assumed to be a good thing. But increasing the number of patient engagements is not the same as improving their quality.

Rather than seeking to replace one medium with another, we should strive for an optimal blend, a balance that optimizes quality of care with the perception of high-quality care. Rather than letting technology dictate that balance, allow patient perceptions to determine the ideal blend. Nudges and association tests can find this balance—simply integrate prospective and retrospective nudges with trending association gradients and embed them into the patient encounter.

We can observe patterns in the quality of communication per encounter, and the effectiveness of digital platforms, for a host of clinical conditions. This would be particularly helpful for patients struggling with substance use disorders. For these patients, telemedicine provides a venue to ease immediate concerns or address acute existential angst that, if not treated early on, can manifest into unnecessary emergency room visits or more overt psychiatric conditions, such as panic attacks.

Early in the COVID-19 pandemic, patients rushed online to

express their fears and concerns—not just about their symptoms, or their perceived risk of being infected, but also about their jobs, livelihoods, and other issues not traditionally associated with medical care. In that moment of fear, mundane everyday topics became medical issues. Telemedicine became the platform to express the associated fear. Telemedicine builds patient trust as much as it treats medical conditions. For many patients who use the platform for urgent mental health needs, trust and treatment are the same.

Telemedicine can also help elderly patients who have dementia. Dementia is a progressive disease, influenced by a patient's social interactions, emotional well-being, and genetic predisposition, all related in a complex balance. With dementia patients, monitoring their perceptions is as important as treating their clinical symptoms. Previously, loneliness, or social isolation, was seen as an effect of dementia. Now it is known that loneliness worsens dementia, too—it is both a cause and an effect.

By understanding the importance of behavior within the context of the presenting symptoms, we can study the relationships among specific behaviors with the main clinical conditions and more effectively treat dementia patients. We can address social isolation through digital platforms by examining perceptions that form through each digital encounter—and provide opportunities for patients to engage with providers based on their behaviors and perceptions instead of through scheduled patient visits. For patients with dementia, this changes care from a discrete set of visits separated in time to an ongoing, evolving relationship between provider and patient.

A patient encounter provides only a snapshot of the entire clinical presentation. After the encounter, it can change based on patient perceptions appearing at different moments in time. The dynamic relationship between a patient's perception and subsequent behavior affects clinical outcomes far beyond the patient encounter. This accounts for limitations in healthcare models that forecast patient outcomes.

Most patient outcome models take input from one or a few clinical studies—largely by focusing on data of a disease's incidence or prevalence—and compare the clinical data from the studies to financial data or patient surveys. The most common example of this is the quality-adjusted life year (QALY) measure, which measures disease burden as derived from samples of patient responses. The resulting outputs from the model are expected values, a mathematical term that calculates the value of something discounted by the probability that it happens.

If a patient needs a follow-up mammogram costing one hundred dollars because the first one was inconclusive, and the incidence of breast cancer is 10 percent for that patient, the expected value is ten dollars. In reality, the expected value is not fixed at ten dollars. It varies based on the patient's changing perceptions. For the woman considering a follow-up mammogram, this equation does not approximate her state of mind. Her perception and subsequent decision-making are based on the uncertainty of the initial result, making the likelihood that she seeks a follow-up exam much greater than 10 percent. Once the fear of an uncertain outcome upwardly shifts the perceived likelihood of that event happening, the perceived value of the follow-up exam also increases, exposing a flaw in predicting behavior by fixed expected value inputs.

Behavioral economists observe that people perceive outcomes differently when faced with the risk of losing versus the likelihood of winning. Expected value models fail to account for perceptions of patients who are presented with clinical information that appears as a potential risk or a possible clinical benefit. The true outcome of a patient decision is influenced by the perception of the outcome relative to how the patient currently perceives his or her health risks. Decisions made in this context are not always rational, and certainly not predictable through the expected value model.

A more appropriate model that best predicts patient behavior in this context comes from prospect theory, which integrates the impact of emotions into decision-making by adjusting the probability of outcomes with decision weights that account for different levels of emotions—negative emotions in response to a potential loss, and positive emotions in response to a possible gain. A decision weight reflects a person's perception of an objective probability, rendering the perceived probability to be higher or lower depending on a person's state of mind. While the modeling can be quite complex, and many permutations have emerged over the years, each model derives from the core premise that people overvalue minor risks and undervalue significant risks. This implies that our perceptions of risk are subject to thought patterns that introduce curves into the model of the perceived value of an outcome.

Take the example of a patient who initially perceives her hypertension to be inconsequential to her overall health. After experiencing a hypertensive crisis requiring an emergency visit to the hospital, she perceives her condition to be serious and changes her lifestyle. That behavioral change is a reaction to her shift in perception, with both known and unpredictable consequences. It is known she plans to take her health more seriously, but it is not known which behavioral changes will reflect the new perceptions and which reflect the original perceptions.

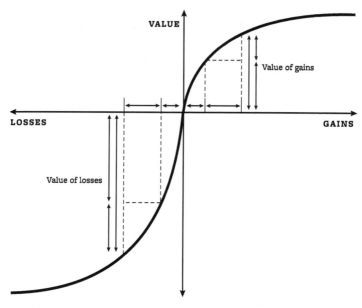

Figure 20.

When modeling the expected value of the above-referenced patient's health, providers must account for her lackadaisical approach to her health before her hypertensive crisis, her behavioral changes after her crisis, and the impact the crisis had on her long-term health. These are three discrete variables, but they are not fully independent, each having a varying impact on the patient's health. The patient's perceived probability of a life-threatening event, and the response to that perception, will shift over time, leading to different likelihoods of complications and requiring different decision weights.

Simply put, healthcare outcomes are a function of a patient's decisions. These decisions are a combination of set actions and changing perceptions. As perceptions change, so do decisions and, eventually, actions. In aggregate, this leads to different patient outcomes. Better predictive models are required, with more realistic approximations of patient behavior.

Early models of healthcare behavior calculated the statistical value of a patient's life by fixing its economic and social value, lumping all the nuanced, dynamic relationships between a person's health and their perceptions into a single term called indirect value. This is a grossly vague and inaccurate term. It fixes the loss of value from reduced economic productivity to the morbidity and mortality associated with a disease.

Recently, more sophisticated models attempt to adjust the loss of value based on trends in the labor market. Even with more realistic inputs, hardly any model attempts to incorporate changing patient perceptions.

Models that study decisions without the proper context of these perceptions frame patient decisions in an unrealistically rational way—and are wrong. Healthcare is dynamic and complex, always in a state of interpretive flux, and should be modeled accordingly. Applied models should analyze decisions in their natural context of irrationality. This is not to disparage patients. Saying patients are irrational is not intended as an insult. Rather, it is a more realistic approach to understanding patient behavior in healthcare, accounting for the unique, unforeseen relationships between perceptions and decisions— the drivers behind patient behavior.

When we account for the different perceptions that influence clinical behavior, patients will have different expected values, because patients prioritize things in their lives differently. Most models calculate the inputs through aggregated feedback surveys. But broad beliefs averaged out are not true at an individual level.

Patient perceptions may be just as complex as aggregate models, but they are distinct per person, and it is not obvious how they impact care or outcomes in various clinical contexts. Moreover, changes in perceptions affect patient behavior in unknown ways and can prompt unpredictable reactions that further complicate how a patient makes decisions. The complexities tend to be ignored in favor of fixed guidelines and inputs. This compromises the ability to predict patient behavior or a patient's response to healthcare policy. No clinician will ever be fully certain of any behavior or decision. The best we can do is optimize the uncertainty in our decisions by structuring the perceptual influences to maximize awareness. This is how we observe trust. And it is the best way to understand patient behavior. Remember, trust is not the absence of uncertainty. It is the lack of sufficient uncertainty needed to overcome the confidence in a decision. Every perception is a balance between uncertainty and known information.

Depending excessively on only what is known leads providers to make reflexive decisions based on default tendencies. But accurate decision-making begins by assuming we are wrong, or starting from the perspective of uncertainty, and approaching decisions by minimizing uncertainty through a structured balance of all perceptions.

When providers observe how a change in perception alters their decisions, they change how they view clinical decisions overall. Every decision, with the right amount of awareness, becomes an opportunity cost with a range of upsides and downsides that represent variations in individual perceptions. This is how we make decisions and how we respond to new medical information—particularly, information from clinical tests.

Clinical decision-making tools rely on parameters known as sensitivity and specificity to determine how accurately a test diagnoses a disease. Sensitivity is the percentage of patients with the disease who have an abnormal test result, indicating the disease is present. Specificity is the percentage of patients without the disease who have a normal test result, indicating the disease is not there. Tests that are more sensitive are better at ruling out a disease, and those that are more specific are better at diagnosing, or ruling in, a disease.

However, much like clinical perceptions, these parameters are not fixed. They change depending on the number of patients who take the test and the prevalence of the disease. Even the accuracy of the test result changes with the changing patient population. This phenomenon was quantified by mathematician Thomas Bayes, who developed simple equations to determine the likelihood that a test result accurately confirms the presence or absence of a disease.

Bayes noted that the accuracy of any test result changes before and after a test. He calculated the changes as a fixed ratio that changed linearly with every test result. It might appear odd that many clinical tests have varying rates of effectiveness that change with the number of tests performed. And not only do the test parameters change, but they also change nonlinearly as both the objective probability of the test and the perception of the test's outcome change. Each of these changes, when combined, produces irrational, unpredictable outcomes. It is no small wonder that so many errors occur in healthcare.

A few decades ago, the Institute of Medicine published a report titled, "To Err Is Human," which revealed that providers have committed hundreds of thousands of errors in recent decades. These errors are usually observed through the most apparent outcomes. But no one ever examines how errors first appear—through perceptions, decisions, and actions that lead up to them. This requires a focus on the uncertainty, to usher in a new way of thinking about error than what we have previously been accustomed to in healthcare.

Take the example of the hypertensive patient who adjusted her behavior after experiencing a hypertensive complication. Her concern over her hypertension determined her behavior, which then dictated her decisions. No one can predict how every patient will respond following a life-threatening complication. No one can predict even how a patient might behave day after day. It comes down to the fluctuating perceptions that drive individual behavior.

Frameworks are needed for providers to fully understand the impact of perceptions in clinical decision-making—to observe the perceived value of a test's changes alongside its statistical value. A good start is to actively include uncertainty in clinical decisions. Colin Powell said that 80 percent certainty is too much when making a decision. Skilled decision-makers use uncertainty as an advantage, by focusing on it and converting it into a conscious ignorance that determines decisions and their potential payoffs. This logic can be applied to clinical decisions.

Uncertainty as a factor in decision-making has been studied in the economic discipline of game theory, which acknowledges uncertainty as a discrete entity that impacts the outcome of any decision. Game theory shows how people make decisions and what factors influence eventual outcomes. It studies how interactions lead to decisions and eventual outcomes, assigning a numerical score to the outcome. Positive outcomes have positive numbers, and negative outcomes have negative numbers. The value of the number indicates how positive or negative the outcome is, with higher value numbers having more extreme outcomes.

Many decisions and outcomes are based on the type of game played. In zero-sum games, decision makers have opposing interests. It is called as much because in two-player, zero-sum games, there is one winner and one loser, so the total score adds to zero. In nonzero-sum games, decision makers have some interests in common, so the total score of each outcome can be a net positive or net negative number. When each decision maker agrees on a plan of action, the game is cooperative, and when decision makers cannot agree, the game is noncooperative. The behaviors of the players, and the decisions they make, are ultimately influenced by the nature of the game and the level of uncertainty.

The most common example cited is Prisoner's Dilemma, a noncooperative game in which two criminals are imprisoned in separate jail cells and told that, if neither confesses, both will receive a mild sentence. If one confesses and one does not, the one who confesses will be freed, and the other will receive a severe sentence. But if both confess, both will receive a moderate sentence. The severity of the sentence can be seen in the absolute value of each payoff—the more negative a number, the more severe the sentence. The payoff for the first prisoner is to the left of the comma, and the payoff for the second prisoner is to the right. Ideally, neither should confess; but in pursuing their own interests, both prisoners confess and receive moderate sentences. It summarizes the conflict between the interests of individuals and the interest of the group.

PRISONER 2

		Confess	Lie
PRISONER 1	Confess	–5, –5	0, –10
	Lie	–10, 0	–1, –1

Figure 21.

Game theory recognizes that people can behave irrationally, so long as it is in their perceived best interests. When applying these principles to healthcare, we see the importance of perceptions in clinical decisions. Perceptions alter the likelihood of clinical outcomes by altering the likely decision and the rules surrounding each decision. They explain the changing perceived value of a test result, of medication compliance, and of behavioral compliance with a chronic disease. It quickly becomes apparent that no perception is as important as trust. Lack of trust in healthcare alters the patient encounter from a cooperative game to a noncooperative game, putting the interests of the players at odds. In such a scenario, providers begin with the notion that they should not trust patients—that the patient must earn their trust.

With the terms of the game set, the perceptions that form shape the course of decision-making. Motivations underlying each individual decision determine whether clinical decisions are made from legal concerns or from true medical need—noncooperatively or cooperatively. The decision made depends on how much trust exists, and it shows how lack of trust increases adverse effects of uncertainty.

When one faces uncertainty, errors are inevitable. But different responses to uncertainty produce different forms of error. A false negative is an error that stems from missing something present, such as failing to detect a disease. This is the most common reason for medical lawsuits. In response to the heightened perceived cost of this error, providers order an excessive number of tests and procedures, often to safeguard against lawsuits. While it is in the individual provider's best interest to prevent a lawsuit, the entire healthcare system shoulders the burden of these excess costs.

During the opioid epidemic, this burden was exacerbated

when providers faced additional risks of criminal prosecution, resulting in even more unnecessary urine drug screens and imaging studies to justify the continued legal use of opioid medications, even if medically appropriate. Providers also face liability through the diversion of prescription medications, even by well-meaning patients. This further skews the game by adding new rules that make the risk of diversion a part of the uncertainty and, therefore, an active player in the decision-making. Soon, the error of a false positive, incorrectly assuming something like opioid misuse is present, becomes greater than the risk of a false negative. These kinds of changes in the rules prompted providers to stop prescribing opioids even when they were medically necessary.

The ramifications that came with this shift in decision-making constitute the cost of distrust in healthcare. They show the importance of integrating the perceptions of trust into healthcare models and correlating the association of trust with patient compliance. If providers perform extra tests because they fear the legal ramifications of not ordering those tests, then those additional services create financial burdens and lead to healthcare waste.

If patients need to exaggerate pain symptoms to obtain clinically necessary pain medication, they have lost trust in the healthcare system. As trust erodes, the cost of care increases, until the rules of the patient encounter become a game between two noncooperative players, each of whom make decisions in his or her own best interest in a zero-sum game. When patients and providers emphasize trust, interests align, and a patient encounter becomes a nonzero-sum game with the provider and patient working together.

PROVIDER

TRUST	Prescribe Pain Medications	Not Prescribe Pain Medications
PATIENT Discuss Pain Exacerbations	10, 10	–5, –10
PATIENT Not Discuss Pain Exacerbations	–10, –5	0, 0

Figure 22.

PROVIDER

LACK OF TRUST	Prescribe Pain Medications	Not Prescribe Pain Medications
PATIENT Discuss Pain Exacerbations	10, –10	–5, 10
PATIENT Not Discuss Pain Exacerbations	–10, –5	0, 0

Figure 23.

In this scenario, the payoff for the patient is to the left of the comma, and the payoff for the provider is to the right. When there is trust, the patient is incentivized to discuss his or her pain exacerbations, and the provider is incentivized to prescribe pain medications accordingly. Absent trust, the provider is incentivized not to prescribe pain medications regardless of whether the patient discusses his or her pain.

Healthcare will never have absolute certainty. By being aware that we do not know every aspect of a patient—and structuring an approach to that uncertainty—we optimize the relationship between perceptions and decisions, creating a balance between trust and uncertainty. This holds true for the individual patient encounter and for healthcare at large.

CHAPTER 21

The prefix *meta-* denotes anything from biological processes to philosophical assumptions, but its Greek root means "after." In the final scene of Leo Tolstoy's novel *The Death of Ivan Ilyich*, the protagonist, after he realizes the end has arrived, spends his final hours reflecting on his life. He realizes the burden he placed on his family. He knows he fought out of fear. As he grows aware, he comes to accept his fate. In his acceptance, he overcomes fear, and goes in peace to the afterlife.

We began with the perceptions that appear throughout healthcare. When we observed them closely, we saw a complex nexus of thought patterns, all emanating from an underlying uncertainty. We saw complexity within this uncertainty. And within that complexity was more uncertainty. On it goes, layer upon layer, all held together in a balance. This dynamic defines healthcare, oscillating between cause and effect and back to cause, between perception and reaction.

Napoleon Bonaparte is credited with saying, "History is a set of fables agreed upon." Similarly, healthcare is an aggregate set of perceptions, built narrative over narrative until the story becomes true. What we perceive becomes what we think. What we think leads to our decisions. Our clinical outcomes are the aggregate of decisions made over time. To fully understand it, we must study the perceptions not through words, but through patterns of complexity.

Physicist Geoffrey West defines complexity as individual parts that, once combined, display collective characteristics that are neither manifested nor predicted individually. In discussing predictive values for clinical tests or expected value models of patient outcomes, we saw the limitations of linear models in predicting outcomes. This is because healthcare is not linear; what is linear is never complex. Yet we rely on these tests, despite their limitations—which, in turn, limit our understanding of healthcare. This approach leads to inconsistent outcomes in patient care. To advance healthcare and make meaningful improvements, we must focus on perceptions—how thought patterns lead to clinical decisions.

This begins by accepting that patient behavior is both irrational and complex. It observes Gaussian curve distributions, commonly known as bell curves. For many grade-school children taking multiple-choice exams, the test score distribution is their first glimpse of complexity. The individual act of answering questions creates a complex pattern that forms when all the test scores are evaluated together, transforming individual responses into nonlinear, bell-shaped patterns. The complexity appears in the distribution of test scores as a complex pattern of dispersion. This is also where we find complex patterns throughout healthcare.

When we examined thought patterns that appear in a clinical encounter, we looked at overlapping patterns as markers of trust. The converging patterns demonstrate that two complex patterns of thought—one from the patient, the other from the provider—can be observed over time relative to each other. Similarly, patterns of dispersion identify trends in behaviors across a range of complex clinical decisions and actions. Patterns reveal tendencies among patients and providers that emerge out of uncertainty in the clinical context where it appears. Patterns show how aggregated perceptions form out of coordinated relationships between complexity and uncertainty that, when observed over time, define clinical decisions and interactions. Together, these patterns form a healthcare ecosystem.

We looked at variables at an individual level in a patient encounter—how we tend to turn those variables into constants, making oversimplified assumptions and focusing on a select few things that transpire in a patient encounter. We identified frameworks that reverse this tendency to reveal the complexity in each patient encounter. But we did so in mostly conceptual terms. To develop an applicable model that studies these patterns across healthcare ecosystems, we must create specific frames of reference that characterize specific clinical behaviors.

To observe referral patterns for patients presenting with skin lesions, we would define the healthcare ecosystem by the number of dermatology practices in a town or metropolitan area. To observe abortion rates per state relative to the birth rate in that state, we would define the healthcare ecosystem as the state itself.

Interactions in each ecosystem are characterized as ratios that tie any two related clinical behaviors together, or tie a corresponding belief to an action. The variance patterns in these ratios reveal fluctuations that define clinically significant interactions within an ecosystem. Each ratio does not necessarily need a linear relationship of cause and effect. It needs only to consist of two behaviors. These behaviors could be a belief and an action or two related actions. When this is applied to the opioid epidemic, we see how perceptions of commonly held notions are refuted.

Law enforcement prides itself on reducing the number of prescription opioids, perceiving that as a victory. Healthcare providers know the reality is more complex. Instead of studying the number of opioids prescribed per provider, studies should focus on the number of opioids prescribed relative to another clinical action—for example, tallying opioids prescribed per physical therapy order, or identifying a belief linked with the act of prescribing opioids.

When we observe trends derived through such a ratio among all providers in a healthcare ecosystem, we see how a provider prescribes opioids as compared to related behaviors among other providers. Such trends offer a more accurate assessment of individual provider behavior and of whether patients truly need the opioids prescribed. While natural variances might occur, those would show similar patterns as long as the underlying interaction between patient and provider are similar. Different patterns of behavior would produce diverging trends in which outlier patterns show different approaches to patient care, isolated examples of substandard patient care, or even medically inappropriate patient-provider relationships.

Figure 24 shows a hypothetical case of ten physicians observed over the course of one year in the same city. The ratio of opioids prescribed to the number of physical therapy orders provided is relatively constant for nine of the ten physicians. The one outlier warrants closer examination to determine underlying behaviors that led to the unique patterns. Is the outlier behavior due to differences in insurance coverage or to available alternatives for pain management for the provider's patient population? Or, is the provider exhibiting substandard care?

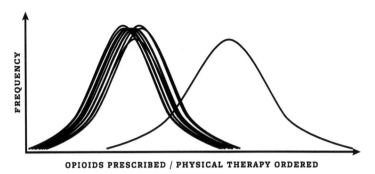

OPIOIDS PRESCRIBED / PHYSICAL THERAPY ORDERED

Figure 24.

Adding more ratios to trend over the same time interval would provide further insights that can answer these questions by comparing various aspects of providers' behavior. These might include the ratio of acetaminophen or other non-opioid medication prescriptions to opioid prescriptions, or the ratio of patients covered by health insurance to uninsured cash-paying patients. We can then superimpose the additional patterns onto one another to observe similarities or diverging trends among the ten providers. Those patterns that form illustrate the complexity in healthcare decision-making. When superimposed patterns are portrayed over a single graph, it reveals the full array of perceptions that form each individual decision.

Using ratios to analyze healthcare frames it as a series of decisions made over time and in relation to one another, depicting medical decision-making in its proper context as an opportunity cost. Remember, no decision in healthcare is made in isolation. It is always relative to another decision, either taken or not.

The table in figure 25 depicts a ratio. The numerator is the evaluative behavior or belief (what we are observing), and the denominator is the reference behavior or belief (what provides the context through which we understand the behavior or belief in the observation). A ratio linking the evaluative behavior relative to the reference behavior provides the necessary context for understanding any action or decision in healthcare.

$$\frac{Numerator \ \textit{Evaluative Behavior}}{Denominator \ \textit{Reference Behavior}} = Clinical \ Metric$$

$$\Sigma \ \textit{Clinical Metric} : [\ \textit{patient} \mid \textit{physician} \mid \textit{pharmacist}\ ]$$
$$\Psi \ (\textit{Clinical Metric}) = \mu/\sigma$$

Figure 25.

Little value comes from studying solely the number of opioids prescribed per year. Instead, the number of opioids prescribed should be studied relative to other actions, such as the number of orders given for physical therapy or for back braces, to evaluate the provider's prescribing behavior in reference to alternative forms of care provided. This creates a frame of reference to see the proper scope of clinical behavior.

This model can be applied to clinically relevant behaviors that extend beyond the patient encounter and into our communities. In McHenry County, Illinois, as in so many counties across the nation, families affected by the opioid epidemic set up community cohesion programs to support one another and provide economic relief for recovering addicts. These programs improve relapse rates and overdose mortality.

Fortunately, we see more examples of these programs as addicted patients are now afforded medical treatments across the country instead of being stigmatized or reflexively criminalized. Many states employ programs that refer patients with addictions to mental health facilities rather than to prisons for crimes deemed less harmful to society. Instead of being castigated to a life of criminal recidivism, these patients get an opportunity to seek medical treatment.

Towns in West Virginia support the opening of guitar shops and other hobby-based businesses that offer people in recovery an opportunity to rehabilitate mentally, socially, and economically from the ravages of addiction. Such measures are more effective long-term than clinical intervention alone. The true value of these programs is their encouragement of behavioral changes, which can be more effectively reinforced through community programs than in a brief patient encounter.

But healthcare professionals continue to obsess over outcomes, as though they are the only accurate gauge of success. Real success comes in structuring the right perception with the best possible clinical decision and optimizing that relationship.

Many continue to falsely believe prescription opioid use correlates with heroin overdoses. But studies have shown that the number of opioid prescriptions has no meaningful relationship to overdose mortality. This perception is nothing more than another heuristic created through an outcome bias— what happens when looking at data based on outcome statistics and extrapolating a cause for those outcomes from data alone.

This is fixed by studying the relationships as they manifest dynamically over time, as a ratio, and modeling the complex patterns of behavior that are both intuitive and nuanced, both rational and irrational. For example, we can model the ratio of unemployment rates to the number of providers offering addiction treatment, or the amount of Medicaid coverage relative to household income levels, or even the varying usage rates of different opioid medications—prescription opioids, opioid addiction medications, and non-opioid alternatives.

These relationships characterize patterns that show how patients become addicts.

Such a model can discern whether medical or social issues in a healthcare ecosystem worsen overdoses. But, more importantly, it finds solutions, such as whether greater benefit would come from treatment centers at specific locations or from more comprehensive insurance coverage for opioid alternatives. Simply model the correct ratios and superimpose the trends. The patterns reveal the defining tendencies that most likely affect healthcare behavior—individual decisions that lead to broad behaviors.

Large settlement funds from class-action lawsuits against opioid manufacturing firms should have helped regions across the country recover from the damage the opioid epidemic caused. But overdoses continue to rise at alarming rates. Lawyers, who do not necessarily understand addiction's nuances, simply accumulated statistics from different data repositories and presented the most grandiose numbers to quantify social and economic impact of a complex process through convenient outcome metrics.

It sounds nice in theory; but when applied, it leads to inevitable conflicts in deciding how to spend the money awarded in the lawsuits. Many government officials who worked together to secure settlements have trouble deciding later how best to manage or disseminate the funds.

Addiction is a complex problem that requires a complex solution. The solution does not appear in the outcomes, but in the individual decisions, which we visualize by structuring ratios specific to each ecosystem and observing the variance patterns. We would first identify characteristics unique to each ecosystem, through specific patterns of behavior. Variances seen at different levels would show how to distribute the funds and which level of government is most fit to oversee recovery efforts.

If there are wide disparities among smaller ecosystems, then local governments are likely better suited to appreciate the smaller nuances and differences. If there are similar trends across multiple towns and counties, this implies that the ecosystem is larger, and a more centralized effort from state or federal officials is better managed at a large scale. The characteristics of the healthcare ecosystem dictate recovery efforts.

Pain Specialist Referrals from Primary Care Physicians per Patient Receiving Chronic Opioids

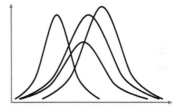

Patients Diagnosed with Substance Use Disorder to the Number of Addiction Treatment Facilities

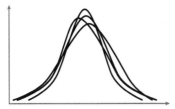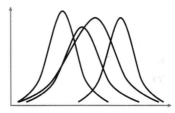

Patients Diagnosed with Substance Use Disorder to the Number of Opioids Written per Patient

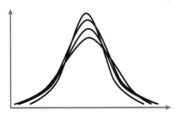

Figure 26.

In figure 26 is a series of graphs. At the top, two graphs side by side compare the ratio of pain specialist referrals from primary care physicians per patient receiving chronic opioids. One graph shows providers with different referral characteristics across different towns, and the other shows providers with similar characteristics. The variances in the graph on the upper right should prompt a review of the pain specialists in the region—specifically, to review why referral rates vary across towns. Perhaps many of the patients struggle with insurance coverage or with excessive wait times to see the specialist.

In the lower four graphs, there are four distribution patterns. The two graphs in the middle compare the ratio of patients diagnosed with substance use disorder to the number of addiction treatment facilities per town within a county, and the graphs on the bottom compare the ratio of patients diagnosed with substance use disorder to the number of prescription opioids written per patient per town within a county. The variances in the hypothetical models indicate whether some correlation can be gleaned from the patterns. For example, it shows whether fewer patients take illicitly obtained opioids when more addiction treatment facilities are available—if so, this would imply that access to treatment facilities helps patients in the model get treatment for their addictions.

On the left is some level of symmetry in the distribution, which implies that with increased access to treatment facilities, fewer patients receive opioid prescriptions. It is presumed, then, that prescription opioids were the principal source of addiction. On the right, there is no such symmetry. Instead, large variances in the number of opioid prescriptions written relative to the number of treatment facilities imply that other factors, such as illicit fentanyl, might be driving addiction, or that patients addicted to prescription opioids are not consistently seeking treatment.

These frameworks and the ratios used to create them can be incorporated into many prominent studies on opioid use and addiction. They can be applied to improve our understanding of general addiction behavior and would provide more in-depth analysis on observed patient behavior.

A widely cited study by Dr. A. S. Venkataramani found an 85 percent increase in mortality in some counties following automotive assembly plant closures relative to the mortality rate expected in similar counties. The study assumed a direct relationship between eroding economic opportunity and opioid overdoses. It is unclear whether this statistic reflects a truly causal relationship or approximates a complex set of behaviors triggered by lack of economic opportunity; but the overall conclusion is obvious: economically empowered patients are less likely to overdose.

If this point is generalized, then the focus might be on providing job opportunities over creating treatment facilities. But the better decision between the two depends on the pattern of responses within each county or designated ecosystem. It is impossible to know what will work until actually implementing a plan of action. But the more we know ahead of time, the more prepared we can be. This starts by going beyond the broad data that reflects the most obvious outcomes and looking granularly at patterns of behavior among patients in response to changes in their community.

Sometimes, however, changes in behavior are observed only after first adjusting our perceptions. Providers treat patients who have chronic pain differently depending on whether the treating provider believes the patient when he or she complains of pain. Pain is a manifestation of multiple factors, including physical injury, mental disorders, and existential stress. We should then also assume that behavioral responses to pain treatment will be similarly varied and complex across different ecosystems.

This was made abundantly clear during the pandemic. The COVID-19 lockdowns revealed a fragile interdependence in healthcare. It became apparent when we observed a rise in deaths of despair. We can trace these outcomes by modeling the patterns of behavior and beliefs through ratios and trend them over the pandemic. Some might characterize the relationship among different clinical perceptions and their corresponding behavior, while others might characterize the relationship between clinical decisions and socioeconomic consequences. When portrayed together, these ratios would provide a gauge of behavioral patterns that appeared throughout the pandemic with both medical and economic causes and consequences.

The more we look at healthcare as an aggregate of these ratios, the more patterns can be discerned. We can refine our existing beliefs to better prepare for unforeseen consequences. While we know opioid overdoses are related to unemployment, we have yet to learn specific patterns of behavior that connect the two. We know opioid overdoses increased during the pandemic, and we attributed that to multiple causes—such as less access to healthcare providers and increasing social isolation, among others. But the true patterns of behavior are more complex.

For patients with substance use dependencies, higher mortality is a combination of factors, each contributing to a shift in behavior that, once aggregated, leads to an overdose. For some, the significant factor related to mortality was a change in drug supply from a traditional heroin mix to one laced with fentanyl. For others, it was the lack of access to in-person care, and the inability to replace the trust and familiarity of an in-person patient encounter through telemedicine.

Overall, it was a deadly mix of many factors best depicted as complex relationships, or ratios interacting over time. When addiction is viewed as patterns of behavior, we find tendencies that are not apparent but that are critical in identifying community-specific solutions.

While opioid-related deaths garner most of the public's attention, a growing number of overdoses stem from illicit drugs like methamphetamine and cocaine. When all the deaths from illicit substances over the past decade are viewed together, it shows the opioid epidemic was never about opioids alone—it was always about the complex nature of addiction. The failure to realize this has led to an evolving addiction and overdose crisis characterized by substitution patterns of drug abuse relative to the changing availability of various illicit substances.

In a few years, people will clamor over the benzodiazepine epidemic, and those outcries will ring just as hollow. Addiction is never about the substance—it is about a pattern of behavior and the thoughts that define the patient's relationship with that substance.

Researchers are discovering a relationship between mental health and opioids. One study found that prescription opioids increase the risk for depression, anxiety, and other stress-related disorders. To those suffering, or to those who know loved ones suffering from addictions, this may seem painfully obvious. But we continue to find disparities among providers, patients, and families who all choose to look at the disease of addiction differently depending on the patient.

These disparities in viewpoints produce disparities in

access to medical care and in perceptions of long-term addiction treatment. They manifest subtlety in the interactions, first in a patient encounter and then in subsequent clinical experiences—first as perceptions and then as patterns of behavior. There is no cause and effect, just variances in patterns in which perceptions influence decisions.

Addiction perpetuates depression as much as depression perpetuates addiction. It is less about which condition leads to the other, and more about the degrees of association. A patient with an opioid dependency may be at higher risk for depression, just as a patient with depression may be at higher risk for substance abuse. Often, a slight change in the tone of conversation or a different clinical decision may be all it takes to determine the path a patient follows.

We can model this through ratios that analyze how patients substitute one drug of abuse for another, or go from using prescribed opioids responsibly to abusing them. Substitution patterns reveal a patient's behavior relative to opioid use. When structured correctly, ratios can model whether a patient uses opioids for pain or for other reasons. We would see particular shifts in behavior in addicted patients who originally used prescription opioids properly.

Suppose a healthcare ecosystem sees fewer opioid prescriptions in response to pressure from law enforcement. We can model ratios over the time when prescription opioids lowered, comparing the percentage change in prescription opioids to the percentage change in prescription benzodiazepines, or even in illicit drugs like heroin.

Figure 27 shows two hypothetical trends throughout a year in which a decrease in prescription opioids saw an increase in prescription benzodiazepines and heroin use, implying that patients who had abused opioids switched to another substance of abuse. But not all patterns of substitution are the same. The graph on the left shows greater convergence, implying a relatively straightforward switch from one substance abuse to another. The graph on the right is less homogenous, implying other factors are involved. These substitution patterns, which appear when patients switch from one form of addiction to another, can help providers adjust their response to tapering medications.

Decrease in Prescription Opioids to Increase in
Prescription Benzodiazepines and Heroin Use per Patient

 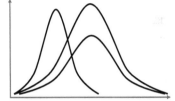

Figure 27.

Law enforcement doggedly holds on to the notion that restricting the quantity of opioids will reduce overdoses. But newer methods of analyzing the epidemic have shown that many tactics used by law enforcement are ineffective and can even worsen these patterns of substitution. Models that depict the opioid epidemic through shifts in patient behavior lead to solutions that are medically appropriate and in line with principles of harm reduction. Reducing the number of prescription opioids has little effect on overdose rates. The greatest impact to improving mortality comes from increasing access to opioid addiction medicine and in reducing relapses among those who have suffered nonfatal overdoses.

When we change the perception of the epidemic from statistical outcomes to a series of decisions and behaviors, we shift our perception of the solutions, as well. When we explore this new mode of thinking, we see that the opioid epidemic is really a series of sub-epidemics unique to each healthcare ecosystem, with each sub-epidemic exhibiting its own patterns of behavior.

These patterns are multilayered and complex. They form trends called emanative and emergent properties, which we can see only when we superimpose patterns across multiple ratios. Emanative properties are directly observable and seen in dispersion patterns among one or two ratios. Emergent properties are more subtle patterns that are difficult to observe, seen only by superimposing multiple patterns after which the additional variance patterns appear.

These second and third order emergent properties in each healthcare ecosystem reflect the uncertainty within the complex patterns. The properties vary based on the unique interactions in each ecosystem. This is why some solutions work in some parts of the country, but not in others. We intuitively understand why physical therapy orders should correlate with opioid prescription rates. But the exact nature of that relationship is a complex array of variables that emerges only when observing specific patterns superimposed on one another. And each ecosystem has its own variations—even when we superimpose the same ratios, different patterns appear.

We struggle to find consistent solutions that apply across different regions of the country when we study the relationship between economic factors like unemployment and opioid overdoses. This is because the relationship that links economic factors with overdose rates comes from subtle emergent patterns instead of any one ratio. No single solution can be generalized, since the nuanced relationships in each ecosystem reflect unique behavioral patterns.

Anthropologist Jared Diamond studies history in much the same way, through trends that may not appear obvious but prove influential in the course of civilization. He describes world history as layers of an onion to be peeled away, through which you see perceived causes that are actually influenced by more subtle forms of cause, and on it goes. Here we characterize that same relationship as ratios revealing complex relationships that make sense out of the uncertainties in healthcare.

Healthcare ecosystems are complex functions consisting of multiple ratios. When we visualize the full extent of these ratios as patterns, we see the effects of individual behavior and perceptions in aggregate. It appears as a composite of many decisions and behaviors, changing our view of healthcare from an objective analysis of patient data to a subjective study of interacting patient perceptions. This is a natural change that arises when we see healthcare through the lens of systemic thinking.

Addiction is no longer just a disease, but a large set of behaviors, with each individual action and decision playing a role in the overall clinical outcome. Ultimately, systems are understood through their component interactions; therefore, clinical behavior is most accurately observed through its component ratios—not any one part, but the interaction of all parts.

The inability to see the opioid epidemic in a systemic way has led to attribution errors in which select individuals or groups are targeted and blamed for a problem that is an inherent aspect of the interactions in healthcare. Sadly, this is not unique to the opioid epidemic. It reflects a fundamental error that spreads across all of healthcare. In this vein, this model of thinking should be applied across all problems in healthcare, and similar frameworks should be used to find solutions unique to each ecosystem.

In recent years, HIV has exploded across rural America, with incidence rates for the first time exceeding those in urban metropolitan areas. Some attribute this to the rise in heroin needles, a secondary effect of the opioid epidemic. Others believe it may be due to a lack of safe sex practices. What is agreed on is that rural America has fewer resources than other parts of the country, and public health is studied less extensively in these regions. The resulting lack of awareness and healthcare infrastructure has created a shortage of resources and education, and an abundance of stigmatization.

To make sense of the patterns and to figure out which are more meaningful in each ecosystem, we can model specific ratios unique to each ecosystem and study the substitution patterns to see how lack of clinical resources hinders individual patient care. For example, in eastern Iowa, the incarceration rate exploded after the sole local mental health facility closed. The lack of access to mental healthcare led to specific patterns of behavior that show how important those resources are to the healthcare needs of that ecosystem. But in other regions, the relationship may not be as stark. And it is important to map those trends to see the relative importance of specific health resources for a given ecosystem.

To study behavioral tendencies relative to available resources, we would create a framework of multiple ratios to study the economic and medical factors influencing patient decisions and behavior. In figure 28, six graphs illustrate six different ratios, all graphed over a one-year period.

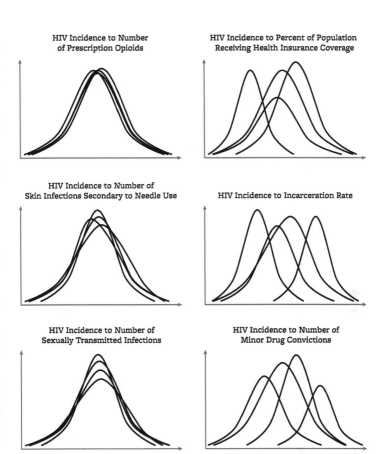

Figure 28.

The three ratios on the left compare HIV incidence to the number of prescription opioids, the number of skin infections secondary to needle use, and the number of sexually transmitted infections. The three ratios on the right compare HIV incidence to the percentage of the population receiving health insurance coverage, to the incarceration rate, and to the number of minor drug convictions.

The dispersion patterns reveal which ratios characterize more clinically meaningful behaviors and the best ways to identify resource constraints. Patterns that show greater levels of convergence are often more likely to influence collective behavior and to define community resource limitations.

This framework can be used to characterize provider behavior across a range of scenarios, as well. It can be used to study patterns of decisions and behaviors that have led to the pandemic of multi-drug-resistant bacteria, which affects over 750,000 lives every year and is poised to worsen in the near future. This complex problem begins from one behavior—prescribing antibiotics to a patient—that has prompted a cascade of consequences, including antibiotic shortages and lives lost.

Despite the global impact of the problem, we remain unsure of how the prevalence of bacterial drug resistance came about. The immediate response has been to blame the overprescribing of antibiotics. But the issue is more complex, arising out of a poorly understood relationship between individual patient care and government policy.

Providers reflexively prescribe antibiotics for symptoms that appear likely to be infectious in origin, as most thought patterns associated with those symptoms center on the interaction between pathogens and antibiotics. As pathogens evolve, they develop resistance to antibiotics, so the same treatments inevitably fail. Antibiotics must similarly evolve with pathogens.

Yet the rate of drug development for multi-drug-resistant bacteria has fallen short of bacterial mutation rates, largely because of the time required and costs of drug development. The limitations at a broad level mirror the limitations at an individual patient level. Our perceptions lead us to reflexively seek the same treatment, despite the growing bacterial resistance. When prompted to try new antibiotics, we fear potential side effects over the new drug's effectiveness and revert to requesting the same antibiotics used before.

To evaluate the factors with the greatest impact on antibiotic resistance, whether they are individual or policy failures, we again model ratios that reflect the clinical context in which decisions will be made and actions taken. In figure 29, the incidence of multi-drug-resistant bacterial infections is compared against the rate of drug development for novel antibiotics, Medicaid costs per region, and additional length of hospital stay per region.

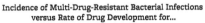

Incidence of Multi-Drug-Resistant Bacterial Infections versus Rate of Drug Development for...

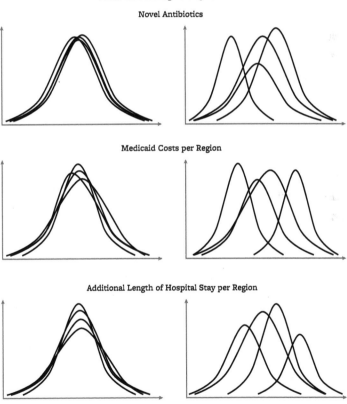

Figure 29.

The hypothetical scenarios show greater convergence on the left side, suggesting a more meaningful relationship to the factors studied when compared to the patterns on the right side. When we apply real data to compare these three factors, we would see how sensitive certain regions are to the financial and medical consequences of bacterial resistance and what influences antibiotic drug development rates. Different regions will display different variances in the patterns—some more clinical, and some more economic. These variances can be used to enact changes in policy or provider practice to address the bacterial resistance based on underlying causes revealed in the patterns.

But policy and perceptions are not mutually exclusive. In fact, health policy is often more a function of perception than of clinical data, as the COVID-19 pandemic proved. Prior to the pandemic, most saw purchasing soap as a consumer decision based on pricing and convenience. During the pandemic, it became a medical decision made by a panicked public who stockpiled sanitation supplies for fear of doomsday scenarios. Decision-making on purchasing soap was different because perceptions changed.

Regardless of policy-makers' clinical expertise, or the extent to which clinical data is available when enacting policies, policy decisions inevitably include subjective perceptions. People naturally react to changes, and those changes reflect the perceptions of the public.

We need to create ratios that integrate those perceptions— the perception that drives a decision—and model those more subjective patterns alongside the other patterns derived through clinical data. Such a ratio would discern whether someone purchased soap out of fear or in a traditional way. These subjective ratios can be modeled alongside other more data-oriented ratios to determine the extent to which prevailing perceptions affect clinical behavior.

Emotions like grit or self-despair have been known to influence patient outcomes for diseases like diabetes. Emotions are far more influential than we might believe, pervading even the most mundane clinical decisions. Healthcare professionals are starting to acknowledge this. But we still do not quite understand how these emotions granularly affect clinical outcomes. The patterns would reveal how emotions affect interactions in healthcare.

The better we understand the complex confluence of perceptions in healthcare, the more we appreciate how perceptions and decisions coalesce into behaviors. We would see the relationship between inner-city violence and average blood pressure values among urban populations, the relative impact of diet and exercise on the effectiveness of medications treating age-related dementia, why a quarter of Medicare recipients must choose between milk or medications, and how pharmacy chains compromise overall quality of patient care by being too efficient.

These interactions drive healthcare, as the component parts of a complex system, fueled by uncertainty and the complex responses to that uncertainty. When we recognize how implicit biases become overt disparities, we can finally reconcile how subconscious thought patterns produce health inequities, particularly concerning subjective matters like race and gender. Any solution to such disparities in healthcare begins by deciding how to view it. Are racial disparities predominantly an economic issue, or a medical one? Do economic factors transform into medical issues if sustained long enough?

By modeling the interactions of Black Americans as ratios,

we would see that racial health disparities are simultaneously an economic and a medical issue defined by specific interactions of individual Black patients. But the interactions overall determine the predominant perception—which would reveal whether the issue is principally economic or medical, relative to each ecosystem. The same exercise applies to gender disparities. The most significant interaction that produces the predominant perception is unique to each ecosystem—just as it is with chronic pain or substance use dependencies.

C. S. Lewis described pain as a duality between its most overt presentation and its secondary consequences, which he called "pain's shadow." That analogy, when applied to this framework, leads to what can be called shadow curves, which define emergent substitution patterns in patients affected by the opioid epidemic. It might be a patient with a substance dependency reacting to the lack of provider access, or a pharmacist uncertain about filling an opioid prescription for a patient dressed in shoddy clothing.

All of healthcare exhibits a shadow, the hidden pattern formed out of the interaction of its complexity and uncertainty. Many emergent factors intuitively assumed to be true, but difficult to define precisely, are shadow curves that expose disparities in healthcare. Defined by changing patient perceptions, these disparities became as clinically significant as hospital capacity constraints during the COVID-19 pandemic. They are responsible for the drop in diagnoses for conditions not linked to COVID-19 early in the pandemic, as patients were too fearful to seek treatment and providers too preoccupied to divert their attention away from COVID-19.

Did the medical importance of diabetic foot ulcers change during the pandemic? No, but the perception of the disease did, and when the perception changed, so did the clinical metrics surrounding it. Shadow curves explain the increase in overdoses during the pandemic. COVID-19 ignited sub-epidemics across the country when different regions were introduced to different illicit substances. This affected each ecosystem through a blend of novel substances of abuse, personal isolation, and abrupt discontinuations in medical care, all with a lingering existential stress of the unknown—pain and its shadow, complexity and its uncertainty.

We will find the right solutions when we become aware of the perceptions we carry about the opioid epidemic—and the decisions we make because of those perceptions. When we view healthcare as a dynamic array of perceptions, we see the opioid epidemic as a systemic problem inherent to healthcare.

This shift in thinking will lead to new, more medically appropriate solutions to help patients with chronic pain and substance use dependencies, two components of a complex disease that eludes our current understanding of healthcare. It encompasses our lives, affecting us economically and socially as much as it does clinically. But for how complex this disease is, at its most fundamental level, it is a series of interactions, like all of medicine.

Healthcare began as an experience between a provider and a patient. Somewhere along the way, as it grew more complex, we forgot about the importance of experience and the role perception plays in clinical decisions. We must now return to the experiential roots of healthcare, recognizing thought patterns that drive clinical decisions, and the interactions that emerge out of those decisions. Healthcare is a series of clinical decisions that emerges from the relationship between each decision and the context in which it is made.

These ratios create patterns that define each healthcare ecosystem: a distinct blend of interactions, consisting of a multitude of decisions with different payoffs. In this vein, healthcare is a game of incomplete dominance in which the relative value of each clinical decision changes with the changing perceptions. There is never an absolute right or wrong decision in healthcare, only a series of relatively beneficial decisions with the value of each benefit derived from the perceptions held. These perceptions, in turn, determine the decisions that form the clinical experience, defining patient care at an individual level and healthcare policy broadly.

Healthcare is a constantly changing fractal, growing in complexity through the same patterns that appear over and over at different scales.

To overcome the opioid epidemic, and indeed the many health crises we are facing and will face, we must be cognizant of how we think and train our minds to be aware of our perceptions. This is not as difficult as one might imagine, since healthcare has always been both an art and a science, two perceptions coming out of the same complex system.

CONCLUSION

Some say prison made me a writer. They would be wrong. Shame and humiliation made me a writer. By putting letters on paper, I display my scars of shame. By forming words from letters, I create an impression of my humiliation. By creating meaning out of words, I transform the alchemy of writing into the science of knowledge framed as solutions to the opioid epidemic.

Much like "rewriting is the essence of writing," the essence of living is redefining our lives. As I write and rewrite my story, I create solutions that turn failure and tragedy into opportunity and learning.

The opioid epidemic formed out of escalating interpretations and reactions, until it became a collection of complexities and uncertainties, that transcended both law and medicine. It permeated our most nuanced decision-making, destroying the belief in healthcare and the fabric of society. So, patch by patch, we will reattach all that we have lost—bonds broken, families razed, and communities fragmented.

When we learn to trust, we start to heal. We replace the fear of uncertainty with the guidance of trust. When we learn the patterns of thought and behavior, we replace hate and malice with awareness and understanding. Interpretation and reaction give way to solutions and achievements. Piece by piece, the world of the opioid epidemic ceases to exist. Screams turn to whispers; whispers turn to silence.

T. S. Eliot concludes his poem "The Hollow Men" with this: "This is the way the world ends. Not with a bang but a whimper." I now leave you with concluding lines of my own, expressing my innermost thoughts written in poem, not prose, because the truest forms of words come in poetry.

FAILURE

I have seen failure.
We met at the end of a journey
which began when I met Kipling's imposters.
I saw Victory but spent the bulk with Disaster.
As I continued on my way, I felt the marks of both.
I noticed the mental block of frustration—
so subtle, yet so impenetrable.
Soon, my strides began to stagger.
It drained and depleted me,
left me with nothing but loss.
Eventually, I had to stop.
This is where I saw failure.
At first, I denied it, tried to hide.
But I had no choice but to accept it.
I stared at it, observing closely.
When I saw it for what it is, I rejoiced.
Suddenly, I found a new perspective.
What appears as a trap of self-despair

can be a shield of self-belief.
Now, I embrace the arrow wounds of glances.
I mock the theatrical eye-play, the contorting lips.
I see I am the Man in the Arena.
A citizen of one, in my own world,
one forged through trials and tribulations.
A marble masterpiece sculpted in sorrow.
I have seen failure.
And I rose from it.

ON MY WALK

On my walk along the rigid shore, watching waves crashing,
I met a free-floating pebble whose reflection gave a shine.
"Look how feeble you are; you cannot fight
against the tide," I said.
In turn, it responded, "Let me show you how strong I can be."
I laughed in disbelief.
"You cannot force the sea tide to relent,
while you sway haplessly back and forth."
"As each tide waxes and wanes, I lose what I started with, true.
But I only shed what I can do without. I give it back," it replied.
I laughed louder, chiding, "The swaying waves will destroy you.
It binds you. You cannot escape, and soon you will disintegrate."
"What holds me captive gives me form. What you
feel holds me is how you perceive me."
"What about when the tide is done?"
"I will leave as I came, call my debts even.
I will shed my burden and then begin anew."
"Another path?"
"No, simply the same, but better directed.
As this path I sway along is the only one for me."

FORGIVENESS

Through faith and forgiveness,
I write the following address.
I forgive you.

On behalf of those who were beaten
until there was nothing left to beat,
I ask you to read closely the words I have written.
I forgive you.

To those bound not by constraints of the Constitution,
but bound to ever expanding spheres of personal ambition,
I forgive you.

For the tears tainted in shame
and humiliations of mourning a lost identity,
lost in the haze of false impressions
formed through the dissemination of
false information, repeated over and over,
until the lies wielded powers of propaganda—
I forgive you.

Should the inevitable time arise
for you to exert undue influence,
I strongly advise:
heed diligence and prudence.
Adhere to the principles of judicial objectivity.
Allow that to guide your behavior accordingly.
But no matter what course of action you decide,
I shall abide and pray upon the following refrain.
I forgive you.

I forgave you yesterday.
I forgive you today.
And I will continue
to forgive you
for all tomorrows to come.

ACKNOWLEDGMENTS

The entirety of the book is dedicated to my patients. But each word is a heartfelt apology to my wife. Thank you, Sonia, my beautiful, amazing wife, for enduring untold stress and keeping our family together. You are the rock of the family. Without your everlasting love, I would not have been able to write this book.

To my son, Shiva: I hope this book makes you proud of Daddy. Everything began when you were only a few days old. I saw your first smile, footsteps, and birthday under the specter of the legal proceedings. I can never remove the stain from those memories, but I will do everything in my power to make your life as happy as possible.

To my parents—my father, mother, and in-laws—your eternal supply of support became my guiding compass. I am where I am because you believed in me. You believed in me when there was nothing to believe in. I pray this book justifies your belief.

Last of all, but most of all, thank you to my editors. Thank you for taking a flier on a fallen physician. You embody the power of friendship and the hope of redemption. You helped make my story and vision a reality. I cannot thank you enough.

OPTIMIZING OPIOID PRESCRIBING AND DOSING THROUGH NUDGES

BACKGROUND

The opioid epidemic has led to significant clinical and economic toll on the United States. Communities have been adversely affected by the human impact from the epidemic. The clinical encounter is a microcosm of the social ramifications of the epidemic. Providers are concerned about clinical and legal consequences that may arise if they prescribe pain medication to patients who may have developed a dependency or are outright abusing the medication. Patients are concerned that their providers will unnecessarily reduce or outright discontinue their medication, impacting their quality of life and their activities of daily living. As a result, there is an inherent lack of trust that builds between the provider and patient. To address this lack of trust and encourage providers and patients to have honest discussions about prescribing and taking opioid medications, we must encourage honest and open conversation.

THESIS

If providers and patients are provided a platform to anonymously express their sentiments, they will honestly convey their concerns. Providers will state their rationale behind prescribing certain opioids to patients, and not prescribing certain opioids. Patients will state their concerns around their use of opioid medications and their concerns around how they communicate with their providers. The feedback will provide meaningful information as to how we can bridge the trust gap that exists between providers and patients with regard to opioid prescriptions.

NUDGES

There are two types of nudges: prospective and retrospective nudges. In prospective nudges, the provider and patient are prompted to behave or converse in a specific way to encourage open discussion. In retrospective nudges, the provider and patient are prompted to review a past action or past event. Both nudges are necessary to optimize the clinical relationship.

PROVIDER PROSPECTIVE NUDGES

Prospective nudges will prompt the provider to consider why and how the patient takes the opioid medication. However, rather than encouraging a one-sided discussion, the nudge will prompt the provider to engage in an open dialogue and discuss his or her concerns about the opioid epidemic with the patient. Revealing the provider's concerns will allow the patient to feel more comfortable expressing his or her concerns, as well. The prospective provider nudge will come through a computer-based or mobile app-based questionnaire that will require the provider to take 1–2 minutes to complete. The nudges will come either monthly or quarterly. The nudges will ask, among other things:

Do you prescribe medically indicated opioids for your patients?

Yes/No

Do you feel comfortable discussing your concerns about prescribing opioids to your patients?

Yes/No

Have you ever decided not to prescribe opioids or prescribe a lower dose of opioids to a patient?

Yes/No

How easy is it for you to obtain imaging studies and urine drug screens for your patients who are prescribed opioids?

Likert Scale—not very easy, not easy, neutral, easy, very easy

Have you ever decided not to prescribe opioids or to prescribe a lower dose of opioids because you did not have access to imaging studies or urine drug screens?

Yes/No

Has your request for imaging studies or urine drug screens ever been denied by a patient's insurance plan or because a patient could not afford it?

Yes/No

Are you likely to continue prescribing opioids for a patient if it is difficult to obtain imaging studies or urine drug screens?

Likert Scale—not very likely, not likely, neutral, likely, very likely

Are you likely to prescribe medically indicated opioids if you have easier access to imaging studies or urine drug screens?

Likert Scale—not very likely, not likely, neutral, likely, very likely

How strongly do the opioid prescribing laws impact your willingness to manage patients who require opioid prescriptions?

Likert Scale—not very strongly, not strongly, neutral, strongly, very strongly

How strongly does your patient-physician relationship impact your willingness to manage patients who require opioid prescriptions?

Likert Scale—not very strongly, not strongly, neutral, strongly, very strongly

If you had better access to imaging studies and urine drug screens, would you feel more comfortable continuing a patient's opioid medication?

Yes/No

How strongly do you believe better access to imaging studies and urine drug screens would improve your clinical decision making in continuing a patient's opioid medication?

Likert Scale—not very strongly, not strongly, neutral, strongly, very strongly

How strongly do you believe better access to imaging studies and urine drug screens would improve your patient-physician relationship?

Likert Scale—not very strongly, not strongly, neutral, strongly, very strongly

The number of questions to ask per nudge and the order in which the questions will be asked can be adjusted per provider. However, all responses must be confidential and stored on a secure database. The prospective nudges will prompt the provider to think about how he or she communicates with patients and how he or she develops trust in his or her patients.

PROVIDER RETROSPECTIVE NUDGES

Retrospective nudges will prompt the provider to review his or her prescription patterns at a broader level as opposed to the individual patient level. The retrospective nudges will be more informative and descriptive, rather than a series of questions. We will send to the provider, either monthly or quarterly, statistics related to the opioid epidemic. Statistics that will be sent in this nudge include:

- nationwide number of opioid deaths within past month and past quarter
- local number of opioid deaths within past month and past quarter
- number of overdoses among patients seen by the provider over the last one year within past month and past quarter

These three data points will inform the provider about the significance of the opioid epidemic and how his or her practice and prescribing patterns compare to the local and national statistics. While sharing data can appear threatening in nature, the goal is to educate providers and prompt them to be more self-aware of how their broader prescription patterns compare to the statistical averages.

Local data will be limited to the specific county that the provider practices.

PATIENT PROSPECTIVE NUDGES

Prospective nudges will prompt the patient to consider why and how the patient takes the opioid medication. However, rather than coming across as if we are interrogating the patient, we want to help the patient feel comfortable discussing their opioid use. The questions will elucidate the patient's rationale for taking pain medications and how comfortable the patient feels communicating that rationale.

The prospective patient nudge will come through a computer-based or mobile app-based questionnaire that will require the patient to take 1–2 minutes to complete. The nudges will come either monthly or quarterly. The nudges will ask, among other things:

Why are you taking pain medications?

Acute pain, Chronic pain

Do you take pain medications regularly, or as needed?

Regularly, As Needed

How often do you take your pain medication as prescribed?

Likert Scale—not very often, not often, neutral, often, very often

How often do you skip a dose?

Likert Scale—not very often, not often, neutral, often, very often

How often do you take more than prescribed?

Likert Scale—not very often, not often, neutral, often, very often

Do you give extra medications to friends/family?

Yes/No

Have you asked for additional pain medication from friends/family?

Yes/No

Based upon your last doctor visit, do you feel comfortable that you will have the same medication dose as before?

Yes/No

Do you feel comfortable discussing your pain medication use with your doctor?

Yes/No

Have you ever asked your doctor for additional pain medications?

Yes/No

Have you ever asked your doctor for fewer pain medications?

Yes/No

How honest can you be with your doctor about your pain medications?

Likert Scale—not very honest, not honest, neutral, honest, very honest

How concerned are you that your doctor will reduce your pain medications without discussing it with you?

Likert Scale—not very concerned, not concerned, neutral, concerned, very concerned

Do you store extra pain medications?

Yes/No

Does your pain medication help with anxiety and stress?

Yes/No

Do you have other symptoms with your pain?

Yes/No

Would you have withdrawals if you suddenly stopped your pain medications?

Yes/No

Do you need to take your medications to function?

Yes/No

How important are the pain medications to your daily livelihood?

Likert Scale—not very important, not important, neutral, important, very important

If you took fewer pain medications, would you still be able to function?

Yes/No

Do you believe you have a dependency on your medications?

Yes/No

Do you believe you have an addiction to your medications?

Yes/No

The number of questions to ask per nudge and the order in which the questions will be asked can be adjusted per patient. However, all responses must be confidential and stored on a secure database. The prospective nudges will prompt patients to think about how they communicate with providers and begin to self-analyze how and why they take pain medication.

PATIENT RETROSPECTIVE NUDGES

Retrospective nudges will prompt the patient to review his or her opioid use at a broader level. The retrospective nudges will be more informative and descriptive rather than a series of questions. We will send to the patient, either monthly or quarterly, statistics related to the opioid epidemic. Statistics that will be sent in this nudge include:

- nationwide number of opioid deaths within past month and past quarter
- local number of opioid deaths within past month and past quarter
- number of prescriptions dispensed at local pharmacies in the area
- number of Schedule I, Schedule II, and Schedule III prescriptions dispensed in the area

Local data and prescription patterns will be limited to the specific county in which the patient sees their provider.

DATA COLLECTION

Data will be collected over a HIPAA certified platform confidential to all participants. Providers and patients will have the option of completing the prospective prompts either on their desktop or mobile platform.

Data for the retrospective prompts will be obtained from publicly available national databases.

DATA ANALYSIS

The duration of this program should be roughly two years. Most clinical recommendations state that opioid tapering should begin after six months, and a two- year benchmark will allow, approximately, four data points in which to review how the nudges affect opioid prescribing rates and opioid mortality.

All responses should be aggregated and de-identified, at a local level and at a national level. The purpose in sharing the aggregated responses is to inform providers or patients of any major deviations or outlier responses they may have provided.

Overall, the data will serve two purposes: (1) inform patients and providers of how their responses vary from the local and national averages, and (2) reduce excessive prescriptions without harming the patient, ultimately reducing opioid-related mortality.

BIBLIOGRAPHY

CHAPTER 12

"About CDC's Opioid Prescribing Guideline." Centers for Disease Control and Prevention. Last reviewed August 16, 2022. https://www.cdc.gov/opioids/providers/prescribing/guideline.html.

Anderson, Robert. "The Rashomon Effect and Communication." *Canadian Journal of Communication* 41, no. 2 (May 2016): 249–70. https://doi.org/10.22230/cjc.2016v41n2a3068.

Berthet, Vincent. "The Impact of Cognitive Biases on Professionals' Decision-Making: A Review of Four Occupational Areas." *Frontiers in Psychology* 12 (January 2022): 802439. https://doi.org/10.3389/fpsyg.2021.802439.

"The Controlled Substances Act." United States Drug Enforcement Administration. Accessed September 23, 2022. https://www.dea.gov/drug-information/csa.

DiSanto, Ronald L., and Thomas J. Steele. *Guidebook to Zen and the Art of Motorcycle Maintenance.* New York: William Morrow and Company, 1990.

Durant, Will, and Ariel Durant. *The Lessons of History.* New York: Simon & Schuster Paperbacks, 1968.

Fassler, Joe. "What It Really Means to Be 'Kafkaesque.'" *The Atlantic*. January 15, 2014. https://www.theatlantic.com/entertainment/archive/2014/01/what-it-really-means-to-be-kafkaesque/283096/.

Gewirtz, Paul. "On 'I Know It When I See It.'" *Yale Law Journal* 105, no. 4 (January 1996): 1023–47. https://doi.org/10.2307/797245.

Gladwell, Malcolm. *The Tipping Point: How Little Things Can Make a Big Difference*. Boston: Little, Brown and Company, 2000.

Goodman, Michael F. *First Logic*. Lanham, MD: University Press of America, 1993.

Grant, Adam. *Think Again: The Power of Knowing What You Don't Know*. New York: Viking, 2021.

Kelly, Joseph. "Letter from Birmingham Jail." Discussion post, HONS 110 Fall 2015 Academic Writing, College of Charleston, September 19, 2015. http://blogs.cofc.edu/hons11006-fa13/2015/09/19/letter-from-birmingham-jail/.

Kinetz, Erika. "China Has Pain Pill Addicts Too, but No One's Counting Them." *Taiwan News*. December 31, 2019. https://www.taiwannews.com.tw/en/news/3847702.

Klein, Ezra. *Why We're Polarized*. New York: Avid Reader Press, 2020.

Kruzel, John. "Judge Blasts FBI Over Misleading Info for Surveillance of Trump Campaign Adviser." *The Hill*. December 17, 2019. https://thehill.com/policy/national-security/474964-surveillance-court-accuses-fbi-agents-of-giving-misleading-basis-for/.

Lampe, Joanna R. *The Controlled Substances Act (CSA): A Legal Overview for the 117th Congress*. Congressional Research Service Report R45948. Updated February 5, 2021. https://sgp.fas.org/crs/misc/R45948.pdf.

MacArthur, Douglas. *Reminiscences*. Annapolis: Bluejacket Books, 2001.

Murphy, Sherry L., Kenneth D. Kochanek, Jiaquan Xu, and Elizabeth Arias. "Mortality in the United States, 2020." *NCHS Data Brief*, no. 427 (December 2021). https://www.cdc.gov/nchs/products/databriefs/db427.htm.

Pei, Mario. *The Story of Language*. Philadelphia: Lippincott, 1965.

Riley, Jack. *Drug Warrior: Inside the Hunt for El Chapo and the Rise of America's Opioid Crisis*. New York: Hachette Book Group, 2019.

"Round-Up of Supreme Court Decisions—June 2022." America's Future. Accessed September 26, 2022. https://www.americasfuture.net/ round-up-of-supreme-court-decisions-june-2022/.

Thornton, Mary. "DEA Agents to Train with FBI Shift." *Washington Post*. May 25, 1985. https://www.washingtonpost.com/archive/politics/1985/05/25/dea-agents-to-train-with-fbi-shift/96e209c5-2653-4f8e-bf68-01ab3267e6de/.

US Department of Justice Office of the Inspector General. "DOJ OIG Releases Report of Investigation of Former FBI Director James Comey's Disclosure of Sensitive Investigative Information and Handling of Certain Memoranda." Press release. August 29, 2019. https://oig.justice.gov/press/2019/2019-08-29. pdf.

Walmart Inc. v. US Department of Justice, et al. 517 F. Supp. 3d 637 (E.D. Tex. 2000). https://casetext.com/case/walmart-inc-v-us-dept-of-justice/.

Wilber, Del Quentin, and Kevin Rector. "There's No National Use-of-Force Policy, and That's Trouble for Police Reform, Experts Say." *Los Angeles Times*. April 30, 2021. https://www.latimes.com/politics/story/2021-04-30/ momentum-growing-to-enact-national-standard-for-police-use-of-force.

"Woman Gets 30 Months for Scheme to Sell Painkillers." *Associated Press*. January 6, 2020. https://apnews.com/article/688e5ce2b12704b5d1919d56f8a00c45.

"What Kind of Training Does an Agent Go Through?" Frequently Asked Questions. FBI. Accessed September 23, 2022. https://www.fbi.gov/about/ faqs/what-kind-of-training-does-an-agent-go-through.

Zapotosky, Matt. "Justice Dept. Concedes It Had 'Insufficient' Cause to Continue Monitoring Former Trump Campaign Adviser in Russia Probe." *Washington Post*. January 23, 2020. https://www.washingtonpost.com/ national-security/justice-dept-concedes-it-had-insufficient-cause-to-continue-monitoring-former-trump-campaign-adviser-in-russia-probe/2020/01/23/2ac20f6a-3e15-11ea-b90d-5652806c3b3a_story.html.

CHAPTER 13

Bazelon, Emily. *Charged: The New Movement to Transform American Prosecution and End Mass Incarceration.* New York: Random House, 2019.

Carr, Emily, and Elizabeth Osborne. "Legal Research: A Guide to Case Law." Library of Congress Research Guides. September 9, 2019. https://guides.loc. gov/case-law.

Chilton, Adam S., and Mila Versteeg. "Courts' Limited Ability to Protect Constitutional Rights." *University of Chicago Law Review* 85, no. 2 (March 2018): 293–336. https://www.jstor.org/stable/26455909.

"Dodd-Frank Act." Commodity Futures Trading Commission. Accessed September 26, 2022. https://www.cftc.gov/LawRegulation/DoddFrankAct/ index.htm.

Dower, John W. *Embracing Defeat: Japan in the Wake of World War II.* New York: W. W. Norton & Company, 1999.

Emerson, Ralph Waldo. *The Essential Writings of Ralph Waldo Emerson.* Edited by Brooks Atkinson. New York: Modern Library, 2000.

Geisst, Charles R. *Wall Street: A History.* New York: Oxford University Press, 1997.

Hayward, Steven F. *Churchill on Leadership: Executive Success in the Face of Adversity.* New York: Three Rivers Press, 1997.

Heisig, Eric. "Cleveland County's Opioid Lawsuits Set as First Cases Against Drug Companies to Go to Trial, Judge Says." Business & Human Rights Resource Centre. April 12, 2018. https://www.business-humanrights.org/ en/latest-news/cleveland-cuyahoga-countys-opioid-lawsuits-set-as-first-cases-against-drug-companies-to-go-to-trial-judge-says/.

"The Interactive Constitution." National Constitution Center. Accessed September 26, 2022. https://constitutioncenter.org/the-constitution.

Kafka, Franz. *The Essential Kafka.* Hertfordshire, England: Wordsworth Editions, 2014.

Kahneman, Daniel. *Thinking, Fast and Slow.* New York: Farrar, Straus and Giroux, 2011.

King, Dr. Martin Luther. "Transcript of Dr. Martin Luther King's Speech at SMU on March 17, 1996." SMU. January 10, 2014. https://www.smu.edu/News/2014/mlk-at-smu-transcript-17march1966.

Linder, Douglas O. "State v. John Scopes ('The Monkey Trial'): An Account." *Famous Trials* (blog). Accessed September 26, 2022. https://famous-trials.com/scopesmonkey/2127-home.

Malcolm, John. *Using Public Nuisance Law to "Solve" the Opioid Crisis Sets a Dangerous Precedent.* The Heritage Foundation. December 20, 2021. https://www.heritage.org/crime-and-justice/report/using-public-nuisance-law-solve-the-opioid-crisis-sets-dangerous-precedent.

Marouf, Fatma. "Implicit Bias and Immigration Courts." *Scholarly Works* (2011): 787. https://scholars.law.unlv.edu/facpub/787/.

Simon, James F. *Lincoln and Chief Justice Taney: Slavery, Secession, and the President's War Powers.* New York: Simon & Schuster Paperbacks, 2006.

Stanford Encyclopedia of Philosophy (Winter 2014). s.v. "The History of Utilitarianism." By Julia Driver. https://plato.stanford.edu/entries/utilitarianism-history/.

State ex rel. Attorney General of Oklahoma v. Johnson & Johnson. 2021 OK 54. Justia US Law. Accessed September 26, 2022. https://law.justia.com/cases/oklahoma/supreme-court/2021/118474.html.

CHAPTER 14

Anderson, Eric C., R. Nicholas Carleton, Michael Diefenbach, and Paul J. Han. "The Relationship Between Uncertainty and Affect." *Frontiers in Psychology* 10 (November 2019): 2504. https://doi.org/10.3389/fpsyg.2019.02504.

Asperin, Alexa Mae. "California to 'Young People' Ignoring Social Distancing: 'Wake Up...Don't Be Selfish." *KRON4*. March 23, 2020. https://www.kron4.com/news/bay-area/california-to-young-people-ignoring-social-distancing-wake-up-dont-be-selfish/.

Atkins, E. M., and Thomas Williams, eds. *Aquinas: Disputed Questions on the Virtues.* Cambridge, UK: Cambridge University Press, 2005.

Britannica Online. s.v. "Hippocratic oath." Last updated September 5, 2022. https://www.britannica.com/topic/Hippocratic-oath.

"COVID-19 Vaccination Dashboard." State of Maine COVID-19 Response Office of the Governor. Accessed September 3, 2022. https://www.maine.gov/covid19/vaccines/dashboard.

Eibner, Christine, and Sarah Nowak. "The Effect of Eliminating the Individual Mandate Penalty and the Role of Behavioral Factors." The Commonwealth Fund. July 11, 2018. https://www.commonwealthfund.org/publications/fund-reports/2018/jul/eliminating-individual-mandate-penalty-behavioral-factors#.

FDA. "FDA Denies Authorization to Market JUUL Products." News release. June 23, 2022. https://www.fda.gov/news-events/press-announcements/fda-denies-authorization-market-juul-products.

"Full Text of the Federalist Papers." Library of Congress Research Guides. Accessed September 26, 2022. https://guides.loc.gov/federalist-papers/full-text.

Flathman, Richard E. "The Theory of Rights and the Practice of Abortion." In *Toward a Liberalism*, 168–205. Ithaca, NY: Cornell University Press, 1989.

Gans, Felicia. "Kennedy Calls Vaping Illnesses a 'Catastrophic Regulatory Failure' and Questions Federal Health Officials About How We Got Here." *Boston Globe.* September 25, 2019. https://www.bostonglobe.com/metro/2019/09/25/kennedy-calls-vaping-illnesses-catastrophic-regulatory-failure-and-questions-federal-health-officials-about-how-got-here/cGYcokC5lvZqjBAijVfo9I/story.html.

Harari, Yuval Noah. *Homo Deus: A Brief History of Tomorrow.* New York: HarperCollins, 2017.

Hasen, Richard L. "Polarization and the Judiciary." *Annual Review of Political Science* 22 (May 2019): 261–76. https://doi.org/10.1146/annurev-polisci-051317-125141.

"Individualism and Collectivism." AFS-USA. Accessed September 26, 2022. https://www.afsusa.org/study-abroad/culture-trek/culture-points/culture-points-individualism-and-collectivism/.

"June Medical Services L. L. C. et al. v. Russo, Interim Secretary, Louisiana Department of Health and Hospitals." No. 18–1323. 591 U.S. (2020). https://www.supremecourt.gov/opinions/19pdf/18-1323_c07d.pdf.

Kean, Sam. *The Violinist's Thumb: And Other Lost Tales of Love, War, and Genius, as Written by Our Genetic Code.* New York: Little, Brown and Company, 2012.

Kentucky Revised Statutes. "Requirement for Performance and Explanation of Obstetric Ultrasound and Auscultation of Fetal Heartbeat Prior to Abortion— Exception for Medical Emergency or Necessity." KY Rev Stat § 311.727 (2019). https://law.justia.com/codes/kentucky/2019/chapter-311/section-311-727/.

Kinghorn, Matt. "Indiana's Life Expectancy Falling Further Behind U.S." *Indiana Business Review* 96, no. 2 (Summer 2021). https://www.ibrc.indiana.edu/ibr/2021/summer/article1.html.

"McCarthyism and the Red Scare." Miller Center. Accessed September 26, 2022. https://millercenter.org/the-presidency/educational-resources/age-of-eisenhower/mcarthyism-red-scare.

Nassar, Matthew R., and Joshua I. Gold. "A Healthy Fear of the Unknown: Perspectives on the Interpretation of Parameter Fits from Computational Models in Neuroscience." *PLoS Computational Biology* 9, no. 4 (April 2013): e1003015. https://doi.org/10.1371/journal.pcbi.1003015.

"National Notifiable Diseases Surveillance System (NNDSS)." Centers for Disease Control and Prevention. Last reviewed September 12, 2022. https://www.cdc.gov/nndss/index.html.

"Oath and Prayer of Maimonides." Dalhousie University Dalhousie Libraries. Accessed September 26, 2022. https://dal.ca.libguides.com/c.php?g=256990&p=1717827#.

"Overdose Death Rates." National Institute on Drug Abuse. January 20, 2022. https://nida.nih.gov/research-topics/trends-statistics/overdose-death-rates#.

Perrone, Matthew, and Dave Collins. "Juul to Pay Nearly $440M to Settle States' Teen Vaping Probe." *Associated Press.* September 2, 2022. https://apnews.com/article/science-health-lawsuits-connecticut-fce3fe4f92066a9068cf50 5ed1fb63b0.

Ravitch, Diane. "William Webster: The Danger to the Rule of Law." *Diane Ravitch's Blog.* December 26, 2019. https://dianeravitch.net/2019/12/26/william-webster-the-danger-to-the-rule-of-law/.

Storer, David Humphreys. "Medical Jurisprudence: Annual Oration 1851." Massachusetts Medical Society. August 8, 2016. https://www.massmed.org/About/MMS-Leadership/History/Medical-Jurisprudence/.

"The Supreme Court & the Second Amendment." Giffords Law Center. Accessed September 26, 2022. https://giffords.org/lawcenter/gun-laws/second-amendment/the-supreme-court-the-second-amendment/.

Teitelbaum, Joel, and Sara Rosenbaum. "Gonzales v. Oregon: Implications for Public Health Policy and Practice." *Public Health Reports* 122, no. 1 (January–February 2007): 122–24. https://doi.org/10.1177%2F003335490712200117.

Whitney, Craig. *Living with Guns: A Liberal's Case for the Second Amendment.* New York: Public Affairs, 2012.

Yang, Tse-Chuan, Carla Shoff, and Aggie J. Noah. "Spatializing Health Research: What We Know and Where We are Heading." *Geospatial Health* 7, no. 2 (May 2013): 161–168. https://doi.org/10.4081%2Fgh.2013.77.

Zin, Che Suraya, and Fadhilah Ismail. "Co-Prescription of Opioids with Benzodiazepine and Other Co-Medications among Opioid Uses: Differential in Opioid Doses." *Journal of Pain Research* 10 (January 2017): 249–57. https://doi.org/10.2147%2FJPR.S122853.

CHAPTER 15

Clegg, Michael, Katherine Ellena, David Ennis, and Chad Vickery. *The Hierarchy of Laws: Understanding and Implementing the Legal Frameworks that Govern Elections.* Arlington, VA: International Foundation for Electoral Systems, 2016.

"Alexis de Tocqueville on the Tyranny of the Majority." EDSITEment. National Endowment for the Humanities. Accessed September 26, 2022. https:// edsitement.neh.gov/curricula/alexis-de-tocqueville-tyranny-majority.

Bomboy, Scott. "Lincoln and Taney's Great Writ Showdown." *Constitution Daily* (blog). May 28, 2022. https://constitutioncenter.org/blog/ lincoln-and-taneys-great-writ-showdown.

Donald, David Herbert. *Lincoln*. New York: Touchstone, 1996.

Ellis, Joseph J. *American Sphinx: The Character of Thomas Jefferson*. New York: Alfred A. Knopf, 1997.

Ellis, Joseph J. *Founding Brothers: The Revolutionary Generation*. New York: Alfred A. Knopf, 2000.

"James Madison and the Federal Constitutional Convention of 1787." Library of Congress Digital Collections. Accessed September 26, 2022. https:// www.loc.gov/collections/james-madison-papers/articles-and-essays/ james-madison-and-the-federal-constitutional-convention-of-1787/.

Jaume, Lucien. *Tocqueville: The Aristocratic Sources of Liberty*. Translated by Arthur Goldhammer. Princeton, NJ: Princeton University Press, 2013.

Maloy, Mark. "The Founding Fathers Views of Slavery." American Battlefield Trust. December 8, 2020. https://www.battlefields.org/learn/articles/ founding-fathers-views-slavery.

Rommen, Heinrich. The Natural Law: A Study in Legal and Social History and Philosophy. Indianapolis: Liberty Fund, 1936. https://oll.libertyfund.org/title/ hittinger-the-natural-law-a-study-in-legal-and-social-history-and-philosophy.

Rossi, William. "Emerson, Thoreau, Fuller, and Transcendentalism." In *American Literary Scholarship: An Annual 2009*, edited by Gary Scharnhorst, 3–22. Durham, NC: Duke University Press, 2009. https://muse.jhu.edu/ article/450033.

Shmerling, Robert H. "The Myth of the Hippocratic Oath." *Harvard Health Blog*. Harvard Health Publishing. November 25, 2015. https://www.health. harvard.edu/blog/the-myth-of-the-hippocratic-oath-201511258447.

"The US Constitution: Preamble." United States Courts. Accessed
  September 26, 2022. https://www.uscourts.gov/about-federal-courts/
  educational-resources/about-educational-outreach/activity-resources/us.

Tucker, Rufus S. "The Distribution of Government Burdens and Benefits."
  American Economic Review 43, no. 2 (May 1953): 518–34. https://www.jstor.org/
  stable/1831515.

Voltaire. *Candide*. New York: Dover Publications, 1991.

Watkins, Martin A. *Henry David Thoreau; Walden, Civil Disobedience*. New York:
  Barnes & Noble, 1968.

CHAPTER 16

Abbott, Brianna. "Vaping-Related Lung Illnesses Appear to Have
  Peaked." *Wall Street Journal*. December 6, 2019. https://www.wsj.com/
  articles/vaping-related-lung-illnesses-appear-to-have-peaked-
  11575660144?mod=article_inline.

Acharya, Viral V., Lasse H. Pedersen, Thomas Philippon, and Matthew
  Richardson. "Measuring Systemic Risk." *Review of Financial Studies* 30, no. 1
  (January 2017): 2–47. https://doi.org/10.1093/rfs/hhw088.

Aubry, Larry, and B. Thomas Carr. "Overdose, Opioid Treatment Admissions
  and Prescription Opioid Pain Reliever Relationships: United States,
  2010–2019." *Frontiers in Pain Research* 3 (August 2022): 884674. https://doi.
  org/10.3389/fpain.2022.884674.

Cochrane, John. "Stock Market Fall and Long-Term Investors." *The Grumpy
  Economist* (blog). January 24, 2022. https://johnhcochrane.blogspot.
  com/2022/01/stock-market-fall-and-long-term.html.

Cohen, Ben. "He's on Fire! What 'NBA Jam''s Hot Hand Reveals About the Power
  of Streaks." *Wall Street Journal*. Updated March 6, 2020. https://www.wsj.com/
  articles/hes-on-fire-what-nba-jams-hot-hand-reveals-about-the-power-
  of-streaks-11583256232.

"Combating the Opioid Epidemic." US Department of Health and Human Services Office of the Inspector General. Updated September 22, 2022. https://oig.hhs.gov/reports-and-publications/featured-topics/opioids/.

Department of Justice Office of the Inspector General. *Audit of the Drug Enforcement Administration's Community-Based Efforts to Combat the Opioid Crisis.* 20-102. September 2020. https://oig.justice.gov/sites/default/files/reports/a20-102.pdf.

Diamond, Jared. *Guns, Germs, and Steel: A Short History of Everybody for the Last 13,000 Years.* New York: W.W. Norton & Company, 1997.

Durschmied, Erik. *The Hinge Factor: How Chance and Stupidity Have Changed History.* London: Coronet Books, 1999.

Fagan, J., and K-L Chin. "Initiation into Crack and Cocaine: A Tale of Two Epidemics." *Contemporary Drug Problems* 16, no. 4 (Winter 1989): 579–618. https://www.ojp.gov/ncjrs/virtual-library/abstracts/initiation-crack-and-cocaine-tale-two-epidemics.

Fidler-Benaoudia, Miranda M., Lindsey A. Torre, Freddie Bray, Jacques Ferlay, and Ahmedin Jemal. "Lung Cancer Incidence in Young Women vs. Young Men: A Systematic Analysis in 40 Countries." *International Journal of Cancer* 147, no. 3 (August 2020): 811–19. https://doi.org/10.1002/ijc.32809.

Healy, Patrick. "The Fundamental Attribution Error: What It Is and How to Avoid It." *Business Insights* (blog). Harvard Business School Online. June 8, 2017. https://online.hbs.edu/blog/post/the-fundamental-attribution-error.

Howe, Catherine Q., and Dale Purves. "The Müller-Lyer Illusion Explained by the Statistics of Image-Source Relationships." *PNAS* 102, no. 4 (January 2005): 1234–39. https://doi.org/10.1073/pnas.0409314102.

Jackson, Phil, and Hugh Delehanty. *Sacred Hoops: Spiritual Lessons of a Hardwood Warrior.* New York: Hyperion, 1995.

Lopez, German. "Jess Sessions's Praise of DARE Shows He Just Can't Quit the 1980s." *Vox.* July 12, 2017. https://www.vox.com/policy-and-politics/2017/7/12/15957490/jeff-sessions-dare-crime.

Mirian, Iman, Mohammad Javad Kabir, Omid Barati, Khosro Keshavarz, and Peivand Bastani. "Deductibles in Health Insurance, Beneficial or Detrimental: A Review Article." *Iranian Journal of Public Health* 49, no. 5 (May 2020): 851–59. PMCID: PMC7475628.

O'Donnell, Jayne. "Is Vaping Safer Than Smoking? Depends Who You Ask, and What Scientific Study They Point To." *USA Today*. October 9, 2019. https://www.usatoday.com/in-depth/news/health/2019/10/09/vaping-safer-than-smoking-studies-differ-lung-injury-cases-rise/3821982002/.

Potts, Natalie, and Genna Reeves-DeArmond. "Re-Evaluation of Laver's Law in the Context of Fashion Trend Revival." Presented at the International Textile and Apparel Association (ITAA) Annual Conference Proceedings, 2014: Strengthening the Fabric of Our Profession, Association, Legacy and Friendships! Charlotte, NC, January 1, 2014. https://core.ac.uk/download/pdf/212845232.pdf.

Sharpe, William F. "The Sharpe Ratio." Reprinted from *The Journal of Portfolio Management* (Fall 1994). http://web.stanford.edu/~wfsharpe/art/sr/sr.htm.

Sommers, Benjamin D., Lucy Chen, Robert J. Blendon, E. John Oray, and Arnold M. Epstein. "Medicaid Work Requirements in Arkansas: Two-Year Impacts on Coverage, Employment, and Affordability of Care." *Health Affairs* 39, no. 9 (September 2020). https://doi.org/10.1377/hlthaff.2020.00538.

Thompson, Derek. *Hit Makers: The Science of Popularity in an Age of Destruction.* New York: Penguin Press, 2017.

u/allenaxie. "Mystery Monday: Week 3 Learning Curve of a Trader." r/trading. Steemit. 2017. https://steemit.com/trading/@allenaxie/mystery-monday-week-3-learning-curve-of-a-trader.

Young, Christen Linke. "Three Ways to Make Health Insurance Auto-Enrollment Work." Brookings Institution. June 13, 2019. https://www.brookings.edu/research/three-ways-to-make-health-insurance-auto-enrollment-work/.

CHAPTER 17

American Medical Association. "Physicians' Progress Toward Ending the Nation's Drug Overdose Epidemic." Accessed September 27, 2022. https://www.ama-assn.org/delivering-care/overdose-epidemic/ physicians-progress-toward-ending-nation-s-drug-overdose-epidemic.

Baker, Nicholson. *The Size of Thoughts: Essays and Other Lumber*. New York: Vintage Books, 1997.

Bartley, E. J., and R. B. Fillingim. "Sex Differences in Pain: A Brief Review of Clinical and Experimental Findings." *British Journal of Anaesthesia* 11, no. 1 (July 2013): 52–58. https://doi.org/10.1093/bja/aet127.

Betsch, Cornelia, Niels Haase, Frank Renkewitz, and Phillipp Schmid. "The Narrative Bias Revisited: What Drives the Biasing Influence of Narrative Information on Risk Perceptions?" *Judgment and Decision Making* 10, no. 3 (May 2015): 241–64. https://sjdm.org/journal/14/141206a/jdm141206a.html.

Blume, Stuart, and Ingrid Geesinik. "A Brief History of Polio Vaccines." *Science* 288, no. 5471 (June 2000): 1593–94. https://www.science.org/doi/10.1126/ science.288.5471.1593#:~:text=DOI%3A%2010.1126/science.288.5471.1593.

Chen, Esther H., Frances S. Shofer, Anthony J. Dean, Judd E. Hollander, William G. Baxt, Jennifer L. Robey, Keara L. Sease, and Angela M. Mills. "Gender Disparity in Analgesic Treatment of Emergency Department Patients with Acute Abdominal Pain." *Academic Emergency Medicine* 15, no. 5 (March 2008): 414–18. https://doi.org/10.1111/j.1553-2712.2008.00100.x.

Dolan, Paul, and Amanda Henwood. "Five Steps Towards Avoiding Narrative Traps in Decision-Making." *Frontiers in Psychology* 12 (August 2021): 694032. https://doi.org/10.3389/fpsyg.2021.694032.

Durant and Durant. *The Lessons of History*.

Emmons, Robert A. *Thanks!: How the New Science of Gratitude Can Make You Happier*. New York: Houghton Mifflin Company, 2007.

Epstein, Joseph. *Charm: The Elusive Enchantment*. Guilford, CT: Lyons Press, 2018.

Fawzy, Ashraf, Tianshi David Wu, Kunbo Wang, Matthew L. Robinson, Jad Farha, Amanda Bradke, Sherita H. Golden, Yanxun Xu, and Brian T. Garibaldi. "Racial and Ethnic Discrepancy in Pulse Oximetry and Delayed Identification of Treatment Eligibility Among Patients with COVID-19." *JAMA Internal Medicine* 182, no. 7 (July 2022): 730–738. https://doi.org/10.1001/jamainternmed.2022.1906.

Gladwell, Malcolm. *Talking to Strangers: What We Should Know About the People We Don't Know.* New York: Little, Brown and Company, 2019.

"Histoplasmosis Statistics." Centers for Disease Control and Prevention. Last reviewed May 22, 2020. https://www.cdc.gov/fungal/diseases/histoplasmosis/statistics.html.

"Identifying Negative Automatic Thought Patterns." Harvard University Stress and Development Lab. Accessed September 27, 2022. https://sdlab.fas.harvard.edu/cognitive-reappraisal/identifying-negative-automatic-thought-patterns.

Kahneman. *Thinking, Fast and Slow.*

"Lyme Disease: Data and Surveillance." Centers for Disease Control and Prevention. Last reviewed August 29, 2022. https://www.cdc.gov/lyme/datasurveillance/index.html.

Lujan, Heidi L., and Stephen E. DiCarlo. "Science Reflects History as Society Influences Science: Brief History of 'Race,' 'Race Correction,' and the Spirometer." *Advances in Physiological Education* 142, no. 2 (June 2018): 163–65. https://doi.org/10.1152/advan.00196.2017.

McEwen, Bruce S. "The Brain on Stress: Toward an Integrative Approach to Brain, Body, and Behavior." *Perspectives on Psychological Science* 8, no. 6 (November 2013): 673–75. https://doi.org/10.1177/1745691613506907.

Meyer, Pamela. *Liespotting: Proven Techniques to Detect Deception.* New York: St. Martin's Press, 2010.

"Pareto Principle." ScienceDirect. Accessed September 27, 2022. https://www.sciencedirect.com/topics/engineering/pareto-principle.

Pletcher, Mark J., Stefan G. Kertesz, Michael A. Kohn, and Ralph Gonzales. "Trends in Opioid Prescribing by Race/Ethnicity for Patients Seeking Care in US Emergency Departments." *JAMA* 299, no. 1 (January 2008): 70–78. https://doi.org/10.1001/jama.2007.64.

Seidman, Dov. *How: Why How We Do Anything Means Everything*. Hoboken, NJ: Wiley, 2007.

Shafer, Leah. "Social Media and Teen Anxiety." Usable Knowledge. Harvard Graduate School of Education. December 15, 2017. https://www.gse.harvard.edu/news/uk/17/12/social-media-and-teen-anxiety.

Stanford Encyclopedia of Philosophy (Spring 2021). s.v. "Maimonides." By Kenneth Seeskin. https://plato.stanford.edu/entries/maimonides/.

Stanford Encyclopedia of Philosophy (Winter 2021). s.v. "Galen." By P. N. Singer. https://plato.stanford.edu/entries/galen/.

Terkel, Studs. *Working: People Talk About What They Do All Day and How They Feel About What They Do*. New York: The New Press, 1972.

"Why Do Positive Impressions Produced in One Area Positively Influence Our Opinions in Another Area?" The Decision Lab. Accessed September 27, 2022. https://thedecisionlab.com/biases/halo-effect.

"Works by Hippocrates." The Internet Classics Archive. Accessed September 27, 2022. http://classics.mit.edu/Browse/browse-Hippocrates.html.

CHAPTER 18

"About CDC's Opioid Prescribing Guideline." Centers for Disease Control and Prevention. Last reviewed August 16, 2022. https://www.cdc.gov/opioids/providers/prescribing/guideline.html.

"Advancing Health Equity: A Guide to Language, Narrative and Concepts." American Medical Association. Accessed September 27, 2022. https://www.ama-assn.org/about/ama-center-health-equity/advancing-health-equity-guide-language-narrative-and-concepts-o.

AJMC Staff. "A Timeline of COVID-19 Developments in 2020." American Journal of Managed Care. January 1, 2021. https://www.ajmc.com/view/a-timeline-of-covid19-developments-in-2020.

Atkins and Williams, eds. *Aquinas.*

Bagassi, Maria, and Laura Macchi. "Creative Problem Solving as Overcoming a Misunderstanding." *Frontiers in Education* 5 (December 2020): 538202. https://doi.org/10.3389/feduc.2020.538202.

Birx, Deborah. *Silent Invasion: The Untold Story of the Trump Administration, Covid-19, and Preventing the Next Pandemic Before It's Too Late.* New York: Harper, 2022.

Browning, Robert. "Porphyria's Lover." Accessed September 3, 2022. https://www.poetryfoundation.org/poems/46313/porphyrias-lover.

Carey, Benedict. "Ronald Melzack, Cartographer of Pain, Is Dead at 90." *New York Times.* January 12, 2020. https://www.nytimes.com/2020/01/12/science/ronald-melzack-dead.html.

Cohen, Steven P. "Benzodiazepines for Neuropathic Back Pain: When the Cure is Worse than the Disease." *Pain* 149, no. 3 (June 2010): 424–25. https://doi.org/10.1016/j.pain.2010.03.038.

"C. S. Lewis Reading Room." Reading Room Archives. Accessed September 27, 2022. https://reading-rooms.tyndale.ca/cs-lewis/.

Cunningham, Chinazo. "Observations of the Opioid Workgroup of the Board of Scientific Counselors of the National Center for Injury Prevention and Control on the Updated CDC Guideline for Prescribing Opioids." Presentation. Scientific Counselors of the National Center for Injury Prevention and Control. July 16, 2021. https://www.cdc.gov/injury/pdfs/bsc/Observations-on-the-Updated-CDC-Guideline-for-Prescribing-6-30-2021-508.pdf.

Dineen, Kelly K., and James M. DuBois. "Between a Rock and a Hard Place: Can Physicians Prescribe Opioids to Treat Pain Adequately While Avoiding Legal Sanction?" *American Journal of Law and Medicine* 42, no. 1 (2016): 7–52. https://doi.org/10.1177/0098858816644712.

Dostoevsky, Fyodor. *The Brothers Karamazov*. Translated by Richard Pevear and Larissa Volokhonsky. New York: Farrar, Straus and Giroux, 1990.

"Effects of TBI." US Department of Veterans Affairs. Updated August 1, 2022. https://www.mentalhealth.va.gov/tbi/index.asp.

Fishman, Scott M. "Pain as the Fifth Vital Sign: How Can I Tell When Back Pain is Serious." *Journal of Pain and Palliative Care Pharmacotherapy* 19, no. 4 (2005): 77–79. PMID: 16431837.

Frankl, Viktor E. *Man's Search for Meaning*. Boston: Beacon Press, 1959.

Gandhi, Mohandas K. *The Story of My Experiments with Truth*. Translated by Mahadev Desai. New York: Dover Publications, 1983.

Gong, Jingjing, Yan Zhang, Jun Feng, Yonghua Huang, Yazhou Wei, and Weiwei Zhang. "Influence of Framing on Medical Decision Making." *EXCLI Journal* 12 (2013): 20–29. PMCID: PMC4803019.

"An Enquiry Concerning Human Understanding." Hume Texts Online. Accessed September 27, 2022. https://davidhume.org/texts/e/full.

Jonsdottir, Thorbjorg, Sigridur Gunnarsdottir, Gudmundur K. Oskarsson, and Helga Jonsdottir. "Patients' Perception of Chronic-Pain-Related Patient–Provider Communication in Relation to Sociodemographic and Pain-Related Variables: A Cross-Sectional Nationwide Study." *Pain Management Nursing* 17, no. 5 (October 2016): 322–32. https://doi.org/10.1016/j.pmn.2016.07.001.

Kanfer, Stefan. "Horatio Alger: The Moral of the Story." *City Journal*, Autumn 2000. https://www.city-journal.org/html/horatio-alger-moral-story-11933.html.

Lahiri, Jhumpa. *Interpreter of Maladies*. New York: Houghton Mifflin Harcourt, 1999.

Lewis, C. S. *An Experiment in Criticism*. Cambridge, UK: Cambridge University Press, 1961.

Loewenstein, David. *Milton: Paradise Lost*. Cambridge, UK: Cambridge University Press, 1993.

Lucy, J. A. "Sapir-Whorf Hypothesis." *International Encyclopedia of the Social & Behavioral Sciences* (2001): 13486–90. https://doi.org/10.1016/B0-08-043076-7/03042-4.

"Major Essays." Henry David Thoreau Online. Accessed September 27, 2022. https://www.thoreau-online.org/major-essays.htm.

Mann, Thomas, and John E. Woods. *Doctor Faustus: The Life of the German Composer Adrian Leverkuhn as Told by a Friend*. New York: Random House, 1994.

Martindale, Wayne, and Jerry Root, eds. *The Quotable Lewis*. Wheaton, IL: Tyndale House Publishers, 1989.

Milton, John. "*Paradise Lost*: Book 1 (1967 Version)." Accessed January 18, 2023. https://www.poetryfoundation.org/poems/45718/paradise-lost-book-1-1674-version.

Purves, Dale, George J. Augustine, David Fitzpatrick, Lawrence C. Katz, Anthony-Samuel LaMantia, James O. McNamara, and S. Mark Williams, eds. *Neuroscience (Second Edition)*. Sunderland, MA: Sinauer Associates, 2001.

"Ralph Waldo Emerson Literary Works." American Transcendentalism Web. Accessed September 27, 2022. https://archive.vcu.edu/english/engweb/transcendentalism/authors/emerson/essays/.

Rich, B. A. "Physicians' Legal Duty to Relieve Suffering." *Western Journal of Medicine* 175, no. 3 (September 2001): 151–52. https://doi.org/10.1136/ewjm.175.3.151.

Richton Park Public Library District. "Eleven Speeches by Rev. Dr. Martin Luther King Jr." Accessed September 27, 2022. https://wmasd.ss7.sharpschool.com/common/pages/UserFile.aspx?fileId=8373388.

Sagan, Carl. *The Dragons of Eden: Speculations on the Evolution of Human Intelligence*. New York: Random House, 1977.

Sandberg, Sheryl, and Adam Grant. *Option B: Facing Adversity, Building Resilience, and Finding Joy*. New York: Alfred A. Knopf, 2017.

Saposnik, Gustavo, Donald Redelmeier, Chrsitian C. Ruff, and Philippe N. Tobler. "Cognitive Biases Associated with Medical Decisions: A Systematic Review." *BMC Medical Informatics and Decision Making* 16, no. 1 (November 2016). https://doi.org/10.1186/s12911-016-0377-1.

Stanford Encyclopedia of Philosophy (Summer 2021). s.v. "Epictetus." By Margaret Graver. https://plato.stanford.edu/entries/epictetus/.

StreetRx: Latest Street Prices for Illicit and Prescription Drugs (website). Accessed September 3, 2022. https://streetrx.com/.

"Symptoms of Mild TBI and Concussion." Centers for Disease Control and Prevention. Last reviewed March 7, 2022. https://www.cdc.gov/traumaticbraininjury/concussion/symptoms.html.

Terkel. *Working*.

Tolstoy, Leo. *The Death of Ivan Ilych and Other Stories*. New York: Barnes and Noble Classics, 2004.

Trollope, Anthony. *The Barsetshire Novels: 6-Volume Set*. Oxford: Oxford University Press, 1989.

Wiesel, Elie. *Night*. Translated by Marion Wiesel. New York: Hill and Wang, 2006.

Whorf, Benjamin Lee. "The Relation of Habitual Thought and Behavior to Language." In *Language, Culture, and Personality: Essays in Memory of Edward Sapir*. Edited by Leslie Spire, A. Irving Hallowell, and Stanley S. Newman. Menasha, WI: Sapir Memorial Publication Fund, 1941.

Xiulu Ruan v. United States. 597 U.S. (2022). https://www.supremecourt.gov/opinions/21pdf/20-1410_1an2.pdf.

CHAPTER 19

Alizon, Samuel, and Mircea T. Sofonea. "SARS-CoV-2 Virulence Evolution: Avirulence Theory, Immunity and Trade-Offs." *Journal of Evolutionary Biology* 34, no. 12 (December 2021): 1867–77. https://doi.org/10.1111/jeb.13896.

Awdish, Rana. *In Shock: My Journey from Death to Recovery and the Redemptive Power of Hope.* New York: Picador, 2017.

Depetris-Chauvin, Emilio, and David N. Weil. "Malaria and Early African Development: Evidence from the Sickle Cell Trait." *Economic Journal* 128, no. 610 (May 2018): 1207–34. https://doi.org/10.1111/ecoj.12433.

Dhondt, Guido. "Orientation." CalculiX CrunchiX User's Manual, version 2.7. March 2, 2014. https://web.mit.edu/calculix_v2.7/CalculiX/ccx_2.7/doc/ccx/node229.html.

Duckworth, Angela. *Grit: The Power of Passion and Perseverance.* New York: Scribner, 2016.

Fauvel, John, Raymond Flood, and Robin Wilson, eds. *Music and Mathematics: From Pythagoras to Fractals.* Oxford: Oxford University Press, 2003.

Han, Paul K. J., William M. P. Klein, and Neeraj K. Arora. "Varieties of Uncertainty in Health Care: A Conceptual Taxonomy." *Medical Decision Making* 31, no. 6 (November–December 2011): 828–38. https://doi.org/10.1177/0272989x11393976.

Harari. *Homo Deus.*

Kahneman. *Thinking, Fast and Slow.*

Lindgren, Kristen P., Jason J. Ramirez, Nauder Namaky, Cecelia C. Olin, and Bethany A. Teachman. "Evaluating the Relationship Between Explicit and Implicit Drinking Identity Centrality and Hazardous Drinking." *Addictive Behaviors Reports* 4 (December 2016): 87–96. https://doi.org/10.1016/j.abrep.2016.10.004.

Lyalin, David. "Applying Euler Diagrams and Venn Diagrams to Concept Modeling." *Business Rules Journal* 21, no. 2 (February 2020): c021. PMCID: PMC9014965.

Malthus, Thomas. "An Essay on the Principle of Population, as it Affects the Future Improvement of Society with Remarks on the Speculations of Mr. Godwin, M. Condorcet, and Other Writers." Electronic Scholarly Publishing Project. 1998. http://www.esp.org/books/malthus/population/malthus.pdf.

McKibben, Bill. *Maybe One: A Case for Smaller Families*. New York: Plume, 1999.

Pastuzyn, Elissa D., Cameron E. Day, Rachel B. Kearns, Madeleine Kyrke-Smith, Andrew V. Taibi, John McCormick, Nathan Yoder et al. "The Neuronal Gene Arc Encodes a Repurposed Retrotransposon Gag Protein that Mediates Intercellular RNA Transfer." *Cell* 172, no. 1–2 (January 2018): 275–88.E18. https://doi.org/10.1016/j.cell.2017.12.024.

Ramanan, Deepshika, Rowann Bowcutt, Soo Ching Lee, Mei San Tang, Zachary D. Kurtz, Yi Ding, Kenya Honda et al. "Helminth Infection Promotes Colonization Resistance Via Type 2 Immunity." *Science* 352, no. 6285 (April 2016): 608–12. https://doi.org/10.1126/science.aaf3229.

Raphael, Melissa. "6: Numerous Experience." In *Rudolf Otto and the Concept of Holiness*, 149–74. Oxford: Oxford University Press, 1997. https://doi.org/10.1093/acprof:oso/9780198269328.003.0016.

Sandberg and Grant. *Option B.*

Shalev-Shwartz, Shai, and Shai Ben-David. *Understanding Machine Learning: From Theory to Algorithms*. Cambridge, UK: Cambridge University Press, 2014.

Spence, D. P., and B. Holland. "The Restricting Effects of Awareness: A Paradox and Explanation." *Journal of Abnormal and Social Psychology* 64, no. 3 (1962): 163–74. https://psycnet.apa.org/doi/10.1037/h0042110.

Stanford Encyclopedia of Philosophy (Summer 2018). s.v. "Phenomenology." By David Woodruff Smith. https://plato.stanford.edu/entries/phenomenology/.

Stanford Encyclopedia of Philosophy (Winter 2020). s.v. "Georg Wilhelm Friedrich Hegel." By Paul Redding. https://plato.stanford.edu/entries/hegel/.

Stangl, Anne L., Valerie A. Earnshaw, Carmen H. Logie, Wim van Brakel, Leickness C. Simbayi, Iman Barré, and John F. Dovidio. "The Health Stigma and Discrimination Framework: A Global, Crosscutting Framework to Inform Research, Intervention Development, and Policy on Health-Related Stigmas." *BMC Medicine* 17, no. 1 (February 2019): 31. https://doi.org/10.1186/s12916-019-1271-3.

Thomas, Robert L. *Evangelical Hermeneutics: The New Versus the Old.* Grand Rapids, MI: Kregel Publications, 2002.

Thompson, William Irwin. *Coming Into Being: Artifacts and Texts in the Evolution of Consciousness.* New York: St. Martin's Press, 1996.

Tversky, Amos, and Daniel Kahneman. "Judgment Under Uncertainty: Heuristics and Biases." *Science* (New Series) 185, no. 4157 (September 1974): 1124–31. https://www2.psych.ubc.ca/~schaller/Psyc590Readings/TverskyKahneman1974.pdf.

CHAPTER 20

"Affective Communication Test (ACT)." Howard S. Friedman, University of California, Riverside. Accessed September 28, 2022. http://www.faculty.ucr.edu/~friedman/act.html.

Agrahari, Shivam. "Monte Carlo Markov Chain (MCMC), Explained." Towards Data Science. July 27, 2021. https://towardsdatascience.com/monte-carlo-markov-chain-mcmc-explained-94e3a6c8de11.

Asim, Yousra, Ahmad Kamran Malik, Basit Raza, and Ahmad Raza Shahid. "A Trust Model for Analysis of Trust, Influence and Their Relationship in Social Network Communities." *Telematics and Informatics* 36 (March 2019): 94–116. https://doi.org/10.1016/j.tele.2018.11.008.

"Best Practice Guides." Telehealth.HHS.gov. Health Resources & Services Administration. Accessed September 28, 2022. https://telehealth.hhs.gov/providers/best-practice-guides/.

"Code of Medical Ethics: Patient-Physician Relationships."
American Medical Association. Accessed September 28,
2022. https://www.ama-assn.org/delivering-care/ethics/
code-medical-ethics-patient-physician-relationships.

"The Controlled Substances Act." United States Drug
Enforcement Administration.

Duke, Annie. *Thinking in Bets: Making Smarter Decisions When You Don't Have All the Facts*. New York: Portfolio/Penguin, 2018.

Fan, Xinxin, Ling Liu, Rui Zhang, Quanliang Jing, and Jingping Bi.
"Decentralized Trust Management: Risk Analysis and Trust Aggregation."
ACM Computing Surveys 53, no. 1 (January 2021): 1–33. https://doi.
org/10.1145/3362168.

Garrett, Neil, Stephanie C. Lazzaro, Dan Ariely, and Tali Sharot. "The Brain
Adapts to Dishonesty." *Nature Neuroscience* 19 (2016): 1727–32. https://doi.
org/10.1038/nn.4426.

Germer, Thomas A. "Modeled Integrated Scatter Tool (MIST)." National
Institute of Standards and Technology. October 2017. https://pages.nist.gov/
ScatterMIST/docs/index.htm.

Gilmore, Jason. "American Exceptionalism in the American Mind: Presidential
Discourse, National Identity, and U.S. Public Opinion." *Communication
Studies* 66, no. 3 (2015): 301–20. https://doi.org/10.1080/10510974.2014.9910
44.

Gladwell. *Talking to Strangers*.

Gladwell, Malcolm. "The Gift of Doubt." *New Yorker*. June 24, 2013. https://www.
newyorker.com/magazine/2013/06/24/the-gift-of-doubt.

Gopal, Dipesh P., Ula Chetty, Patrick O'Donnell, Camille Gajria, and Jodie
Blackadder-Weinstein. "Implicit Bias in Healthcare: Clinical Practice,
Research and Decision Making." *Future Healthcare Journal* 8, no. 1 (March
2021): 40–48. https://doi.org/10.7861/fhj.2020-0233.

Holt, Charles A., and Alvin E. Roth. "The Nash Equilibrium: A Perspective." *PNAS* 101, no. 12 (March 2004): 3999–4002. https://doi.org/10.1073/pnas.0308738101.

Isaacson, Walter. *Steve Jobs.* New York: Simon and Schuster, 2011.

Jensen, David G. "The Law of Reciprocity." *Science.* February 15, 2013. https://www.science.org/content/article/law-reciprocity.

Kahneman, Daniel, and Amos Tversky. "Prospect Theory: An Analysis of Decision Under Risk." *Econometrica* 47, no. 2 (March 1979): 263–92. https://doi.org/10.2307/1914185.

Klosterman, Chuck. *But What If We're Wrong? Thinking About the Present As If It Were the Past.* New York: Blue Rider Press, 2016.

National Academies of Science, Engineering, and Medicine. *Reproducibility and Replicability in Science.* Washington, DC: The National Academies Press, 2019. https://doi.org/10.17226/25303.

Newport, Cal. *Deep Work: Rules for Focused Success in a Distracted World.* New York: Grand Central Publishing, 2016.

Otto, Rudolf. *The Idea of the Holy: An Inquiry into the Non-Rational Factor in the Idea of the Divine and Its Relation to the Rational.* Translated by John W. Harvey. London: Oxford University Press, 1923.

Parikh, Rajul, Annie Mathai, Shefali Parikh, G. Chandra Sekhar, Ravi Thomas. "Understanding and Using Sensitivity, Specificity and Predictive Values." *Indian Journal of Ophthalmology* 56, no. 1 (January–February 2008): 45–50. PMCID: PMC2636062.

Popova, Maria. "Leo Tolstoy on Emotional Infectiousness and What Separates Good Art from the Bad." The Marginalian. September 9, 2013. https://www.themarginalian.org/2013/09/09/leo-tolstoy-what-is-art-infectiousness/.

Räty, Lena, and Barbro Gustafsson. "Emotions in Relation to Healthcare Encounters Affecting Self-Esteem." *Journal of Neuroscience Nursing* 38, no. 1 (February 2006): 42–50. https://doi.org/10.1097/01376517-200602000-00009.

Stanford Encyclopedia of Philosophy (Fall 2021). s.v. "Game Theory." By Don Ross. https://plato.stanford.edu/entries/game-theory/.

Snow, Richard. *I Invented the Modern Age: The Rise of Henry Ford.* New York: Scribner, 2013.

"Take a Test." Project Implicit. Accessed September 28, 2022. https://implicit. harvard.edu/implicit/takeatest.html.

Thaler, Richard H., and Cass R. Sunstein. *Nudge: Improving Decisions About Health, Wealth, and Happiness.* New Haven, CT: Yale University Press, 2008.

Verigin, Brianna L., Ewout H. Meijer, Glynis Bogaard, and Aldert Vrij. "Lie Prevalence, Lie Characteristics and Strategies of Self-Reported Good Liars." *PLoS One* 14, no. 12 (December 2019): e0225566. https://doi.org/10.1371/journal.pone.0225566.

CHAPTER 21

Brooks, David. *The Second Mountain: The Quest for a Moral Life.* New York: Random House, 2019.

Burns, Lawton Robert, ed. *The U.S. Healthcare Ecosystem: Payers, Providers, Producers.* New York: McGraw Hill, 2021.

Cornforth, Daniel M., and Kevin R. Foster. "Antibiotics and the Art of Bacterial War." *PNAS* 112, no. 35 (August 2015): 10827–28. https://doi.org/10.1073/pnas.1513608112.

Dalio, Ray. *Principles: Life and Work.* New York: Simon & Schuster, 2017.

Diamond. *Guns, Germs, and Steel.*

Dower. *Embracing Defeat.*

Durant and Durant. *The Lessons of History.*

"Health Information Privacy" (home page). US Department of Health & Human Services. Accessed September 28, 2022. https://www.hhs.gov/hipaa/index. html.

Hefner, Jennifer L., Tory Harper Hogan, William Opoku-Agyeman, and Nir Menachemi. "Defining Safety Net Hospitals in the Health Services Research Literature: A Systematic Review and Critical Appraisal." *BMC Health Services Research* 21, no. 278 (2021). https://doi.org/10.1186/s12913-021-06292-9.

"A Just Recovery to Achieve Economic Security and Health for All" (home page). County Health Rankings & Roadmaps. Accessed September 28, 2022. https://www.countyhealthrankings.org/.

King. "Transcript of Dr. Martin Luther King's Speech at SMU."

Kochenderfer, Mykel J. *Decision Making Under Uncertainty: Theory and Application.* Cambridge, MA: MIT Press, 2015.

Kutner, Michael H., Christopher J. Nachtsheim, John Neter, and William Li. *Applied Linear Statistical Models.* 5th ed. New York: McGraw-Hill/Irwin, 2005.

Okuda, Takuya, and Diego Trancanelli. "Spectral Curves, Emergent Geometry, and Bubbling Solutions for Wilson Loops." *Journal of High Energy Physics* 2008 (September 2008). https://doi.org/10.1088/1126-6708/2008/09/050.

108th Cong. 2nd Session. *The Constitution of the United States of America: Analysis and Interpretation—2004 Supplement.* Killian, Johnny H., George A. Costello, and Kenneth R. Thomas, eds. Y1.1/3. Washington, D C: Congressional Research Service Library of Congress, 2004. https://www.govinfo.gov/content/pkg/GPO-CONAN-2002/pdf/GPO-CONAN-2002.pdf.

Pink, Daniel H. *Drive: The Surprising Truth About What Motivates Us.* New York: Riverhead Books, 2009.

Pollan, Michael. *The Omnivore's Dilemma: A Natural History of Four Meals.* New York: Penguin Books, 2006.

Sagan. *The Dragons of Eden.*

Sinek, Simon. *Start with Why: How Great Leaders Inspire Everyone to Take Action.* New York: Penguin Group, 2009.

Stanford Encyclopedia of Philosophy (Winter 2021). s.v. "Emergent Properties." By Timothy O'Connor. https://plato.stanford.edu/entries/properties-emergent/.

StreetRx: Latest Street Prices for Illicit and Prescription Drugs (website).

Taleb, Nassim Nicholas. *Antifragile: Things That Gain from Disorder.* New York: Random House, 2012.

Thompson. *Coming Into Being.*

"Three Generations of Health Research" (home page). Framingham Heart Study. Accessed September 28, 2022. https://www.framinghamheartstudy.org/.

Venkataramani, Atheendar S., Elizabeth F. Bair, Rourke L. O'Brien, and Alexander C. Tsai. "Association Between Automotive Assembly Plant Closures and Opioid Overdose Mortality in the United States: A Difference-in-Differences Analysis." *JAMA Internal Medicine* 180, no. 2 (2020): 254–62. https://doi.org/10.1001/jamainternmed.2019.5686.

Made in the USA
Las Vegas, NV
29 May 2023

72696487R00199